Paths

Commands
Commands F1

Brushes

The
Essential
Photoshop™
Book

Other Prima Computer Books

AVAILABLE NOW!

Build a Web Site: The Programmer's Guide to Creating,
  Building, and Maintaining a Web Presence
The CD-ROM Revolution
CompuServe Complete Handbook and Membership Kit,
  Second Edition (with CD-ROM)
Create Wealth with Quicken, Third Edition
Cruising America Online 2.5
Cruising CompuServe
Cruising The Microsoft Network
Data Security
The Essential Book for Microsoft Office
Excel for Windows 95: The Visual Learning Guide
Interactive Internet: The Insider's Guide to MUDs, MOOs,
  and IRC
Internet After Hours, 2nd Edition
Internet Information Server
The Internet Warp Book: Your Complete Guide to Getting
  Online with OS/2
Introduction to Internet Security
Managing with Microsoft Project
Microsoft Works for Windows 95: The Visual Learning Guide
Migrating to Windows 95
Moving Worlds (with CD-ROM)
Netscape Navigator 3 Complete Handbook
PowerPoint for Windows 95: The Visual Learning Guide
Quicken 5 for Windows: The Visual Learning Guide
Researching on the Internet: The Complete Guide to Finding,
  Evaluating, and Organizing Information Effectively
Sound Blaster: Making WAVes with Multimedia
Stacker Multimedia
UnInstaller 3: Uncluttering Your PC
Visio 4: Drawing Has Never Been Easier!
Web Advertising and Marketing
Web After Hours
Web Browsing with America Online
Web Browsing with Netscape Navigator 1.1
Web Browsing with NETCOM NetCruiser
Web Browsing with Prodigy
Web Browsing with The Microsoft Network
Windows 3.1: The Visual Learning Guide
Windows 95: The Visual Learning Guide
Windows 95: A to Z
Windows 95: Easy Installation Guide
The Windows 95 Book: Your Definitive Guide to Installing
  and Using Windows 95
WinFax PRO 7 for Windows: The Visual Learning Guide
Word for Windows 95: The Visual Learning Guide
WordPerfect 6.1 for Windows: The Visual Learning Guide

How to Order:

For information on quantity discounts contact the publisher: Prima Publishing, P.O. Box 1260BK, Rocklin, CA 95677-1260; (916) 632-4400. On your letterhead include information concerning the intended use of the books and the number of books you wish to purchase. For individual orders, turn to the back of this book for more information.

Paths

Commands

Commands F1

Brushes

The
Essential
Photoshop™
Book

The Get-It-Done

Tutorial for Professionals

Eileen Mullin

PRIMA PUBLISHING

P is a registered trademark of Prima Publishing, a division of Prima Communications, Inc. Prima Publishing is a registered trademark of Prima Communications, Inc. Prima Publishing, Rocklin, California 95677.

Adobe Photoshop™ is a trademark of Adobe Systems Incorporated.

Publisher: Don Roche, Jr.
Associate Publisher: Ray Robinson
Senior Acquisitions Editor: Alan Harris
Senior Editor: Tad Ringo
Acquisitions Editor: Julie Barton
Project Editor: Kelli Crump
Copy Editor: Hilary Powers
Technical Reviewer: Vincent Freeman
Interior Design and Layout: Danielle Foster
Cover Design: Vanessa Perez and Mike Tanamachi
Color Insert Design and Layout: Rick Wong
Production Manager: Dan Foster
Indexer: Emily Glossbrenner

Important: If you have problems installing or running Adobe Photoshop 3, notify Adobe at (206)628-2040. Prima Publishing cannot provide software support.

Prima Publishing and the author have attempted throughout this book to distinguish proprietary trademarks from descriptive terms by following the capitalization style used by the manufacturer.

Information contained in this book has been obtained by Prima Publishing from sources believed to be reliable. However, because of the possibility of human or mechanical error by our sources, Prima Publishing, or others, the Publisher does not guarantee the accuracy, adequacy, or completeness of any information and is not responsible for any errors or omissions or the results obtained from use of such information. Readers should be particularly aware of the fact that the Internet is an ever-changing entity. Some facts may have changed since this book went to press.

ISBN: 0-7615-0695-0

Library of Congress Catalog Card Number: 96-68060

Printed in the United States of America

96 97 98 99 BB 10 9 8 7 6 5 4 3 2 1

*To my mom and dad, for all the good
things they taught me.*

Contents at a Glance

Contents

8 Filter Essentials   221

9 Scanning Essentials   271

10 Retouching Essentials   291

Acknowledgments

First, let me give heartfelt thanks to all my friends and family for their support. Most of all, I want to thank Ross Rubin for his thoughtful advice, irrepressible good cheer, and all the good bits. His devotion and attention, willingness to fetch Diet Coke, and do impressions on demand is also deeply, deeply appreciated.

My warmest thanks go to Neil deMause for his eagle-eyed reading of the manuscript and unfailing ability to lift my spirits. Lee Steele was invaluable for brainstorming about Web graphics and considering what Barbie would get out of the book. I'd also like to thank Eadie Adamson, Joanne Chernow, and the other Webgrrls who offered suggestions for improving the manuscript and ideas for topics to include.

My sincerest thanks go to Karen Whitehouse, who started me down the slippery slope of computer book authorship. Also deserving of thanks are Kelli Crump, project editor; Alan Harris and Julie Barton, acquisitions editors; Hilary Powers, copy editor; Vincent Freeman, technical editor; and Emily Glossbrenner, indexer. Credit on the design end belongs to Danielle Foster for the design and layout of the interior, and Mike Tanamachi and Vanessa Perez for the cover art.

Thanks and extra kibble to my furry companions Starsky and Hutch, who provided many hours of entertainment and middle-of-the-night companionship.

Thanks to Tom Lehrer, Squeeze, Elvis Costello, and Razor & Tie Music's *Everything '80s* CD for the soundtrack. Vast quantities of Juba's coffee was also instrumental in making this book possible.

And thanks to Adobe for giving graphic designers such wonderful tools!

Eileen Mullin

July 1996

About the Author

Eileen Mullin is an editor and graphic designer. Currently a technical editor for *Web Week* magazine, she has extensive experience in print production, Web graphics, and technical writing. Eileen resides in Manhattan with her boyfriend and cats.

Introduction

This book is designed to help you learn effective Photoshop techniques from the ground floor up so you can approach your graphic design projects in a smart, creative way. It's intended to help you expand your core design skills so you can successfully complete professional-quality assignments for print publications, online projects, or your own portfolio.

Becoming proficient in Photoshop is like learning how to swim—there's a certain amount you can do with no problem at the shallow end, but you have to take a lot of initiative if you want to become really good at it. The greatest barriers to taking the plunge, so to speak, include information overload—because there's such a confusing array of user manuals, books, online documents, instructional CD-ROMs, courses and seminars about Photoshop—and the intimidation factor of hoping to keep up with the ever-changing world of new technologies.

My approach is one I developed after reading one of Calvin Trillin's wonderful columns from *The Nation*. In it, Trillin described how he and his wife, Alice, dealt with their information anxiety about current events. Specifically, he was worried about appearing ill-informed at dinner parties and the like when asked to give his opinion about the state of affairs in parts of the world about which he knew nothing. His solution was to divide with his wife the responsibility for keeping up to date about different topics, each providing the other with relevant information on a need-to-know basis. Thus, he could blissfully ignore news reports on "her" topics without fearing he might miss something, knowing he would be apprised on events as he needed to know them.

Similarly, I organized the material in this book on a need-to-know basis. There is a lot of introductory material in the first few chapters that will increase your understanding of the more advanced features—which sounds obvious, I know, but it's something that's really lacking in many Photoshop books that showcase special effects or single-use tips and tricks. As you may have found already, there's almost always more than one way

to achieve a particular effect in Photoshop—so the best method to use should depend more on your level of Photoshop expertise and your ultimate use for a particular graphic function than on any single shortcut.

For example, I describe several different ways you can create drop shadows. The first way is a fine solution if you're brand-new to Photoshop and wouldn't know what the Layers feature was if it came up and bit you on the nose. Later on, an explanation of the Layers feature shows what a powerful capability Photoshop has added in letting you edit objects independently of one another, and what great potential that adds for letting you edit shadows further, move them around, and change their opacity. Later still, an overview of Photoshop filters explains the differences among blur filters that you can use to make realistic blurred shadow edges, and how you could put the advanced Lighting Effects and Offset filters to work in creating shadows. In short, while I give step-by-step information on how to achieve certain effects, I want to emphasize that there's a continuum of Photoshop techniques and various methods are suited to different skill levels and the final use of your graphics.

In short, I'm leery of tips-and-tricks techniques that show you just one way of doing things. I hope you'll use the exercises in this book to get up to speed on using Photoshop's features and that you'll continue to explore—for example, by tweaking combinations of filters and figuring out how the elaborate images you see in other print publications were created. The examples in this book demonstrate a range of real-world uses of Photoshop features, and are designed to extend to situations or assignments far beyond those shown here.

What's Inside

Here are the topics you'll find addressed in the chapters ahead:

Chapter 1: System Essentials affords you an opportunity to assess whether your computer setup is equipped to handle your Photoshop work. An overview of third-party software, printers, and scanners is included, as are resources for obtaining source artwork.

Chapter 2: File Format Essentials addresses the range of graphics formats and Photoshop image modes available to you, depending on what your ultimate uses for your graphics will be.

Chapter 3: Toolbox Essentials is a tour of Photoshop's most functional tools and some accompanying power-user techniques. This chapter includes the book's first hands-on exercises for creating a couple of all-purpose effects: drop shadows and a 3-D sphere.

Chapter 4: Color Essentials guides you through the optimization of your images' colors both onscreen and in print, and offers a quick run-through of the basics of color theory. Exercises include how to create an indexed color palette—which is especially useful for creating Web graphics—and a walkthrough of how to save graphics using such a custom palette.

Chapter 5: Layering Essentials explains Photoshop's powerful layering feature and some of its potential uses. In this chapter's exercises, you'll use layering to create type masks for graphics—that is, type outlines that contain other images—and create objects and shadows on their own layers for editing independently of the rest of an image.

Chapter 6: Path Essentials provides a step-by-step guide to creating paths and Bézier curves with the Pen tool. The chapter exercises include a hands-on use of clipping paths, which are essential for creating silhouette images in Photoshop for exporting to page layout programs.

Chapter 7: Channel and Mask Essentials breaks down Photoshop's powerful but confusing-at-first channel capabilities into manageable steps that you can use to create unique composite images.

Chapter 8: Filter Essentials demonstrates the range of unusual special effects you can create with Photoshop filters. Exercises include tryouts of two of the most difficult filters, Lighting Effects and the Displace filter.

Chapter 9: Scanning Essentials explores the steps you can take to ensure your scanned images will look good. This chapter offers

tips on using different kinds of scanner controls, adjusting gamma, and avoiding problems when you're scanning halftoned images (that is, images that have been printed previously).

Chapter 10: Retouching Essentials covers a prominent real-world application of Photoshop—retouching and correcting less-than-perfect images. This chapter's exercises will help you create stunning "after" artwork for all your "before" photographs.

Chapter 11: 3-D Essentials shows you how to add depth to two-dimensional objects with realistic textures and shadow effects. The images you create with this chapter's exercises include 3-D geometric shapes, raised lettering effects, and the kind of button graphics popular on many Web sites.

Chapter 12: Print Production Essentials includes the hard-and-fast, need-to-know rules for ensuring that your Photoshop creations look as good in print as they do onscreen. The chapter covers RGB to CMYK conversion, duotones for two-color printing, and examples of putting clipping paths to use.

Chapter 13: Web Graphics Essentials offers eye-opening material on how designing for a Web audience greatly differs from designing for print. Coverage includes how to design images that reduce display time while retaining image quality, how to create seamlessly tiling background images, and how to use Photoshop to create images with transparent or interlaced backgrounds.

Chapter 14: Multimedia Essentials teaches you how to edit images in Photoshop for use with video and presentation software. The chapter discusses formats, importing and exporting, and touches upon specific uses with programs like Macromedia Director and Adobe Premiere.

Appendix A: Sources for Further Information includes a bibliography of other useful Photoshop books, general design books, and computer magazines. There is also a listing of related professional organizations, prominent Web sites that offer Photoshop-related tips and techniques, and a listing of relevant Usenet newsgroups.

Appendix B: Vendor Directory lists contact information for many hardware and software manufacturers whose products can be used with Photoshop.

Conventions Used in This Book

Photoshop's menus contain many submenus and commands. I try to give directions in the order in which you'd navigate the menus yourself. For example, "Choose Adjust from the Image menu, then select Brightness/Contrast… from the Adjust submenu." This might sound like quite a mouthful, but I find it more readable than a purely hierarchical description.

The vast majority of screen shots in this book show the Macintosh version of Photoshop. But the content of the screens and dialog boxes are what's important to focus on—not the minutiae of the interface windows. The instructions given should prove just as useful for PC users as for Mac users. Wherever necessary, I've included separate steps for what to do if you're running Photoshop on a PC or if you're using a Mac. For the most part, this only affects instructions for pressing key commands. Wherever a Mac user would press the Command or Option key, a Windows user would press the Control or Alt key.

Getting Additional Help

I've tried to answer in this book as many of the pressing questions that come up for professional Photoshop designer as possible, but there are always more that will crop up—some that require exhaustive detail, others that involve emerging technologies yet to come. To that end, the listings for online resources in Appendix A should prove more helpful than any print publication.

Sometimes finding the right answer is a matter of knowing where to look, but all too often it's also a matter of building up the courage to ask.

"Did you hear they discovered the gene for shyness?" comedian Jonathan Katz once said. "They would've found it years ago, but it was hiding behind a couple of other genes."

Don't hide behind a couple of other Photoshop designers. If you're struggling with a thorny what-scanner-should-I-buy question or puzzling over creating a certain effect, chances are that others are too. Start by asking your circle of acquaintances for help, but you can also get a wider perspective by seeking help on an online forum.

There are many online resources where you can get a quick answer to a specific question, or a push in the right direction if your query is more broad-based. The Usenet newsgroup **omp.graphics.apps.photoshop** is a good first stop; for Web graphics, **comp.infosystems.www.authoring.images** covers a wide range of Internet graphics topics. On America Online, you can post messages in the Photoshop Special Interest Group folder (keyword: Photoshop) for Photoshop help; on CompuServe, help is available by typing GO ADOBE. Appendix A also contains pointers to many additional online resources where you can find the answers to specific Photoshop questions.

Before you post to a newsgroup or online message board, there are three rules of netiquette to follow that will save you from unwittingly raising your fellow readers' hackles. First, check to see if the group has a FAQ (Frequently Asked Questions) list and read it to see if your query is answered within. Secondly, catch up on the messages and topics currently in circulation; you'll be forgiven if your question was discussed and answered a month ago, but not if it just came up two days ago.

The third rule relates not to the content of your question but how you ask for replies. Many fledgling Internet users post help requests in so many areas—including many newsgroups they don't visit regularly—that they ask for responses sent via e-mail, not posted to the online forum itself. This will infuriate many other users, though, because it violates the spirit of the group as a forum for shared information, and you'll stand the risk of being perceived as a taker, not a giver. If you decide you must ask for responses via e-mail, make it clear in your original post that you will summarize the most helpful hints and post accordingly—and then do it!

Feedback

If you have any comments or suggestions about this book, I look forward to receiving e-mail about it; please write me at **eileen@interport.net**.

1

System Essentials

IN THIS CHAPTER

Hardware and Memory Needs

👁

Printers

👁

Scanners

👁

Calibration

👁

Images

You're all set to put Photoshop to work for you in preparing graphics for print publication, GIFs for your Web site, or touching up images for interactive presentations, but first you need to make sure—sooner rather than later—that your computer system is up to the task.

This chapter covers some getting-started topics to think about, including:

👁 How to determine your hardware and memory needs and get the best performance out of the system you have.

👁 What printing and scanning capabilities are available to you—whether you're looking to buy your own equipment or just need to call your service bureau to conduct some printing tests.

👁 How to make sure your monitor is properly calibrated, and what kind of difference that really makes.

👁 How to find good source materials for your images.

If you're already using Photoshop in your daily work, you may be familiar with some of this material. If that's the case, keep this chapter in mind as a ground-level reference and feel free to skip ahead to Chapter 2, which explores the different real-world applications where Photoshop can be put to use.

Hardware and Memory Needs

Whether your interest in Photoshop is driven by a personal motivation to become a computer graphics expert or by fast-approaching deadlines at your job, you should take to heart the Boy Scout motto and be prepared. One of the first things you need to do is ensure that your computer's infrastructure—its hardware and memory—is up to the task.

It may surprise you at first, particularly if you're new to computer graphics in general, how far you have to extend most out-of-the-box computer setups to optimize for professional design use. If you add up memory upgrades, third-party filters, utilities and tools, scanner software, Photoshop and other graphics software packages, you could spend as much on extras as you did on your CPU, hard drive, and monitor.

Outfitting a computer system for intensive Photoshop use is like decorating a brand-new apartment: there's simply an enormous range of things you need. Right after I moved into my new place last year I had a shopping list that began—and at the time it didn't seem strange to me at all—as follows:

corkscrew

light bulbs

sofa

The remainder of this section addresses how to get a handle on the same kinds of juxtaposed needs, that is, picking up the simpler stuff while you're also up against more pressing problems. Let's focus on your system components—including your CPU, RAM, and hard disk space—and see if any major purchases should be in your near future.

CPU

A computer's *CPU*, or central processing unit, is the main chip that processes software instructions. Typically, the CPU will be the most significant factor in determining a computer's price.

 note

Since this book covers running Photoshop on Macintosh OS-based and Windows computers, this overview of microprocessing chips is limited to those from Motorola and Intel. Although Windows NT can run on different families of processors, Adobe currently supports Photoshop for Windows NT only on Intel-based systems. Photoshop is also available for Sun and Silicon Graphics workstations, but maintaining a Unix workstation is not a chore suitable for the average user.

To make it easier for you to follow along the discussion of microprocessor chips if you're only familiar with one system, Table 1.1 shows rough equivalents for the chips found inside Windows and Mac OS-based computers.

The faster your computer processes your commands, the faster you'll be able to complete operations in Photoshop and knock off work early

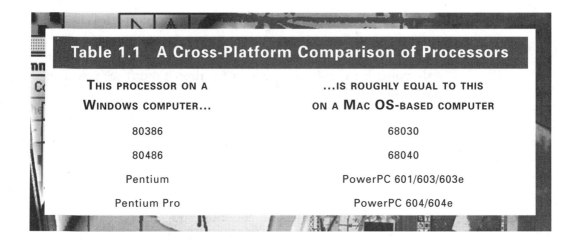

Table 1.1 A Cross-Platform Comparison of Processors	
THIS PROCESSOR ON A WINDOWS COMPUTER...	...IS ROUGHLY EQUAL TO THIS ON A MAC OS-BASED COMPUTER
80386	68030
80486	68040
Pentium	PowerPC 601/603/603e
Pentium Pro	PowerPC 604/604e

for the day. If your processing speed is less than optimal, you'll feel every extra second of processing time as it creeps by.

If you have the opportunity to run Photoshop on two different computer models, it should be an eye-opening experience—and drive home the difference in operating speed that a faster microprocessor chip makes. Currently, the fastest machines for running Photoshop are the Daystar Genesis MP on the Mac side and the Intergraph TD-400 on the Windows side. Both take advantage of multiple processors in the same computer to achieve their speed. Be aware, though, that both of these muscle machines cost well over $20,000!

While Macintosh users can run Photoshop on a Mac II with a 68020 microprocessor, regular use will warrant at least a 68040 microprocessor like those in the Quadra series. For hard-and-heavy use, you'll be much happier running Photoshop on a PowerMac. Similarly, Windows users can run Photoshop on a 80386 machine, but will be more productive with an 80486—or better yet, a Pentium.

Additionally, your computer's ability to run Photoshop at a fast clip is partly determined by its CPU's operating speed, or *clock speed*, which is measured in megahertz (MHz). For example, a 150MHz Pentium chip is faster than a 75MHz one. This number isn't, as some people might assume, a true measure of your processor's speed, however. A 90MHz Pentium will still outgun a 100MHz 486. Clock speed is also not a valid way of comparing the speeds of Pentium and PowerPC systems to each other. A 100MHz Pentium is not necessarily faster than an 80MHz PowerPC 601.

Since it's hardly practical to replace your computer every time a new model with a faster CPU is announced, there are a couple of ways you can improve your existing machine's clock speed and thus its performance: upgrade your computer's motherboard, or install a commercial Photoshop accelerator board. Let's take a look at these below.

Motherboard Upgrades

A computer's motherboard, or logic board, is the main component to which the CPU, RAM, hard disk, and other peripheral devices connect.

There are a number of vendors who sell motherboard upgrades. Upgrading your motherboard means you'd take your machine to a dealer where they'd remove the old motherboard and put in a new one. The rate at which prices for new computers drop, though, rarely makes such an upgrade a good value—especially if you need to replace your RAM. Windows users should check the back of *Computer Shopper* and Mac users can peruse the back of *MacWeek* for the names of vendors who sell motherboard upgrades.

Windows users can also often take advantage of chip-level upgrades where only the CPU is replaced. Intel also sells a line of OverDrive processors that can achieve a speed boost by adding a chip to a designated slot on the motherboard. The Mac world has not embraced the CPU upgrade concept as strongly, although many recent desktop models now wisely place the processor on a daughtercard for easier upgrading.

Custom Photoshop Accelerator Boards

These boards are specifically targeted to speeding up Photoshop operations; they use a chip series called Digital Signal Processor (DSP). For Macintosh users, the Radius PhotoEngine and Thunder series and the Adaptive Solutions PowerShop boards will speed up some Photoshop functions such as color mode conversions and the application of certain filters—although not all functions—as much as 30 times. The

speed differences are more noticeable on 680x0 machines than on PowerMacs, and are more substantial if you have as much RAM installed as possible.

Note that these DSP accelerators actually calculate filter effects differently than Photoshop does. Adobe has a certification process whereby DSP accelerators whose filter outputs look the same as those produced by native Photoshop filters get to display an "Adobe Charged" logo.

RAM

RAM, or random access memory, is where your computer stores the information it is currently using. Accessing information from RAM is much faster than accessing it from even the fastest hard disk, so the more RAM you have the faster your machine will run. After the CPU, the amount of RAM in a computer is typically the second most expensive factor in a computer's price. It is usually easier—and sometimes cheaper—to upgrade a computer's RAM than its CPU.

Photoshop's operation in particular is inextricably tied to how much of your computer's RAM it can use. Before you save a file for the first time, that data is stored in your computer's RAM. But with Photoshop files, even after you save a file to disk, the program keeps a copy in RAM. This is what quickly allows you to undo a step.

Photoshop's use of memory is so funky that I want to take time out from this buyers' discussion here to cover the basics of how the program's memory-caching scheme, called *virtual memory*, works.

Virtual Memory

Virtual memory is a technique Photoshop uses to substitute hard disk space for RAM. If Photoshop doesn't have enough RAM to complete an operation, it makes use of free hard disk space on your computer. This will get the job done, but since accessing hard disk space is much slower than accessing RAM, Photoshop will operate much more slowly.

Both Windows and Apple's System 7.x have their own virtual memory schemes built into their operating systems. It's a good idea for you to understand the fundamentals of how your computer's operating system uses virtual memory, so you can prevent it from working at cross-purposes with Photoshop's scheme.

If you're a Windows user, you can improve Photoshop performance on your machine by setting your virtual memory to one-and-a-half to two times your physical memory (i.e., the amount of RAM installed on your machine).

For Windows 3.1 users:

1. Open up your Main program group.

2. Double-click on Control Panel.

3. Double-click on the Enhanced icon. The Enhanced dialog box appears.

4. Click on the Virtual Memory button.

5. Click on the Change>> button. The Virtual Memory dialog box expands.

6. In the part of the expanded dialog box that says "New Swap File Settings," choose None from the list box.

7. Click on OK.

8. At the "Do you want to make changes to the virtual-memory settings?" prompt, click on Yes.

9. Quit and restart Windows.

For Windows 95 users:

1. Click on the Start button, then choose Settings from the Start menu. Choose Control Panel from the Settings submenu.

2. The Settings folder opens, revealing a number of icons. Double-click on the Control Panel icon and double-click on System.

3. Click on the Performance tag in the System Properties dialog box.

4. Click on the Virtual Memory… button.

5. In the resulting Virtual Memory dialog box, click on the radio button that reads "Let me specify my own virtual memory settings." Enter equal values for the Minimum and Maximum sizes.

6. Click on OK.

7. Answer Yes to the Confirm Virtual Memory Settings dialog box.

8. Click on OK in the System Properties dialog box.

Figure 1.1 shows the dialog box for changing your virtual memory settings under Windows 95.

If you're a Macintosh user, you may already know that under System 7 virtual memory can let you open more applications than the amount of RAM you have would normally allow. On PowerMacs, virtual memory also reduces the actual amount of RAM each application needs to run if you've turned on the Modern Memory Manager in the Memory control panel.

However, there can be instances in which Apple's virtual memory scheme will directly conflict with Photoshop's. There's been little agreement over whether to turn off virtual memory when running Photoshop.

In most cases, you'd do well to just turn off Apple's virtual memory when you're using Photoshop—it's the path of least resistance. However, if you really have insufficient RAM and it's cramping your ability to use Photoshop, turning on System 7's virtual memory or using Connectix's RAM Doubler could alleviate the problem.

Figure 1.1

Optimizing the Windows virtual memory scheme

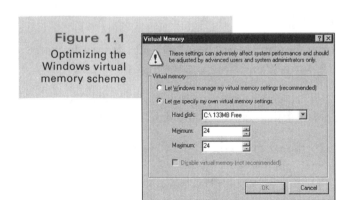

If you're going to use System 7's virtual memory, remember that you should never allocate more RAM to Photoshop than you physically have. And don't allocate *all* the RAM you have just to Photoshop—you have to account for what your system software uses and subtract at least that much from your total RAM before assigning RAM to Photoshop.

The following tip will walk you through allocating RAM to Photoshop on a Mac. It may look familiar to you—it's the same way you'd increase the memory for any Mac application—so you should feel free to skip it if you already know how to take care of giving a program more RAM.

tip

How to Increase RAM Allocated to Photoshop under the Mac OS

1. Make sure that you've quit Photoshop and are working from your Mac desktop. Select your Photoshop application icon and choose the Get Info command from the File menu (or press ⌘-Ⓘ).

2. Once you launch the Adobe Photoshop Info dialog box, enter a higher number in the Preferred size box to allocate more RAM to the application.

3. Remember the warning about not allocating more RAM to Photoshop than you physically have. If you have 24MB of RAM chips installed in your machine and your System software uses 6MB of RAM, don't make Photoshop's Minimum or Preferred size larger than 18MB. You can check the amount of RAM your system software uses by choosing "About This Macintosh" from the Apple menu in the Finder.

Figure 1.2 shows the dialog box for allocating more memory to Photoshop directly.

Figure 1.2
Allocating more RAM to Photoshop via its Get Info dialog box

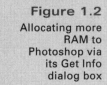

Adobe Photoshop™ 3.0 Info

Adobe Photoshop™ 3.0

Kind: application program
Size: 5.9 MB on disk (6,208,689 bytes used)
Where: Hard Drive: Adobe Photoshop 3.0:

Created: Sat, Sep 10, 1994, 11:33 PM
Modified: Mon, Aug 14, 1995, 8:05 PM
Version: 3.0.1 ©1989–94 Adobe Systems Incorporated
Comments:

—Memory Requirements—
Suggested size: 13284 K
Minimum size: 10500 K
☐ Locked Preferred size: 16000 K

Note: Memory requirements will decrease by 5,092K if virtual memory is turned on in the Memory control panel.

tip

● ●

General Suggestions for Speeding Up Photoshop

In addition to optimizing RAM and virtual memory, there are a few other instant fixes short of a major hardware purchase that can help your performance. Here are some everyday, all-around tips to help you on the spot when Photoshop suddenly goes sluggish:

👁 **Partition or defragment your drive.** Photoshop runs most smoothly when information on the hard disk is contiguous and unfragmented.

👁 **Turn off background printing.** Background operations can occupy CPU time and slow down Photoshop.

👁 **Remove unnecessary utilities, plug-ins, and extensions.** You can help free up memory by removing unused plug-ins, and this can extend the functionality of Photoshop. On a Mac, you can try rebooting with unnecessary extensions turned off before launching Photoshop. On a PC, you can switch to custom CONFIG.SYS and AUTOEXEC.BAT files to load only the most essential programs and utilities before loading Windows and Photoshop.

👁 **Cut down on your fonts.** How many different typefaces do you really need at any one time in Photoshop, anyway? A font management program like Suitcase (for Mac users) or Font Minder (for Windows users) can help track your font usage.

● ●

Scratch Disks (Hard Disk Space)

Since Photoshop will start using up your hard disk space when it runs out of RAM, what happens if you don't have that much free disk space to sparc? Photoshop calls the hard disk it's using for virtual memory a scratch disk. When that's no longer available, Photoshop will display an error message that says the scratch disk is full (see Figure 1.3).

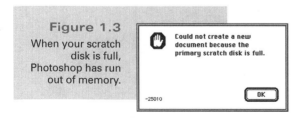

Figure 1.3
When your scratch disk is full, Photoshop has run out of memory.

Note that you can speed up working from the scratch disk by using a faster hard disk. Yes, it's time to take notes for your shopping list again. Heavy users may benefit from installing a disk array using a system called *RAID*, which stands for redundant array of inexpensive disks.

Photoshop requires that you have at least as much free hard disk space as you have RAM allocated to run the program. If you've allocated 32MB of RAM to Photoshop, you must have at least 32MB free on your scratch disk—even if you're only trying to open a tiny file.

To avoid running out of scratch disk space while working in Photoshop, however, you should keep considerably more than that available—at least three to five times as much free hard disk space as you have RAM. So if you're using 16MB of RAM, try to keep 48MB of free hard disk space available before launching Photoshop.

Check Your Memory Use on the Fly

There's an easy way within Photoshop to check your scratch disk efficiency and keep track of how much RAM your commands are using up: let your status line display it for you. The status line is a little text blurb that shows up in the lower-left corner of your document window in Photoshop. The default line reads "Document Size," but you can click on the status line to display a pop-up menu with your other options. You can select "Scratch Size," which shows how much RAM Photoshop is using and how much you have allocated—as shown in Figure 1.4. If the amount of RAM used (the first number shown) is larger than the amount allocated (the second number), then you'll know that Photoshop's virtual memory has kicked in.

How to Switch Your Scratch Disk

If you have a secondary hard disk connected to your computer with a large amount of free disk space or one that runs faster than your primary one, you might want to designate that drive as your scratch disk. To do so, you need to take the following steps.

1. After launching Photoshop, choose Preferences from the File menu. Macintosh users will select Scratch Disks from the Preferences

Figure 1.4
Changing your status line to "Scratch Size" will display a running count of how much memory is being used.

submenu; Windows users need to select Memory from the Preferences submenu. The Scratch Disk Preferences dialog box will appear (see Figure 1.5).

2. Click on the Primary pop-up menu and select the drive you want. Repeat this for the Secondary pop-up menu as needed.

Monitor Basics

A large color monitor is another must-have asset in your daily Photoshop work. Its screen size, sharpness, and color accuracy are all crucial factors in how comfortably and efficiently you'll be able to produce your designs.

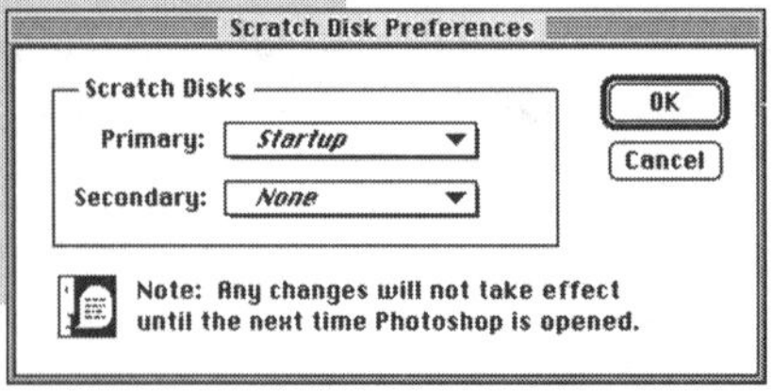

Figure 1.5
The Scratch Disk Preferences dialog box on a Mac

Again, there's a difference between the bare minimum Photoshop requires to run and what makes sense for day in, day out usage. If you're considering buying a new monitor, you'd do well to conduct some hands-on tryouts at a local computer dealer. You'll also be able to judge for yourself if you really need a 20- or 21-inch monitor (if you can afford it) or if you can live with a 17-incher.

You'll find more details on how colors are stored in computer memory in the "Filling in the Bits" section in Chapter 2.

Other features to look for in a monitor are a high refresh rate (at least 70Hz), which will help prevent screen flickering, and a small dot pitch (under 29 mm), where reducing the amount of space between the dots on your screen produces a sharper image.

Video Display Cards

Video cards determine several factors in conjunction with your monitor. First is the maximum resolution of the screen image, measured in the number of pixels displayed horizontally by the number of pixels displayed horizontally, such as 1280x1024 or 1600x1200. Note that certain monitors may place real or practical limitations on how high a resolution you can display. For example, using a 17" monitor at 1600x1200 will result in on-screen objects that are very hard to see. Second is the number of colors that can be displayed at a given resolution, such as 8-bit color (256 colors), 16-bit color (65,536 colors) or 24-bit color (16.7 million colors). If your video card allows you to add more memory, you can increase the number of colors it can display at higher resolutions.

Note that many Macintoshes have the functions of the video card on the computer's main logic board; most higher-end Macs can even accommodate more memory for their built-in video. However, you can always add a third-party video card if the built-in video capabilities don't meet your needs.

Some leading video card manufacturers include ATI, Diamond Multimedia, Radius, Matrox, Miro, and Imagine. Many newer video cards work on both Macs and PCs.

Video Accelerators

Some vendors sell accelerated video cards that help speed up screen redraws, but they may not do much to significantly enhance Photoshop's performance beyond that. If you have or purchase an accelerated video card, you should install the maximum amount of video RAM allowed for the card for best performance. The memory on the card affects only maximum resolution and bit depth, not speed.

Assessing Your System

Now that you've had a chance to review the various components in your system, you should have a good sense of whether you're well-equipped to do intensive Photoshop work with your current setup.

At some point, most computer owners wish for a bigger hard drive, more RAM, or a larger monitor. Photoshop users probably reach that point sooner—and start wishing more fervently—than almost anyone else.

Photoshop can place the kind of heavy-duty strain on your computer's memory resources that messy children do on their clothes in those laundry detergent commercials on TV. You don't need a top-of-the-line computer to run Photoshop—but you'll find that the amount of RAM you have, your processing speed, and the amount of free space on your hard disk will directly affect how much work you can accomplish and how quickly.

Table 1.2 shows an at-a-glance checklist for you to make sure you have at least the minimum system requirements for running Photoshop; some additional system recommendations are also listed.

Printers

As a Photoshop designer, you'll find that complicated printing demands come with the territory. You may have an office (or home office) laser printer to take care of checking designs-in-progress on paper, but still need full-color printouts for a client presentation. Or you may have to send out to your service bureau for color proofs, but also need to determine what option will save money while providing good color accuracy.

Table 1.2   System Requirements for Running Adobe Photoshop

	SYSTEM REQUIREMENTS IF YOU'RE USING A MACINTOSH...	SYSTEM REQUIREMENTS IF YOU'RE USING A PC...
CPU	Any 68020 microprocessor or later model, although at least a 68030 or 68040 is recommended. Any PowerPC model will be more than adequate.	An 80386 microprocessor or later model; a Pentium is recommended.
RAM	At least 6MB of free RAM is required (11MB for PowerMac users) but it's really not practical to try to get by with anything less than 16MB of RAM (24MB for PowerMac users).	Minimum requirements are at least 8MB of free RAM for Windows 3.1 users; 16MB for Windows NT. However, Adobe recommends 16MB of RAM (32MB for Windows NT users).
Hard disk space	At least 20MB of free hard disk space. On a practical level, though, you'll probably need much more.	At least 20MB of free hard disk space. On a practical level, though, you'll probably need much more.
System software	System 7 or higher; Adobe recommends at least System 7.1.2.	DOS 5 or later (DOS 6 is recommended) with Windows 3.1, Windows 95, or Windows NT.
Monitor	A 256-color monitor is required, but 24-bit color or a 32-bit video display card is even better, of course. You can still use images with more colors on a 256-color monitor, but you won't get an accurate screen display.	VGA+ display (256 colors at 640 by 480 resolution) is required. A 24-bit color display adapter is recommended.

At some point you may debate purchasing a new laser printer. A definite sign is if you engage in much freelance design—or work you'd rather take home at the end of the day—yet find yourself at your (or your client's) offices at godforsaken hours of the day or night, just to use the equipment!

Comparing printer models is beyond the scope of this book, but there are a number of more timely resources that can help you out. Periodicals for graphic designers, such as *Publish* and *PC Graphics & Video,* include product roundups and reviews of new printers; computer magazines like *MacWeek* and *PC Week* offer similar help for the specific platform you want. Once you've narrowed down your choices, a magazine like *Computer Shopper* can help you compare prices.

Laser Printers

Like a photocopier, a laser printer transfers finely powdered toner—please try to avoid breathing the stuff when you change the cartridge!—to paper to recreate the original image, then applies heat to hold it in place. One of the important factors that determines print quality is the resolution, or how many dots per inch the printer can create. A minimum resolution of 300 dpi is standard; an increasing number of models now offer 600 dpi and higher.

Color Printers

If you're lucky enough to own or have access through your job to a color printer, you know how many uses you can find for color printouts, despite their relatively high per-page cost. When you're outsourcing your color work, you should know the basic differences between the various categories of color printers:

- 👁 Color laser printers use toner cartridges like their black-and-white counterparts, but use separate cartridges for cyan, magenta, yellow, and black in separate passes to produce full-color pages.

- 👁 Inkjet printers produce colored dots from disposable ink cartridges.

- 👁 Thermal-wax printers run each page through multiple passes to apply wax-based colors.

- 👁 Dye-sublimation printers are the highest quality (and priciest) of the color printers described here, although color laser printers have begun to rival dye-sub printers in quality. Dye-sub printers use four separate dyes—cyan, magenta, yellow, and black—to produce a continuous-tone image with good color accuracy.

Imagesetters

A service bureau's imagesetters, or typesetters, typically output photo-sensitive paper or film that then needs to be developed in a separate step, like film from a camera. Imagesetter output is usually at a high resolution such as 1,270 or 2,540 dpi.

If you have a full-color print job to send to film, your service bureau will output a separate piece of film for each color—cyan, magenta, yellow, and black (these four are collectively called *process colors*), and any additional colors (called *spot colors*)—in your job. This film can be used to generate an *off-press proof* (so-called because they're making it from film alone, and not on the press) that will give a good indication of the final color output. These proofs are used by commercial printers at press time to help color-check the final product. If you're asked to look at and approve color for off-press proofs of your work, you'll probably see laminated proofs, such as Matchprints, FujiArt proofs (for process color work), or Chromalins (for spot color jobs).

Scanners

Scanners will widen considerably the range of source materials for your Photoshop graphics. With a scanner, you're free to copy old photographs, hand-drawn or painted artwork, textures from fabric swatches and household objects, doodles on napkins—almost anything you can put on a flat surface.

There are quite a few scanners in the home office category, generally priced from several hundred dollars up to about $1,200. Many low-end models aren't suitable for high-resolution Photoshop use, however, because they tend to produce muddy colors or dark overcasts on every scan—problems that will take valuable time to correct. Before you make a scanner purchase, solicit as much feedback as you can (for example, if you have Internet access, through the comp.graphics.apps.photoshop newsgroup) from other users who've had experience with the model you've chosen.

Depending on the level of design work you'll be doing, you may be able to contract out your scanning to a service bureau. You may really just need to work with low-resolution scans to position type and photos in a

magazine layout, let's say, while leaving it to your service bureau to swap in high-resolution scans that they produce before going to film output.

Whether you plan to purchase a scanner yourself or you simply write up purchase orders to have others do your scanning for you, you'd do well to understand the fundamentals of how scanners work and what quality you can expect from different kinds of scanners.

Flatbed Scanners

Most scanners sold for office and home office use are flatbed scanners, which resemble copying machines to a certain extent. After you place your artwork under the machine's cover, thousands of light beams pass over the original and reflect back information for a digitized reproduction. Some of the leading manufacturers of flatbed scanners include Agfa, Hewlett-Packard, La Cie, Microtek, Howtek, Relysis, Sharp, Epson, and Umax.

Resolution is just as important in scanning as it is in printing. The greater the *resolution* (measured here in pixels per inch, or ppi), the sharper your final image. Lower-cost scanners generally produce 600-ppi output; some boast 1200-ppi resolution but really use *interpolation*—filling in more colors and pixels after an initial scan—to approximate the claimed resolution.

Slide Scanners

If you ever have to digitize slides, you'll need a slide scanner to get the job done. These tend to have much better resolutions than flatbed scanners, up into the 5,000- to 6,000-ppi range. Some of the leading slide scan manufacturers include Nikon, Kodak, BarneyScan, and Polaroid.

Drum Scanners

The most professional scan output you can get is from a drum scanner, which rotates the original material on a drum and uses a stationary light source to scan the image. Since a drum scanner can cost $30,000—and is pretty massive, to boot—you'll probably have your service bureau produce these high-quality scans (at $25 to $100 a pop) for you.

tip

● ●

Show Your Scanner a Little TLC

To produce the sharpest scans, it's very important to keep your scanner as spotlessly clean as possible. Ideally, it should be clean enough to eat off of (not that I'd recommend doing so). Every time you lift the cover and use your flatbed scanner, the glass platen is vulnerable to dust, fingerprints, and grime. Try to keep a container of glass cleaner and a soft cloth handy to wipe off the platen as needed; a can of compressed air is also handy for getting rid of dust. If you ever need to scan something heavy or metallic that might scratch the platen, it's a good idea to put down a sheet of clear plastic first.

● ●

Further details on good scanning techniques appear later—in Chapter 12, "Print Production Essentials."

Calibrating Your Monitor

Calibrating your monitor will help you match the colors in an image called up on your computer screen with those in a full-color print piece using that image. Chapter 4, "Color Essentials," will cover in greater detail what monitor calibration can—and can't— do for you. For example, there are a great number of colors that can be displayed on computer monitors, which use the RGB (red, green, blue) color gamut, that are simply impossible to reproduce on press because they have no counterpart in the CMYK (cyan, magenta, yellow, black) color range. Therefore, there's no way to guarantee that the colors you see on your monitor can be reproduced in print. However, calibrating your monitor will go a long way toward ensuring that the contrast and grayscale also match. This is especially crucial because many images that seem vivid and sharp viewed on uncalibrated monitors will appear much too dark in print—and nothing ruins a printed piece faster than a dark overcast on all graphics that obscures all detail.

Monitors are also subject to a lot of variance every time you turn them on and off and as they warm up. They wear out over time, so the monitor you bought two years ago is probably a lot dimmer than it was when you first got it.

Despite all the good reasons to calibrate your monitor, it's something that many designers just never get around to doing. Many art directors and entire professional art staffs never fine-tune their monitors but still manage to get by. Maybe it's human nature, but it's the way people treat their television sets too: through careful tweaking you can add never-before-seen vivid and realistic colors, yet almost everyone settles for just plugging the thing in and turning it on.

Calibration programs judiciously reduce the brightness of your monitor's red, green, and blue channels. As a result, your monitor will be somewhat dimmer after you've calibrated it than before.

You can calibrate your monitor either through the program that's included with Photoshop (kind of a pain, but doable), or with any of a number of commercial monitor calibration programs like Radius's SuperMatch. There are also Web sites that will walk you through monitor calibration on the spot, as shown in Figure 1.6.

No matter which calibration method you use, there are some good all-purpose steps to take beforehand:

Figure 1.6

Stanley Rowin Photography maintains one of a number of Web sites that help readers calibrate their monitors on the fly.

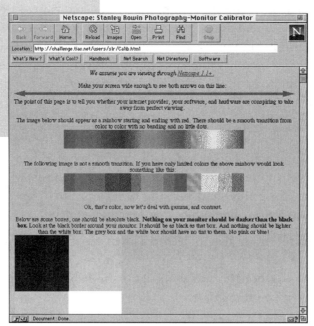

👁 Leave your monitor turned on for at least half an hour to stabilize the monitor display.

👁 Make sure the room lighting is set to the ordinary conditions you plan to maintain. It's best to close off all outside lighting as much as possible, because natural light tends to make colors look different on the screen at different times of day.

👁 Set your desktop pattern to a solid gray. Dithered gray or colored patterns can play tricks on your eyes during the calibration process. Mac users can change this by using the General Controls control panel. Windows 3.1 users can go to the Control panel and double-click on the Color icon to change their settings. Under Windows 95, background color is changed through the Display control panel.

👁 Fine-tune your monitor's brightness and contrast to the levels that look best to you.

Crash Course in Calibration Terminology

Here are the basic settings that you're tweaking when you calibrate your monitor. The next section—on using Photoshop's own built-in calibration—will walk you through how to refine these settings.

👁 *Gamma* is a numerical representation of an image's contrast. As the gamma increases, the contrast gets higher and the images get lighter. Lower gamma means less contrast and darker images.

👁 Your monitor's *white point* should be set to display the same color white of the paper stock you print on. Uncalibrated monitors tend to have a blue overcast that can be difficult to compensate for when you're trying to picture what an on-screen image will look like in print. Your monitor's white point is measured in degrees.

👁 Your monitor's *black point,* similarly, is the heaviest shade of black that can be displayed. Setting the black point helps ensure that shadows and dark areas display properly on your screen.

👁 Your monitor's *phosphors* are the values for its pure red, green, and blue hues.

Using Photoshop to Calibrate Your Monitor

If you're a Mac user, follow these steps:

1. Make sure that the Gamma control panel, which is included in Photoshop's Goodies folder, has been placed in your Control Panels folder. If it's not, you'll have to move it there and restart your machine. The Gamma control panel appears in Figure 1.7.

2. Double-click the Gamma control panel. Make sure that the On radio button in the lower-left corner of the dialog box is clicked.

3. Notice the various settings for Target Gamma near the top of the Gamma dialog box. Keep the default, 1.8. (It's only necessary to change this if you plan to output to video or slides, when it should be 2.2.)

4. Setting your monitor's gray levels is next. Click the Gamma Adjustment slider near the top of the Gamma control panel. Move the slider left or right until the strip looks as much like a single shade of gray as possible.

5. Next, you'll turn your screen's whites even whiter. Hold up a piece of white paper—the kind of paper stock you print on—beside your screen. In the Gamma control panel, click the White Pt radio button to select it. Drag the red, green and blue slider controls until you're happy with how your monitor's white matches the paper. If you use different paper stocks, you can save different calibration settings for each one.

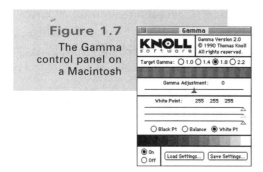

Figure 1.7
The Gamma control panel on a Macintosh

6. Now click the Balance radio button, to the left of the White Pt button. Dragging the red, green, and blue sliders can help you eliminate color casts that appear in the gray strip at the bottom of the dialog box.

7. Here's where you'll set the black point for your monitor. Click the Black Pt radio button, which is to the left of the Balance button. Drag the red, green, and blue sliders to eliminate any remaining color casts in the gray strip at the bottom of the dialog box, while maintaining definite gradations or bandings between each swatch. You should double-check your settings for White Pt, Balance, and Black Pt, because changes in all three affect the others' settings.

8. Close the Gamma dialog box by clicking the small square in the upper-left corner of the window. You will now need to launch Photoshop to finish the calibration process. Choose Preferences from the File menu, then select Monitor Setup from the Preferences submenu.

9. Your final settings are all made here within the Monitor Setup dialog box. First, click the Monitor pop-up menu and highlight your monitor on the list. The target gamma you set in the Gamma control panel reappears here. You can leave the White Point set at 6500° K. Click the Phosphors pop-up menu and choose a value that matches the arrangement in your monitor. If your monitor isn't on the list, you can get the right numbers from the manufacturer and enter them as custom settings. Click the Ambient Light pop-up menu and select the lighting setting that best describes the room you're in. Click OK when you're done.

Here are the steps to follow if you're a Windows user:

1. Make sure that Photoshop is launched, because you're going to access the calibration utility from within the program.

2. Choose Preferences from the File menu, then select Monitor Setup from the Preferences submenu. Click on the Calibrate button.

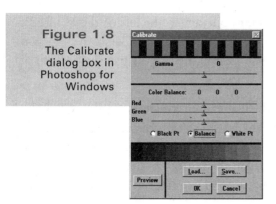

Figure 1.8

The Calibrate dialog box in Photoshop for Windows

3. Setting your monitor's gray levels is next. Click on the Gamma Adjustment slider near the top of the Calibrate dialog box, shown in Figure 1.8. Move the slider left or right until the strip looks as much like a single shade of gray as possible.

4. Next, you'll turn your screen's whites even whiter. Hold up a piece of white paper—the kind of paper stock you print on—beside your screen. In the Calibrate dialog box, click on the White Pt radio button to select it. Drag the red, green, and blue slider controls until you're happy with how your monitor's white matches the paper. If you use different paper stocks, you can save different calibration settings for each one.

5. Now click on the Balance radio button, to the left of the White Pt button. Dragging the red, green, and blue sliders can help you eliminate color casts that appear in the gray strip at the bottom of the dialog box.

6. Here's where you'll set the black point for your monitor. Click on the Black Pt radio button, which is to the left of the Balance button. Drag the red, green, and blue sliders to eliminate any remaining color casts in the gray strip at the bottom of the dialog box, while maintaining definite gradations or bandings between each swatch. You should double-check your settings for White Pt, Balance, and Black Pt, because changes in all three affect the others' settings.

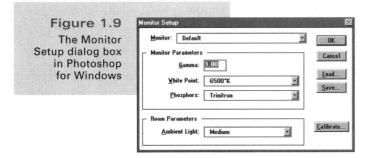

Figure 1.9

The Monitor Setup dialog box in Photoshop for Windows

7. Click on OK to close the Gamma dialog box. You should be back at the Monitor Setup dialog box, shown in Figure 1.9.

8. Your final settings are all made here within the Monitor Setup dialog box. First, click on the Monitor pop-up menu and highlight your monitor on the list. Set Gamma to 1.8; it's only necessary to change this if you plan to output to video or slides, when it should be 2.2. You can leave the White Point set at 6500° K. Click on the Phosphors pop-up menu and choose a value that matches your monitor. If your monitor isn't on the list, you can get the right numbers from the manufacturer and enter them as custom settings. Click on the Ambient Light pop-up menu and select the lighting setting that best describes the room you're in. Click on OK when you're done.

note Apple's ColorSync 2 technology—which lets Mac users get more predictable and accurate color from applications and input and output devices—came after the release of Photoshop 3, so there's nothing built into the current version of Photoshop to take advantage of ColorSync 2. Apple now offers ColorSync 2 Plug-ins for Photoshop for maintaining accurate color when importing and exporting across devices.

Acquiring Images

While Photoshop is an incredible image editing program, it doesn't usually do well as an image creation program. The following methods

describe some of the main ways designers get hold of the base images they use in creating their stunning compositions.

Scanning

As mentioned earlier, most designers regard scanning as a prime method for obtaining source material for new digital compositions. Typical uses include scanning photographs or original artwork, but a little brainstorming will help you come up with additional effects. For example, if you need an image of a household object like a safety pin or a textured pattern like denim, you can place the object right on the scanner's glass and scan the original. I've seen people scan telephone receivers, dinner napkins, leaves, and a roll of metallic wrapping paper. Please take care, though, not to scratch the scanner's glass and not to try scanning anything that could get inside the scanner and damage it—for example, a pile of sand!

Drawing Tablets and Software

If you're adept at traditional illustrating or cartooning, you can sketch straight into Photoshop. You'll probably be able to draw faster and more accurately with a pen-based graphics tablet than with a mouse or trackball, however. Wacom is a leading manufacturer of pressure-sensitive drawing tablets, which let you draw thicker lines by pressing harder on the tablet; CalComp and Kurta also offer pressure-sensitive graphics tablets.

Many artists also use other software such as Fractal Design Painter, Adobe Illustrator, CorelDraw, or Macromedia Freehand to create images that they later edit in Photoshop.

Video and Digital Cameras

If you're going to shoot a lot of your own photos for use in your Photoshop work, it might be worthwhile for you to invest in a video or digital camera to create electronic images on the spot.

Video cameras work with a video card installed in your computer. Many Macintoshes already have built-in video capabilities. For example, if you have an AV Macintosh, such as the 8500, you can attach the camera directly to the computer. Windows users may want to check out a device that grabs images from video such as the Snappy from Play, Inc. Most video cameras capture images at a resolution of only 72 ppi.

Digital cameras look like ordinary 35mm cameras for the most part, but save their images within the camera's built-in storage or to an attached hard drive. Leading vendors include Kodak, Casio, Logitech, Apple, Epson, and Nikon.

Photo Clip Art

Packaged clip art and stock photos can provide a quick fix if you need, say, a photo of a typewriter or a Stetson in a hurry. There are a great number of software vendors who sell clip art on CDs and all manner of packaged art collections. These clip art CDs can contain graphics in many different formats, such as Kodak's proprietary PhotoCD format or TIFF; the PhotoCD format is especially useful for stock art purposes, because you can open PhotoCD files in several different sizes and resolutions. Check your mail-order catalogs for Mac or PC software collections.

The best advice here is to view for yourself as much of the collection as you can before buying it. You'll feel gypped if you wind up purchasing a lot of cheesy images that don't really suit your needs.

Online Image Archives

If you have Internet access, you'll find there are a great many image archives at your disposal. There are Web sites that specialize in providing images devoted to a specific genre—say, scientific illustrations or celebrity photos. Many of these sites make public domain images available for free downloading, use, and alteration. Appendix B lists the URLs for some noteworthy image archives on the Web.

The large commercial online services like America Online and CompuServe also have graphics file libraries with a wide range of user-supplied, readily downloadable images. One nice feature about these file libraries is that they are searchable—if you need a photo of a frog in a hurry, let's say, you can do a search on the word "frog" and generate a list of all the images in the library that include "frog" in their file description.

 note Not all of the images you'll find in online archives are in the public domain. Some are uploaded by graphic designers advertising their services; others are copyrighted images that belong to companies or commercial photo archives. The "do unto others" rule is always a good one to live by: much as you wouldn't want others to reproduce your artwork with obtaining your permission first and giving you credit, don't take advantage of others by passing off their work as your own.

Summary

In this chapter you've learned about your system requirements for running Photoshop as smoothly and consistently as you'd like, the basics of printing and scanning terminology, what monitor calibration can and can't do for you, and obtaining source material for your Photoshop creations.

Straight ahead in Chapter 2, we'll look at the basics of opening and saving files in Photoshop.

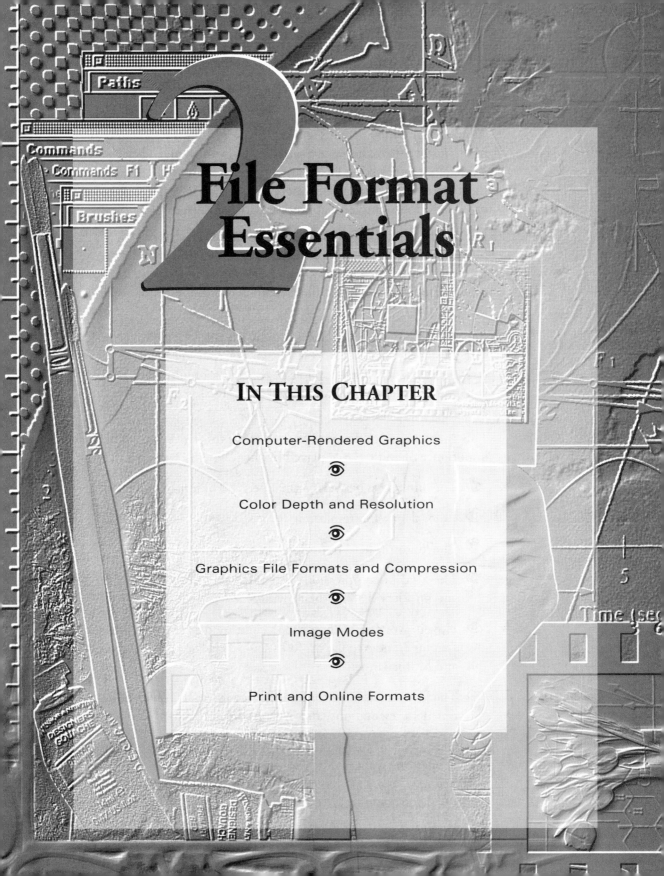

2 File Format Essentials

IN THIS CHAPTER

Computer-Rendered Graphics

◉

Color Depth and Resolution

◉

Graphics File Formats and Compression

◉

Image Modes

◉

Print and Online Formats

Whenever graphic designers and art directors discuss exchanging files, they constantly ask the same question: "How do you want me to send that?" We're not talking FedEx here—rather, the question is which of the many available graphics file standards and which color mode (RGB or CMYK, for example) is appropriate for your needs.

Like many other graphics applications, Photoshop has its own native file format, which shows up in your Save As... options under the File menu as Photoshop 3 (or the previous version, Photoshop 2). If you're using Windows 3.1, then a file in native Photoshop format will have the extension .PSD.

In practice, though, you'll probably only use the native Photoshop format during the creative process. When you're ready to send off your images to a client or use them in a page layout or multimedia program, you'll turn to one of the acronymized file standards: TIFF, EPS, JPEG, and GIF, among others.

This chapter aims to demystify graphics file formats by explaining the importance of and the role played by the following factors:

- 👁 The differences between bitmapped and object-oriented graphics

- 👁 Color depth and resolution

- 👁 The kinds of files Photoshop can save and open

- 👁 The kind of compression best suited to your particular images, and how it will affect their quality

- 👁 How to work with Photoshop's eight modes: Bitmap, Grayscale, Duotone, Indexed Color, RGB Color, CMYK Color, Lab Color, and Multichannel

- 👁 The file formats most commonly used for print publication, multimedia presentations, and Web graphics

You'll find that this chapter really only introduces the file formats and color modes; the real get-down-to-business examples and exercises are still to come in later chapters. If you have a burning graphic file format question, you should feel free to turn ahead to the appropriate section now. But do come back and read this chapter all the way through, because it will give you a good grounding in the underlying considerations to take into account when choosing from the variety of graphics format options you have as a Photoshop user.

Computer-Rendered Graphics: Bitmapped vs. Object-Oriented

Your graphics software uses two methods to store your images: *bitmapped* (or *raster-based)* and *object-oriented* (or *vector-based).*

From a designer's perspective, the terms also describe the different ways you would edit these graphics—with bitmapped graphics you edit the picture dot by dot, whereas with object-oriented graphics you can move lines, curves, and shapes independently of other image elements.

Bitmapped Graphics

Bitmapped graphics use a matrix of dots, or picture elements *(pixels),* to present the image (See Figure 2.1). The number of dots in a bitmapped graphic can vary, as can the number of colors available to each pixel. Scanned images are always bitmapped, as are graphics you

Figure 2.1

A sample bitmapped graphic; a close-up look reveals the dots that form the image.

get from paint or image-editing programs (like Photoshop), screen shots, and images captured on video. There are several standard file formats for bitmapped graphics, both platform-specific like PCX and BMP (for PCs) and PICT (for Macintosh), or cross-platform like GIF (Graphics Interchange Format), TIFF, and JPEG. You can save your Photoshop images in any of these file formats, depending on what's most appropriate for your needs.

Object-Oriented Graphics

When you draw a shape in a program like Adobe Illustrator that uses object-oriented graphics, you designate its size, border, fill colors, and so on. You can edit and move each shape around onscreen or between documents without affecting the other shapes. It's kind of like playing with Colorforms; you can layer your image's elements, then move them, then place them somewhere else—all without disturbing the rest of the scene.

Other programs using these kinds of graphics include Macromedia Freehand, CorelDraw, and AutoCAD. Object-oriented graphics files tend to be much smaller than bitmapped ones, which makes sense if you think about it—describing an object's general properties and dimensions is more efficient than storing all of an image's information on a pixel-by-pixel basis (see Figure 2.2).

Figure 2.2
A sample object-oriented graphic; a close-up still shows the image's curves.

Treating Bitmaps as Objects

It's possible to import a bitmapped image into an object-oriented graphics program as an independent object. For example, you can include a scanned image saved as an EPS (Encapsulated PostScript) file in an Illustrator file. You'll be able to rotate and stretch the object but not touch up individual pixels—those aren't editable within Illustrator.

There's another situation where it's useful to treat a Photoshop graphic like an object-oriented graphic, and that's when you want to use a Photoshop image as a *silhouetted image* in a page layout program. Silhouetted images let you overlap the object with other separate images or make text run around the image easily. You will need to save these files within Photoshop in EPS format, incidentally.

Chapter 6, "Filter Essentials," will describe the intricate but manageable process of creating *clipping paths* that let you treat bitmapped graphics like object-oriented ones.

Bringing Object-Oriented Graphics into Photoshop

The only kinds of object-oriented graphics that Photoshop will easily recognize and open are Adobe Illustrator and Dimension files in EPS format. If you use other kinds of drawing programs, you might be able to convert them to an Illustrator format and open them that way.

And while you can open up Illustrator EPS files in Photoshop, the program will *rasterize* the image elements—that is, turn them into pixels, so you won't get access to their object properties. There are three basic ways to bring Illustrator EPS files into Photoshop:

1. You can open an Illustrator EPS file from within Photoshop by choosing Open from the File menu, then selecting the file you want. This will call up the Rasterize Adobe Illustrator Format dialog box shown in Figure 2.3. From this dialog box, you can change the image's width, height, resolution, and color mode before you load it.

   You can also choose *anti-aliasing,* which will apply blended shades of gray to the edges of the image's objects to simulate the smooth curves in the original.

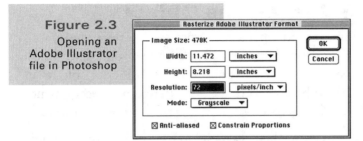

Figure 2.3

Opening an
Adobe Illustrator
file in Photoshop

2. You can place an Illustrator EPS file within an existing Photoshop document by choosing Place from the File menu, then selecting the file you want. The file will appear as a floating selection onscreen, and you can click and drag to reposition the graphic.

3. If you're using Illustrator 5, you can simply copy selections from an Illustrator document and paste them into Photoshop. The only shortcoming to this method is that quality will degrade if you need to resize the rasterized Illustrator object. To avoid that, return to Illustrator, do your resizing there, and only then cut and paste to Photoshop.

Color Depth and Resolution

One reason for the variety of graphics formats in current use is that different kinds of images lend themselves to different methods of information storage. Two properties that come into play here are color depth (how many colors an image has) and resolution (how many pixels it uses).

Filling in the Bits

Bitmapped file formats differ in terms of how many colors each pixel can carry. At this point it's necessary to digress a little into the fundamentals of computer memory. Each byte of computer memory includes 8 bits, and each bit has a value of 1 or 0. Thus, 1-bit graphics can only contain pixels with one of two values—black or white. In an 8-bit graphic, each of the 8 bits could have a value of either one or zero;

totaling up the potential combinations gives you 2^8, or 256 possible colors. In 24-bit graphics, each pixel has three bytes—that's a whole byte (8 bits) of information each for red, green, and blue hues. This yields 2^{24} or 16.7 million possible colors—which, as it turns out, are too many colors for the human eye to process. A 24-bit graphic, therefore, should appear very realistic to the viewer.

Naturally, 24-bit or larger images use a lot of memory—see Figure 2.4. To reduce those memory requirements, in certain circumstances Photoshop can employ a *color look-up table*—a CLUT—to display or convert your image to 8-bit by distilling the closest 256 colors. We'll revisit the CLUT scheme later in this chapter in the section on Indexed Color mode.

Resolution

We've already discussed how a bitmapped image really comprises a large collection of pixels laid out on a grid. When you measure a bitmapped

Figure 2-4

Different amounts of memory are allocated to graphics of different color depths.

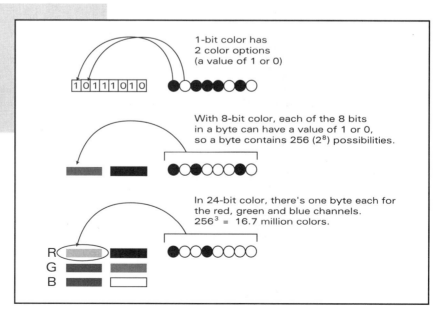

1-bit color has 2 color options (a value of 1 or 0)

With 8-bit color, each of the 8 bits in a byte can have a value of 1 or 0, so a byte contains 256 (2^8) possibilities.

In 24-bit color, there's one byte each for the red, green and blue channels. 256^3 = 16.7 million colors.

R
G
B

image, it's not enough to know how many inches tall or wide the picture is—you also need to know its *resolution*, or how many pixels fit in a certain unit of measurement, usually pixels per inch (ppi).

Let's say you have a 72-ppi image that measures 3 inches square. If you restrain the file size, you could resize that image to only 1.5 inches square without changing the number of pixels in it—instead they'll just double up to 144 pixels per inch. Doubling the physical measurements—6 inches across now, instead of 3 inches—will lower the resolution to 36 pixels per inch.

Figure 2.5

Resizing an image to change the resolution. With the "File Size" option checked, the number of pixels per inch changes, but not the number of pixels *altogether*.

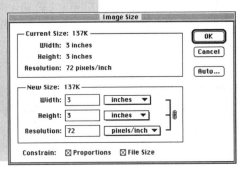

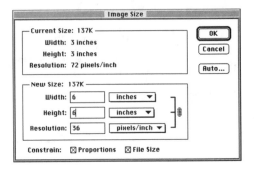

You can see this for yourself by creating your own sample RGB image in Photoshop measuring 3 by 3 inches with a resolution of 72 ppi. Choose Image Size… from the Image menu, as shown in Figure 2.5, and note how the resolution changes if you alter the height and width.

Here's a real-world example using your 72-ppi image measuring 3 by 3 inches. Service bureaus and professional printers will output your job using one of several standard line screens and for best results your graphics' resolution should roughly double that line screen. If the job will print using a 150-line screen, the general rule for you is to use a 300-ppi resolution for all your graphics. (Chapter 12, "Print Production Essentials," will cover this process at much greater length.)

So now you need to convert your 72-ppi image to a 300-ppi one. The math used here is a simple ratio, but Photoshop will take care of it all for you when you choose Image Size… from the Image menu, as shown in Figure 2.6, and enter your projected resolution (300 ppi). Make sure the File Size check box is checked. As you can see, your original 3-by-3 graphic now measures .72 of an inch on each side.

note

What happens if you don't restrain the file size—that is, you don't check the File Size check box—when you change the dimensions of the image? As you might expect, increasing width and height will boost the file size and reducing width and height will decrease your file size. However, this will cause resampling, which means Photoshop will add or subtract pixels in your image to meet whatever ratio you've imposed—and this can adversely affect the quality of your final image, as Figure 2.7 demonstrates.

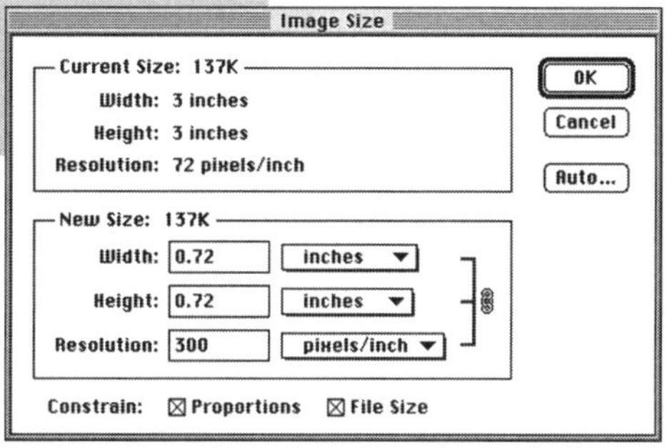

Figure 2.6
The Image Size dialog box

```
                           Image Size
 ┌─ Current Size: 137K ──────────────────┐      ┌──────┐
 │     Width:  3 inches                   │      │  OK  │
 │     Height: 3 inches                   │      └──────┘
 │     Resolution: 72 pixels/inch         │      ┌──────┐
 └────────────────────────────────────────┘      │Cancel│
                                                  └──────┘
 ┌─ New Size: 137K ──────────────────────┐       ┌──────┐
 │    Width:  [0.72]   [inches    ▼]  ─┐  │       │Auto..│
 │                                     ├  │       └──────┘
 │    Height: [0.72]   [inches    ▼]  ─┘  │
 │    Resolution: [300]  [pixels/inch ▼]  │
 └────────────────────────────────────────┘

   Constrain:  ⊠ Proportions   ⊠ File Size
```

Figure 2.7
After resampling, the image on the right loses the clarity of the image on the left.

Graphics File Formats

We've mentioned some file formats for bitmapped images but haven't yet talked about what these different formats will mean to you in your Photoshop work. Before we go any further, then, it's important to introduce the different kinds of file formats you can save and open in Photoshop.

Photoshop—which originated, incidentally, as a file format translation program—has over 20 graphics formats built in. It also lets you add plug-ins so you can open and export even more graphics file formats.

Here we'll just touch on the formats that you're most likely to use and the common applications where you'll find them. The sections that follow contain more practical information for how you'll use and think about these file formats—some contain compression schemes for keeping the images' physical file size low, and some should have certain color models (things like RGB or CMYK) assigned depending on what their end use is. Figure 2.8 shows some of the file formats we'll look at next.

Native Photoshop

While you're editing and tweaking your images, you'd do well to save all your files in Photoshop's native format. It lets you use all of the program's editing tools, commands, and filters. The Photoshop 3.0 format includes features unsupported by the earlier Photoshop 2.0 format, such as *layers* (discussed extensively in Chapter 5) and a compression scheme.

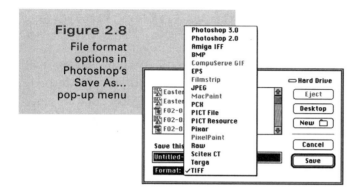

Figure 2.8

File format
options in
Photoshop's
Save As...
pop-up menu

Print Formats

When you're ready to finalize your images for use for print publication,
you'll want to save in one of the following major graphic file formats:

Encapsulated PostScript (EPS)

The main advantage of the EPS format is how it lets you use graphics
with clipping paths—images that can be silhouetted against others or
against other elements in a page layout program. As mentioned earlier,
EPS is a popular file format for object-oriented graphics, but you can
also open EPS files in Photoshop by rasterizing them (see "Bringing
Object-Oriented Graphics into Photoshop," earlier in this chapter).

Tagged-Image File Format (TIFF)

TIFF is a scanning standard for high-resolution grayscale images. It is a
very flexible file format, with options for compression and byte order—but it is also a platform-specific setting; Macs and PCs store TIFFs
in slightly different ways. TIFF is well-suited for manipulating large
images. Along with EPS, it's one of the two main formats for preparing
graphics for page layout programs.

Online Standards

If you're creating graphics for Web sites or other online distribution,
you'll need to save in one of the following formats.

CompuServe Graphics Interchange Format (GIF)

CompuServe originally designed GIF to enable users to transfer graphics files across its online service. Available on nearly all computer platforms, it's currently a standard format for Web graphics. It uses compression and limits the number of colors that can be displayed—two features that make it a logical choice for online transmission and display.

The format's widespread use was threatened in late 1994 and early 1995 because the compression scheme that CompuServe chose for GIF, called LZW (for Lempel-Ziv-Welch), is patented. After Unisys, one of the patent holders, discovered the use violation, it eventually reached an agreement with CompuServe over licensing software that displays GIFs. Unisys mainly wanted to collect royalties from developers who sell commercial programs using LZW that can create and display GIFs; it's OK for designers to create and distribute GIF files.

Figure 2.9

An interlaced GIF, shown in mid-display and as a completed image

A popular variant of the format called GIF89a displays graphics as interlaced—first a rough preview of the image appears, then gradually more detail emerges. With version 3.0.5, Photoshop began to include support for the GIF89a format.

Joint Photographic Experts Group (JPEG)

The JPEG format is named for the group seeking a compressible format for high-quality images that collaborated on its design. JPEG shrinks files down by using a lossy compression method, one that differs from the methods employed by the other compressible formats described here; you'll find more information on it later in this chapter, in the "Understanding Compression" section.

JPEG is a popular Web graphics format that has gradually gained wider acceptance by Web browsers. There is also an interlaced JPEG format, called progressive JPEG. There isn't yet a process built into Photoshop for creating progressive JPEGs, but there are several third-party plug-ins that can accomplish this including ProJPEG from BoxTop Software and JPEG Transmogrifier from inTouch Technologies.

Portable Network Graphics (PNG)

The PNG format was designed by a number of software developers after the licensing flap over GIF. PNG has a couple of advantages over GIF—it supports 64-bit images and uses a better and unpatented compression scheme. PNG also supports interleaving. It is not a standard file format included with Photoshop, but PNG plug-ins are available. Few Web browsers currently support PNG, however, which limits its usefulness so far.

On-screen and Multimedia Standards

The following low-resolution formats are optimized for on-screen viewing; Adobe supplies plug-ins for viewing these and several other file formats. For the most part, these formats have been in wide use with platform-specific paint programs.

PICT

PICT is the Macintosh native image resource format; if you take a screen capture on a Mac, it's saved as a PICT file. You can import PICT files into page layout programs—but it's not recommended for print production because it's a low-resolution format; PICTs have a resolution of 72 ppi.

You can also open and save a Photoshop file as what's called a *PICT resource*. This is a preview of a PICT image that can be stored in the resource fork of a Macintosh file. EPS files, for example, all contain a PICT preview in their resource forks.

BMP and PCX

BMP is the Windows native bitmap format; it is supported by many applications for Windows and OS/2. It can save up to 24-bit images, and has optional compression capabilities.

PCX originated as the native format for PC Paintbrush, the first paint program to run under DOS. The PCX format evolved and accumulated quite a bit of redefinition in a less-than-orderly way; as a result, the BMP format generally replaces it.

Filmstrip

This format is for opening and resaving a collection of frames from a video editing program like Adobe Premiere. You can only open an existing Premiere document in Photoshop, however—there's no way to save a file created in Photoshop as a Filmstrip document.

Special Interest Formats

A number of file format plug-ins come bundled with Photoshop, and we've already looked at a couple of them (GIF, BMP, Filmstrip). Most of the others, though, are of limited use to designers in general, and need only the briefest of mentions just in case the question "What're these for?" ever comes up. You can use these formats if you need to open (and sometimes save) files sent to you by anyone using one of these systems.

◉ **Amiga IFF**   The native file format for the now-defunct Amiga from Commodore.

◉ **MacPaint**   The file format for the Mac's first paint program. At best, you can use it to open old 1-bit MacPaint clip-art files; you can't save in this format.

◉ **Pixar**   Remember Pixar, the brains behind *Toy Story?* This format is for opening and saving still images for use with one of their 3-D rendering programs, like Typestry or RenderMan.

◉ **PixelPaint**   The file format for PixelPaint 1 and 2, the first 8-bit Mac paint application. (Its commercial success bit the dust about the time Photoshop entered the graphics scene, although the program is still around as PixelPaint Professional.)

◉ **Scitex CT**   A format used by high-end Scitex computers, which professional service bureaus use to produce color separations; the CT stands for *Continuous Tone.* Check with your service bureau first before sending images in this format; they'll probably tell you not to bother and just use TIFF instead.

◉ **Targa**   This format for TrueVision's video boards really belongs with the multimedia category, but its proprietary nature limits its use. You'd use it to superimpose still images and animation graphics onto live video.

When You're Left Guessing: Photoshop's Raw Format

Has this ever happened to you? You've received an image from a client for a project, but there's no indication what file format it's saved in and Photoshop won't open it for you. In desperation, you click the Show All Files checkbox in the dialog box you get when you choose Open from the File menu; now you can choose from a pull-down menu of file formats and try to open the file in specific file formats. After unsuccessfully trying to open the image in BMP, PICT, or other formats, you try Raw. A Raw Options dialog box appears and your heart soars—

you're going to be able to read this picture after all—but your hopes are soon dashed when you see the garbled mess that displays next.

The Raw format is designed as a free-for-all format for reading image data that's unknown as any other file format. It may be possible for you to recover the image data, although it helps if you know ahead of time what the image's dimensions should be. The Raw Options dialog box asks for several general kinds of information common to all graphics files. It first asks for the image's width and height in pixels; if you don't know them, leave both boxes blank and press the Guess button. The Photoshop program will then figure out likely dimensions. The Raw Options dialog box also asks you to identify how many channels are in the image, so it helps if you know if this should be an RGB file (with three channels: red, green, and blue) or a CMYK graphic (with four channels: cyan, magenta, yellow, and black). Finally, the dialog box prompts you to answer if the image file has any header information at the beginning of the file, as some graphics do. As you can see, though, if you already knew this kind of information about your file at hand, you'd probably already know what kind of graphics program you should be using to display or edit it!

Understanding Compression

It's not unusual for even a single Photoshop image to take up a significant amount of storage—10MB, 20MB, or even more, especially if you're dealing with 24-bit color images. Most graphics seem to travel in herds—you might have to wrangle dozens or hundreds of images for a full-length magazine, brochure, or book project. As a result, compression is a crucial feature built into many graphics formats.

Lossy Compression

Lossy compression shrinks an image by discarding information that is less important to visual perception—hence, there will still be a loss of data, though a virtually imperceptible one, after it is decompressed. The JPEG method is the main lossy compression scheme. For scanned and photographic images like that shown in Figure 2.10, lossy compression will create a significantly smaller file without much degradation of image quality. It's less suitable for graphics of line drawings or containing only a few solid colors. Since lossy compressed files can't be totally reconstructed, it's a good idea to save an uncompressed version of the image if you plan to edit it any further in the future.

Lossless Compression

Formats that use lossless compression, such as TIFF or GIF, have only moderate levels of compression—but retain image data in its entirety. Although the resulting file size of a lossless compressed image is larger than the equivalent file saved as a JPEG, it will display more quickly onscreen. Lossless compression formats are better for reducing file sizes of uncomplicated images such as icons or logos than for detailed photographs.

Figure 2.10

Lossy compression is better suited to photos than to simple line art. Compare the highest-quality JPEGs on the left with their low-quality JPEG counterparts on the right. The quality of the line art image on bottom right suffered much more than the photo of the puma at top right.

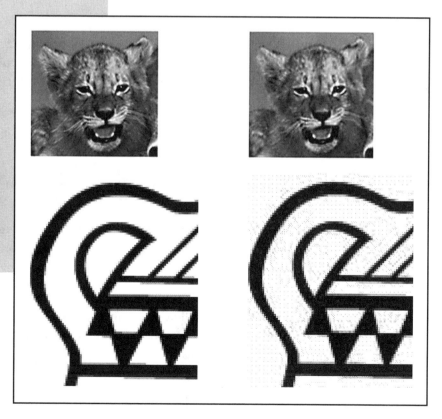

Figure 2.11

The TIFF format's LZW compression scheme is optional.

TIFF Options

Byte Order
○ IBM PC
◉ Macintosh

☐ LZW Compression

OK
Cancel

There are several popular schemes for lossless compression. Photoshop's native format and BMP use one called *Run-Length Encoding (RLE)*. GIF uses the general-purpose LZW (described earlier in this chapter), which is not specifically tailored to compress graphic images. TIFF can use a variety of compression methods.

For most of these formats, there's no way to turn this compression off; with TIFF, however, you do have the option not to use any compression at all, as the dialog box in Figure 2.11 attests.

Image Modes

As you create new documents in Photoshop, you'll notice that its default image mode is RGB Color. Many of your design projects, however, will probably require you to convert to another color mode. Some examples include:

👁 When preparing graphics for four-color printing, you'll need to convert to CMYK color mode.

👁 When you're designing a series of icons for a Web site using the same color palette, you'll need to save in Indexed Color mode.

👁 When using duotones, (images with two inks, usually black and one other color, superimposed on each other), you'll need to switch to Duotone mode.

Additionally, to make use of some file formats or apply various Photoshop filters, you'll need to convert to a different image mode. For example, to save in GIF format you'll need to convert to either Indexed Color mode or Grayscale.

I've included some brief descriptions and features of Photoshop's color modes. You can find and experiment with them by choosing each item

Figure 2.12
Sample Bitmap
image

separately under the Mode menu. These descriptions are very intro-ductory—you'll get a better look at each mode's features as you progress through these pages.

Bitmap

Photoshop's Bitmap mode really describes 1-bit images—black-and-white only, no colors or grays. This mode is the most limited; you can't use any filters and you can't scale or distort images in Bitmap mode. Since you can't use any shades of gray, any features that would compel their use—like anti-aliasing, the Smudge tool, and the Blur tool—are unavailable.

Since 1-bit graphics are pretty basic by nature (see Figure 2.12), there aren't really any restrictions in terms of what file format you can save them in.

Grayscale

In Grayscale documents, you have access to all of Photoshop's filters and editing and painting tools. Most of the time that you're in Grayscale mode you'll be working with 8-bit images including up to 256 shades of gray (see Figure 2.13). If your final printed piece is one-color, how-ever, the number of visible shades of gray will be cut way down.

Like Bitmap mode, Grayscale mode lends itself to saving in any of Photoshop's available file formats.

Figure 2.13
Grayscale images, like that shown at left, have greater depth and dimension than their bitmapped counterparts, like the one shown at right.

Duotone

Duotone mode lets you enhance grayscale images so you can print them using one, two, three, or four different colors of ink (called monotones, duotones, tritones, and quadtones, respectively).

If you work on two-color print pieces, then Duotone mode will be your friend. It lets you produce a greater range of tones than would be available with either single ink alone. Let's say you're designing a two-color newsletter in black and one other ink, or spot color. Your range of possibilities for introducing color include all shades and blends of the black ink, all shades and blends of your second color, and—with duotones—combinations of both inks together.

Before you can convert an image into a duotone, it must first be in Grayscale mode. To save your duotones for use with page layout programs, you'll need to save them as EPS files. (The only other file formats available are Photoshop's native format and Raw.)

Chapter 12, "Print Production Essentials," gives step-by-step details for converting a grayscale image into a duotone.

Indexed Color

Indexed Color mode is useful if you specifically want to create 8-bit, 256-color images—for example, if you want to guarantee how images will appear to users whose monitors have limited color capabilities. One very popular use for this mode is in designing Web graphics; it's also a natural for multimedia and on-screen presentations.

Indexed-color images draw from a table of 256 colors, called a color look-up table (CLUT), chosen from the full 24-bit palette. You can create a new CLUT every time you convert an RGB or CMYK image to Indexed Color. However, it's also useful to save a CLUT if you want to create a number of related graphics that all use the same color palette—say, a number of very well-coordinated, related icons.

There are some limitations in editing in Indexed Color mode. Anti-aliasing, the Smudge tool and the Blur tool are unavailable, because that could introduce new colors not in the CLUT.

You can save indexed-color images as CompuServe GIF, PICT, Amiga IFF, BMP files, or in Photoshop's native format. If you need to export an indexed-color image to a page layout program, you should convert it to CMYK mode; the image will still only contain 256 colors at most, though.

See Chapter 13, "Web Graphic Essentials," for some roll-up-your-sleeves details for working with Indexed Color mode and creating a CLUT.

RGB Color

The RGB color model, which is what your computer monitor is based on, defines all possible colors as percentages of red, green, or blue. Devices like televisions and computer monitors produce color by emitting red, green, and blue light beams. As a result, RGB mode is appropriate for any kind of on-screen graphics viewing or editing.

As mentioned earlier, RGB Color is Photoshop's default mode. With an RGB Color document open, you have access to all of Photoshop's image-editing menus, filters, and commands.

RGB Color is one of several modes where you can view the separate color components, or channels, that make up the format. Here's how to use the Channels palette:

1. Open or create any document in RGB Color mode.

2. Choose Palettes from the Window menu, then choose Show Channels from the Palettes submenu.

3. After the Channels palette opens, you should see four channels: each of the RGB channels, and a composite channel on top (see Figure 2.14).

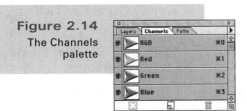

Figure 2.14
The Channels palette

4. You can look at and edit each channel individually, if you like. Toggle among channels by clicking on the name of the channel you want in the Channels palette. You can also toggle between channels by pressing their assigned key combinations, which show up next to the channel names. To view the red channel alone, for example you'd press ⌘-1 on a Mac (or Ctrl-1 on a PC). Press ⌘-2 (Ctrl-2 on a PC) for the Green channel, and ⌘-3 (or Ctrl-3) for Blue. Go back to the composite view by pressing ⌘-0 (or Ctrl-0). Notice that the listings for the channel(s) that are viewable at any given time appear colored in gray in the Channels palette.

• •

Channel Palette Shortcuts

You can choose to view and edit more than one channel at a time. Highlight the first channel you want to view by clicking on its name in the Channels palette, then hold down Shift as you click on the second name. Figure 2.15 shows an image with just the Red and Blue channels in view.

• •

Chapter 7, "Advanced Filter Essentials," includes a much more extensive discussion of channels.

Figure 2.15
Selecting several channels to view at once

CMYK

If you create graphics for four-color print production, you'll need to save your images in CMYK format. CMYK divides an image into four channels—one each for cyan, magenta, yellow, and black, corresponding to the inks used in four-color printing.

You can convert from CMYK to RGB and back again, but you should try to avoid this because there are some hues in each mode that don't exist in the other—and this can cause you to lose some colors along the way. For that reason, if you obtain an image to edit that's already in CMYK mode—for example, if your service bureau returns high-end, drum-scanned CMYK images—you're better off keeping CMYK even if you've already calibrated your monitor for RGB.

CMYK images can be saved in many formats, including TIFF, EPS, JPEG, native Photoshop format, Scitex CT, and Raw. For four-color printing and exporting to page layout programs, TIFF and EPS are the most common.

Lab Color

Lab Color is a device-independent mode, designed to display consistent colors no matter what kind of computer system or monitor is in use. It's actually the internal color model that Photoshop uses when converting between RGB and CMYK.

Although not as well-known as RGB or CMYK, it's really the safest color mode choice when you need to export an image for editing on another computer system, since you won't risk converting any information or changing how it looks. Files in Lab Color mode can be saved in TIFF, EPS, native Photoshop, or Raw format.

Multichannel

Multichannel is a general-purpose mode that can contain a number of 8-bit channels. If you delete a channel from an RGB, Lab, or CMYK image, Photoshop automatically switches over to Multichannel mode.

If you want to experiment with channel conversions or import extra channels into your images, you'll probably find Multichannel very useful

for intermediary steps. Otherwise, you may never find uses for Multichannel in your daily work.

Images in Multichannel mode can be saved only as native Photoshop or Raw files.

Print and Online Formats

When you're ready to distribute your artwork, you need to know which file formats make the most sense for your purposes, and save and distribute your images accordingly. To that end, this section covers how to make your images readable whether they'll appear in print, in an on-screen presentation, or displayed online.

Putting It on Paper

Whenever you create graphics for use in a page layout program like QuarkXpress or Adobe PageMaker, you should convert them to CMYK and save them in TIFF or EPS format.

I mentioned earlier that if your Photoshop graphics use clipping paths to simulate object-oriented graphics, you'll need to save your files as EPS; this is the main reason for choosing EPS over TIFF as a file format for images in print publications. Actually, there's now a method for saving clipping paths in TIFF files that can be read by Adobe PageMaker 6, but I wouldn't recommend it unless QuarkXpress supported it as well.

TIFF has a lot of advantages over EPS. With a TIFF, you can make some changes in QuarkXpress or PageMaker, such as applying a new background color to or changing the halftone frequency of the graphic. EPS doesn't let you do that; its file information is a self-contained unit that simply gets downloaded straight to the printer when called upon.

The second reason affects processing time when your print job is output. If your printing needs use only a fraction of your graphic information—say, only one corner of an enormous graphic will appear on the page—then using TIFF will speed things along. An EPS must be processed in its entirety even if only a small portion will actually print. Similarly, TIFF is a little more efficient in printing when the settings call for a lower resolution than the image is optimized for, and in color separation (although it needs to take time out to generate an image preview, which EPS files already contain).

Another common use for EPS is practiced by service bureaus that make high-resolution scans for their customers. When they save these high-resolution CMYK images in EPS format, they turn on an EPS option called DCS (Desktop Color Separation) that saves one image in five different files—one for each color channel, and a low-resolution, composite file. The service bureau will return the much smaller, low-res composite file to the customer to work with; when the time comes to print the job, the service bureau makes use of the other image files. Service bureaus like this EPS format because it will make graphics print faster, instead of tying up their imagesetting equipment for many hours.

The different uses for TIFF and EPS formats are discussed further in Chapter 12.

Multimedia Applications

If you plan to use your images in presentations viewed onscreen—for example, in slide shows or demos—your requirements are less demanding than for print output. You can keep the image mode at RGB because you're still adhering to an on-screen format; bitmapped file formats like PICT, BMP, or PCX are usually suitable. Your best guide is to find out what file formats the multimedia software you're exporting to can accept.

As mentioned earlier, Photoshop also has a Filmstrip file format option that's included specifically to let you open and save files from multimedia authoring programs like Adobe Premiere. You can use a number of other common formats to create and edit images as single from frames for Macromedia Director or Adobe Premiere, including PICT.

Serving Up Web Graphics

If you plan to serve up your graphics to the Web, your most likely choices come down to the two most popular Web graphics formats: GIFs (using lossless compression) or JPEGs (using lossy compression), until PNG gets wider support.

Table 2.1 Matching Uses with Image Modes and File Formats

REAL-WORLD USE:	USE THIS IMAGE MODE:	SAVE IN THIS FILE FORMAT:
Artwork for full-color printing	CMYK	TIFF or EPS
Black-and-white line art	Bitmap	BMP (for PC users) or PICT (for Mac users). Resolution must be very high to prevent jagged edges.
Grayscale halftones for printing	Grayscale	TIFF
Simple Web graphics	Indexed Color	GIF
Highly detailed, photorealistic Web graphics	RGB	JPEG
Graphics for slide shows and digital video	RGB	TIFF, BMP, PCX, or PICT for single frames; Filmstrip (for a collection of frames); Targa (if you're using a TrueVision video board)

The discussion earlier in this chapter about which kinds of graphics are better suited for lossy vs. lossless compression should help simplify your decision for your Web design efforts. You should also consider that GIF is an 8-bit format, so it can only represent up to 256 colors. If you save a 24-bit color TIFF with millions of colors to a GIF, you'll obviously lose some clarity as the system *dithers* the colors—that is, mixes pixels in the available color range in an attempt to reproduce all the actual colors in the 24-bit image.

Table 2.1 summarizes the potential applications for your graphics and what the most appropriate color modes and file formats are for each situation.

Summary

This chapter covered a lot of ground to prepare you for working with all kinds of graphic file formats with various color models, compression schemes, and end uses. With all this material for common ground, you're well-equipped to start planning what shape your creations will take.

Coming up in Chapter 3, we'll dip into Photoshop's tool palette and get started on some tips and techniques for painting and image editing.

Toolbox and Palette Essentials

IN THIS CHAPTER

Toolbox Overview

Hand and Zoom Tool Shortcuts

Selection Tools

Moving Pixels and Cropping Selections

Type, Painting, and Drawing Tools

When you're ready to start tooling around in Photoshop—literally—you'll want to take a good, long look at the Toolbox and experiment with your options there. Most Photoshop tools can be really easy to understand, but their best features are not very intuitive. This chapter aims to help you discover the powerful uses you wouldn't find through casual dabbling.

Straight ahead, we'll cover the following topics to give you a thorough grounding in how to manipulate Photoshop's tools, their associated palettes, and the other icons represented in the Toolbox:

- What each of the tool icons stands for, and what additional options for controlling these tools are available to you

- Other Toolbox controls, including changing the foreground and background colors

- Using the selection tools

- Creating typographic effects with the Type tool

- Painting and drawing tips, using tools, and the Brushes palette

- Using the editing tools for image touch-ups

When you first launch Photoshop, the Toolbox should appear by default on the upper left side of your screen; however, you can move it anywhere on the screen you like. If you moved or hid the Toolbox the last time you'd used Photoshop, it'll remain moved or hidden until you change its position. In other words, you can always find your tools just where you left them.

The Toolbox is one of a number of *palettes* in Photoshop. Similarly, the other Photoshop palettes—which can be accessed by choosing Palettes from the Window menu—can be repositioned anywhere you want onscreen. These *floating palettes* will remain in those positions until you move them, or choose a menu command from the Palettes submenu of the Window menu to hide them. The palettes are also highly customizable; each is represented by a folder-like display. You can pick up these folders by the tabs and reposition them into groupings with other palettes. As you grow more accustomed to using Photoshop, you may find that there are certain palettes you use more frequently; you can then take advantage of their customizable design to keep together the palettes you like to use the most.

You'll encounter these extremely useful palettes as you progress through this book. For now, it's enough for you to take a look at the menu commands you'll see listed under the Palettes submenu of the Window menu. These let you view and hide the following palettes: Brushes (used by the painting tools); Options (which relates to whichever tool is currently highlighted); the Picker, Swatches, and Scratch palettes (all involve choosing colors); Layers (covered in Chapter 5); Channels (covered in Chapter 7); Paths (covered in Chapter 6); Info (a highly useful reference palette); and Commands (which displays current keyboard shortcuts).

note   **You can press the Tab key to toggle between showing and hiding the Toolbox. This also hides and reveals any floating palettes.**

Toolbox Overview

A couple of the positions in the Toolbox actually contain more than one tool. For the icons that contain more than one tool, Mac users can hold down (Option) (Windows users can press (Alt)) as they click on an icon to toggle to the next option. For example, (Option)-clicking the Marquee tool key will toggle between the Rectangular and Elliptical Marquee tools.

Figure 3.1 shows the Toolbox and its parts.

● ●

tip   ### Using the Keyboard to Select Tools

In addition to just clicking the tool you want, you can also select an icon by pressing its assigned key on the keyboard. Each key assignment is a single letter without using any modifier keys, so the instructions given here apply to both Mac and Windows users. Figure 3.2 shows the keystroke you would press to select each tool.

For the icons that contain more than one tool, pressing that icon's keystroke again will toggle you to the next option. For example, pressing (O) three times will select the Dodge, Burn, and Sponge tools in turn.

● ●

Figure 3.1

The icons that make up the Toolbox

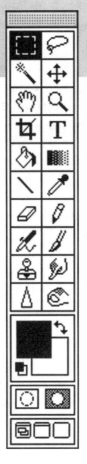

Double-clicking an icon will call up that tool's Options palette, where you can specify more settings for using that tool. (You can also call up the Options palette from the menu bar: choose Palettes from the Window menu, then choose Show Options from the Palettes submenu.)

note   If you switch tools while the Options palette is on the screen, the palette's display will change to show the correct options for whatever tool is currently selected.

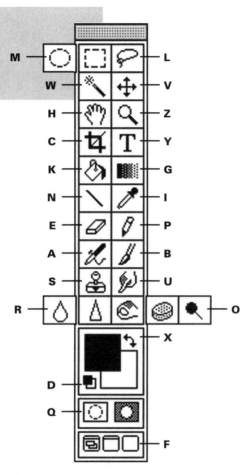

Figure 3.2

The Toolbox icons and their associated keystrokes

tip Any modifications you make to a tool's options remain in memory until you actively change them again. There is a pull-down menu on the right side of the Options palette you can use to either reset a specific tool's settings or to reset all the tools to their default values (see Figure 3.3).

Before discussing the tools themselves, let's look at the bottom of the Toolbox—it contains some special controls that affect the whole process:

👁 **Color control box** This area controls the current foreground and background colors. If you delete an area onscreen, it will fill with

Figure 3.3

Resetting a tool's options to its default values

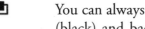

the background color you've chosen. If you add anything to an image, such as drawing a line or filling in a selected area, you'll apply the foreground color. We'll cover masks at great length and with gusto in Chapter 7, "Channel and Mask Essentials."

Clicking on either the foreground or background color will call up Photoshop's color palette, where you can click to choose from a dazzling array or type in a color's numeric value from one of several color modes—i.e., RGB, CMYK, or Pantone color models.

You can always quickly revert to Photoshop's default foreground (black) and background (white) colors by clicking the Default Colors icon (or pressing D).

The Switch Colors icon lets you reverse your foreground and background color selections. You can click the icon or press X to activate this.

Mask mode box In Quick Mask mode, you can use painting tools to extend the boundaries of a selection area—that is, you can make a selection on a pixel-by-pixel basis if you're having difficulty defining a precise area onscreen with just the ordinary selection tools (Marquee, Lasso, or Magic Wand). Don't worry, you don't need to understand at this point how or when to use this option; I just feel compelled to mention the Quick Mask mode here because it does appear in the Toolbox. When no document is open onscreen, this option is unavailable. We'll cover masks in fuller detail in Chapter 7, "Channel and Mask Essentials."

Clicking here will bring you into Quick Mask mode.

Clicking here will return you to Normal mode.

👁 **Screen display mode box** Photoshop gives you several options for hiding or displaying whatever stuff is on your screen besides the image you're editing.

The leftmost icon shows the standard window, which is your default display. With this option, your document's title bar, scroll bars, and status line (for showing memory usage) are all shown onscreen; you also see your menu bar at the top of the screen.

The center icon activates a setting Photoshop calls "full screen with menu bar." This hides all the accouterments about your image—the title bar, scroll bars, and status line. The menu bar remains at the top of your screen, and a gray background fills the rest of your screen. Figure 3.4 shows the same image in standard view and as full screen with menu bar.

The rightmost icon activates a setting Photoshop calls "full screen without menu bar." Now even the program's menu bar is hidden, and a black background fills in behind your image. Figure 3.5 shows the image used in Figure 3.4 in this mode.

Hand and Zoom Tool Shortcuts

Need to look at different parts of your image and it takes too long to use the scroll bars to move around? You can use the Hand or Zoom tools to change what part of your image is shown onscreen without affecting its placement.

The Hand Tool 🖐

The Hand tool drags your image so you can see a different portion of it onscreen. It's helpful for scrolling through an image that's too large to fit in the active window. No matter what tool is selected, you can always temporarily access the Hand tool by pressing the spacebar on your keyboard.

●●●

tip A quick way to fit the entire image in your window at once after looking at a magnified view is to double-click the Hand tool. (Unlike the other

Figure 3.4

A document in standard view, and hiding interface elements in the "full screen with menu bar" mode

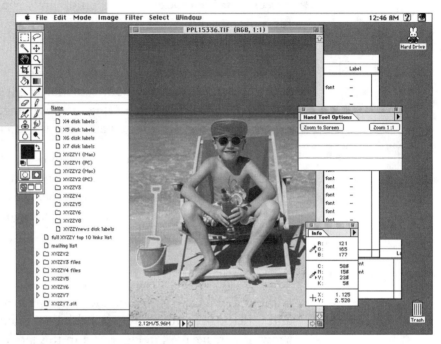

Figure 3.5

Hiding all interface elements—including the menu bar. You can still toggle floating palettes on and off.

tools, double-clicking the Hand won't call up the Options palette.) If you have the Options palette open already, you can accomplish the same effect by clicking the Zoom to Screen button. There's also a Zoom 1:1 button that will create 100 percent view size—that is, one screen pixel for one image pixel. Figure 3.6 shows the Hand tool's Option palette.

• •

The Zoom Tool

With the Zoom tool, you can change the magnification of the image you're working on. Select the Zoom tool and click anywhere in your image to double the magnification size. Your document's title bar gives

Figure 3.6

The Hand tool's Option palette

information about what magnification level you're at. For example, if it reads 1:2, that means one screen pixel represents two of your image's pixels. If you click in this image a couple of times with the Zoom tool, you could see a ratio of 4:1 on the title bar; here, four screen pixels represent just one of your image's pixels (see Figure 3.7). You can also use the Zoom options under the Window menu to set the screen-to-image pixel ratio.

tip

Here are some useful shortcuts I've found for zooming in and out of images:

1. You can click and drag with the Zoom tool, creating a marquee on a portion of your image, to magnify just that selected area.

Figure 3.7

Two views of the same image after magnification with the Zoom tool

2. It's easier to use the keyboard commands for zooming (⌘-+ and ⌘-– for Mac users; Ctrl-+ and Ctrl-– for Windows users) than either the Zoom tool or the menu commands.

3. You can zoom out to the maximum magnification possible by pressing ⌘-Option-+ (for Mac users) or Ctrl-Alt-+ (for Windows users). Similarly, ⌘-Option-– (for Mac users) or Ctrl-Alt-–(for Windows users) will zoom in to the minimum possible magnification.

4. When another tool is selected, you can zoom in quickly by pressing ⌘-Spacebar (for Mac users) or Ctrl-Spacebar (for Windows users), while adding Option (for Mac users) or Alt (for Windows users) lets you zoom out.

Selection Tools

Making selections in Photoshop is what gives you so much control over editing parts of an image; the selection feature lets you apply effects like blends and filters to portions of your image while leaving other parts completely untouched. The areas you select are displayed onscreen within a crawling, blinking border of *marching ants.*

tip   **Hiding the Marching Ants Border**

After you apply a special effect to a selection, you may want to see what your image looks like without the marching ants border in place. You could deselect the border (Mac users, press ⌘-D; Windows users, press Ctrl-D), but what if you still need to have that area selected for other effects? You can just hide the marching ants (Mac users, press ⌘-H; Windows users, press Ctrl-H), instead of deselecting them entirely.

Marquee Tips 🔲 ⬭

When you select the Rectangular or Elliptical Marquee tool, your cursor will change to a crosshair. Clicking on your image creates a starting point for your selection, and you can drag your pointer in any direction to enlarge your selection area.

You can also make your first click the center of the selection instead of an edge point. To accomplish this, Mac users can hold down Option

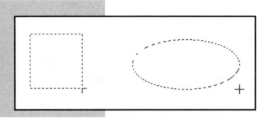

Figure 3.8
Clicking and dragging to create rectangular and elliptical selections

(Windows users hold down (Alt)) before clicking. Figure 3.8 shows the results of clicking and dragging to create a selection.

● ●

tip   **Adding To or Subtracting From a Selection**

Let's say you want to apply a filter or some other effect to two separate, noncontiguous areas. It's possible for you to make multiple selections at once by holding down (Shift) after you make your first selection; you can then use one of the selection tools to grab another portion of your image while the first selection remains highlighted.

Alternatively, you can subtract a portion of your current selection by holding down (⌘) (for Mac users) or (Ctrl) (for Windows users) as you carve out a second selection.

It's even possible for you to create a selection that includes just the overlapping area between two selections; hold down (⌘)-(Shift) (for Mac users) or (Ctrl)-(Shift) (for Windows users) as you select both areas. I think of these as

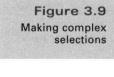

Figure 3.9
Making complex selections

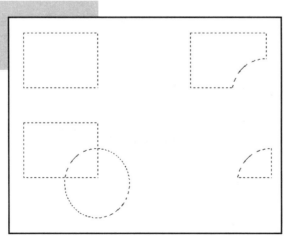

Figure 3.10

Setting options for the Marquee tool

"subset" selections because they remind me of those illustrations of sets and subsets from math class in grade school. Figure 3.9 demonstrates how to add and subtract from selections and create "subset" selections.

● ●

Double-click the Marquee icon to call up the tool's options, as shown in Figure 3.10. From this option palette, you can control your selection's shape, size, and *feathering*—an effect to smooth the transition between the areas inside and outside the selection's border.

Drawing a Perfect Square or Circle

The simplest method is to press ⟨Shift⟩ as you click and drag your selection. This will constrain your selection's height and width to identical dimensions.

You can also constrain the selection's dimensions using the Marquee options. Type 1 in both the Width and Height boxes to draw a perfect square or circle. The Constrained Aspect Ratio setting is also useful if you're creating a design that requires shapes with the same proportions but different sizes. Figure 3.11 shows how to set a constrained aspect ratio in the Marquee tool's option palette.

Creating a Selection of Fixed Dimensions

The Marquee options also let you indicate in pixels the exact size of the selection you want. Choose Fixed Size from the Style pull-down menu

Figure 3.11

The Constrained Aspect Ratio setting for the Marquee tool

and type in the desired Width and Height. Among other uses, this comes in handy if you need to create several objects with the same size dimensions for a tile or brick pattern.

Feathering a Selection

As I mentioned earlier, feathering is used to soften the transition boundaries between a selection and the rest of your image. It's a great technique for adding shadows to type and objects in an image, and for creating vignette effects. Figure 3.12 shows an example of adding a vignette effect to a photograph; here, I've cropped the image with the Marquee tool set to 10 pixels of feathering. This softens the edges and makes them look like they're disappearing gradually into the background.

Lasso Tips

The Lasso is the tool of choice for more free-form selections. You can use it to select irregularly shaped areas that other tools can't get hold of easily.

The Lasso is tricky to use, however. Unless you have very, very steady hands, the boundaries of your selection tend to wobble all over the place. Another disadvantage: If you stop clicking as you drag your cursor, the beginning and end points will connect and automatically close the selection. This is particularly frustrating if you accidentally stop clicking as you drag your cursor.

You can, however, use the modifier keys to gain greater control over the Lasso tool. For example, you can draw a straight line with the Lasso tool by holding down Option (for Mac users) or Alt (for Windows users). You can take advantage of this effect if you need to stop clicking and lift the cursor for any reason; as long as you've got Option (or Alt) pressed, you can stop clicking your mouse and reposition your cursor to a better spot.

After you make a selection, you may sometimes find that you want to add to it. You can do this by holding down Shift while you outline another selection with the Lasso tool, as shown in Figure 3.13. Here, after selecting the face and neck area, we begin a second selection over the ear.

Figure 3.12

Setting a
selection's
feather radius to
10 pixels

Similarly, you can subtract from a selection by using another modifier, ⌘ (for Mac users) or Ctrl (for Windows users). This is just how you added to and subtracted from selections with the Marquee tool earlier in this chapter. In Figure 3.14, we've selected too wide an area for the second selection, so we have to press ⌘ or Ctrl in conjunction with

Figure 3.13
Using Option
(or Alt) with the
Lasso tool

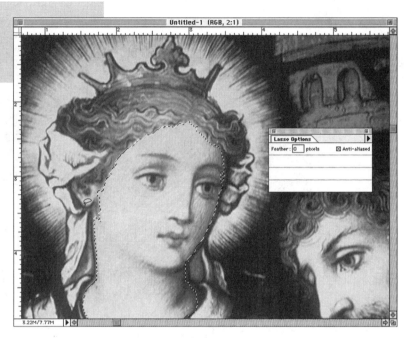

Figure 3.14
Using ⌘ (or Ctrl)
with the
Lasso tool

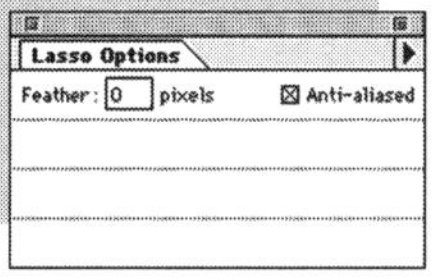

Figure 3.15

The Lasso tool's option palette

the Lasso tool to reduce our second selection to just the ear—we don't want to select any of the hair.

Feathering vs. Anti-Aliasing

The only options to set in the Lasso tool's option palette (see Figure 3.15) include feathering and anti-aliasing. Both are useful when creating a composite image by blurring the boundaries between an irregularly shaped object and the background. The difference: feathering blurs pixels on both the inside and outside of a selection, while anti-aliasing only introduces blurred pixels on the outside of the boundary.

Magic Wand Tips

It's not just for Tinkerbell anymore. With the Magic Wand, you can select areas of your image based on the colors they contain. For me, this often turns out to be the most useful selection tool. It's especially easy to use if you need to select parts of an image bounded by a border in a clearly contrasting color. You can specify how choosy the Magic Wand tool should be in selecting pixels by setting its tolerance level.

Setting Tolerance Levels

It sounds like it should describe the limits you set for how long you can stand being around people you don't like, but tolerance levels really just define how many similarly colored, contiguous pixels the Magic Wand will pick up after you click in an image. You can enter a numeric value for your tolerance settings in the Magic Wand's Option palette; the default is 32. If you choose a tolerance level of 0, the Magic Wand selects only pixels that have the same color as the one you first click on. The higher the tolerance setting, the greater the range of pixels the wand will select for you.

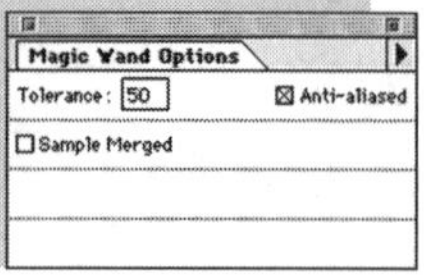

Figure 3.16
The Magic Wand tool's Option palette

> **Magic Wand Options**
> Tolerance: 50   ☒ Anti-aliased
> ☐ Sample Merged

In many cases, you probably won't be able to guess the best tolerance level for grabbing the exact selection you want on the first try. Photoshop uses its own calculations, based on hue and luminance, to figure out what pixels will and will not be selected. For example, if you set your tolerance settings to 20 and click on a pixel with a value of 100, the wand will pick up all pixels that have a value between 80 and 120. Figure 3.16 shows the Magic Wand's default settings including anti-aliasing, which smooths out the edges of your selections.

tip

● ●
Making Smart Tolerance Settings

There can be a lot of trial and error in using the Magic Wand to select the exact area you want. If your first selection doesn't grab enough of the right area, it's easy to raise the tolerance level to allow a wider range. Most of the time, however, this can backfire by grabbing much more of your image than you really want. You can retain more control by keeping the tolerance levels low, holding down (Shift), and just adding a separate selection based on a new color value.

● ●

The Magic Wand in Action

The image in the upper half of Figure 3.17 shows a straightforward use of the Magic Wand tool: you can select just the irregularly-shaped collection of Easter eggs in this image by first clicking on the light-colored background, then choosing Inverse from the Select menu to select the opposite of your original selection.

What if you need to select not just a solid object, but an image of something like a doughnut or a block of type where part of the background shows through? After you click the Magic Wand on the background, choose Similar from the Select menu—it will pick up all

Figure 3.17
Selecting objects by slightly roundabout means with the Magic Wand tool

other instances of the background color—and then choose Inverse from the Select menu. Figure 3.17 shows an example in the bottom half of the picture. To select just the coffee cup, I clicked on the background area with the Magic Wand tool; I then chose Inverse from the Select menu, and the small background area inside the cup handle became highlighted too. I was then able to choose Inverse from the Select menu to get just the selection I wanted. This technique is especially helpful for hard-to-select items like a doughnut but not the hole, or an entire sky background including small patches between tree branches.

See the transparent drop shadow exercise in Chapter 5 for another method of creating this effect using layers.

Moving Pixels and Cropping Selections

Now that you've learned some techniques for selecting parts of an image, you're ready to start applying some effects to them. A couple of the most straightforward applications here are moving parts of an image and cropping an image.

EXERCISE 3.1

Using the Magic Wand to Create Fuzzy Drop Shadows

Since the Magic Wand is such a nifty tool, we'll use it here in the book's first hands-on exercise. In these steps, we'll use the Magic Wand tool to trace an object's outline. We'll then use menu commands to blur that outline's edges, clear the selection, feather the edges, fill it with 50 percent black to create the shadow backdrop, and paste the original object back in place. Later, in Chapter 5, I'll show you a more complicated way to create a transparent drop shadow that's good for objects you want to place on a textured background, and for creating duplicate objects with their own drop shadows.

For this exercise you'll need a source image that you're going to add the drop shadow to. If you don't have such an image, you can use a simple geometric shape you create and fill with the Marquee or Lasso tool.

②

③

1. Make sure that the image background is the same color as the one that you want to appear in the finished image. The shadow we're creating will look like it's blending away into that background color, so you don't want to change that in a later step. If your final background is going to be textured, skip ahead to the "Good-to-Know" version of this exercise.

2. Select the object that you want to add the shadow to. If your object is a single color, you can just click it directly. Otherwise, you may have to click the background with the Magic Wand and then choose Inverse from the Select menu.

3. Choose Copy from the Edit menu to copy your object to the Clipboard. You'll use it to paste in later.

4. Now you'll need to fill the selection with the same color as the background color. Make sure the foreground color is set to the right color, then choose Fill from the Edit menu.

5. Now we're going to add the fuzzy shadow effect. With your object still selected, choose Feather from the Select menu. Here we're setting the Feather value to 5, but you should note the blurred shape that this creates for your object and judge for yourself how much feathering to add.

6. Set your foreground color to black. A quick way to do this is to click the Default Colors icon on the Toolbox.

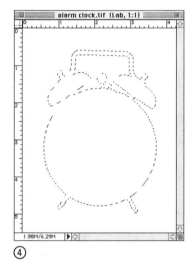

④

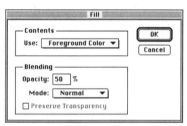

⑤

7. Choose Fill from the Edit menu and select a 50 percent fill in Normal mode. You can choose a different value for a lighter or darker shadow.

8. Now you can deselect your object. Choose None from the Select menu, or press ⌘-D (for Mac users) or Ctrl-D (for Windows users).

9. Paste your original object back in place. Choose Paste from the Edit menu, or press ⌘-V (for Mac users) or Ctrl-V (for Windows users).

10. Your original object appears right on top of the shadow. Use the arrow keys on your keyboard to move it into position above and to the left of the shadow. Click ↑ and ←‧ five times each. You can move the object closer or further from the shadow to alter the illusion of lighting and depth.

⑦

Figure 3.18
Creating a drop shadow: the finished effect

After you make a selection with one of the Selection tools described earlier in this chapter (the Marquee, Lasso, or Magic Wand tool), your cursor turns into an arrow-shaped pointer when positioned over your selection. With this pointer, you can click once on your selection and move it around anywhere on your image. A more useful trick is to use the arrow keys on your keyboard to move your selection up, down, left, or right. Your selection will move one pixel at a time with each press of an arrow key.

The Move Tool

The Move tool is the only tool that lets you reposition part of an image without needing to make a selection first; it's used for moving whole layers or channels (for example, just the red channel in an RGB document) at a time.

The Cropping Tool

With the Cropping tool, you select part of an image and discard the remainder. This is a useful feature if you've scanned a large image but only wanted to capture a smaller portion. I also use this a lot for sectioning part of an image for use in a page layout program when I don't want to compel the program to load a huge graphics file.

You can also crop an image by making a selection and then choosing Crop from the Edit menu. When you use the Cropping tool, though, you have extra options for specifying the image's height, width, and resolution. Click the Fixed Target Size check box in the Cropping tool's Options palette to make these extra options available.

Here are a couple of instances where you might find it useful to take advantage of the Cropping tool's size-specification features:

👁 You need to resize a number of images to a certain height, width, and resolution. Open a document that has the dimensions you want to match, then click the Front Image button in the Cropping tool's Options palette. The height, width, and resolution of that image will automatically show up in the Options palette. Any images that you crop afterward will resize to those dimensions.

Cropping Tool Options	▶
☒ Fixed Target Size	Front Image
Width: 320	pixels ▼
Height: 480	pixels ▼
Resolution: 72	pixels/inch ▼

👁 You want to presize a number of images to fit a certain column width after you export them to a page layout program. Choose Preferences from the File menu, then choose Units from the Preferences submenu. You can enter the dimensions for the column and gutter size in your destination document and click on OK when you're done. Back in the Cropping Tool's Option palette, you should then select columns from the pop-up menu next to the Width box. After you denote how many columns the image will need to run across, any cropping you apply to that image will automatically resize the image to fit that number of columns.

The Cropping tool gives you corner handles so you can further refine your selection before you actually crop the image. Click inside the

Figure 3.19
Using the
Cropping tool

marching ants to effect the cropping change. You can even rotate your selection by holding down [Option] (for Mac users) or [Alt] (for Windows users), then clicking and dragging one of the corner points.

Type T

The Type tool lets you add text and text effects to your images. It can be hard to produce really good-looking text in Photoshop because you're working with bitmapped pixels instead of smooth curves (this is what was at the heart of our discussion of bitmapped vs. vector-based graphics in Chapter 2). Photoshop's type also lacks kerning capabilities for letter pairs, that is, it won't let you nudge pairs of letters closer together or further apart for greater readability.

Unlike many other programs, Photoshop doesn't let you add type directly in your open document. After you select the Type tool and click in your document, the Type Tool dialog box launches. Here you can select your typeface, type size, *leading* (the amount of space between lines of type), and *kerning* (letter spacing) for the entire text selection, and also get a preview of what your text will look like.

Clicking the anti-aliasing check box in the Type Tool dialog box (see Figure 3.20) can create smoother edges that blend better into the rest of your image. This is a good solution if the images you're working on are intended for on-screen viewing, so you should remember to always anti-alias your type if your graphics' end use is for the Web or multimedia applications. For print production, however, this will just make your type look fuzzy at the edges. If you really need crisp, clean type in your finished work, export your Photoshop image to either an illustration or page layout program and add the type at that later stage.

tip

• •

Importing Text from Adobe Illustrator

If you're an adept Adobe Illustrator user, you'll probably find it easier to create many type effects (such as a specialized color blend) in Illustrator and then import that text into Photoshop. As we've seen, though, your Illustrator file will rasterize and become a bitmapped selection.

• •

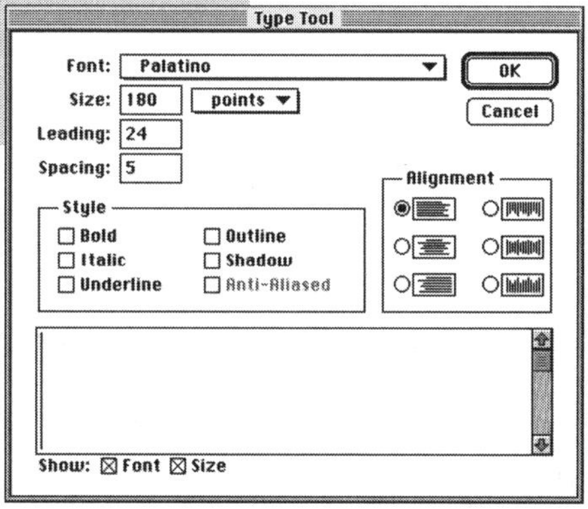

Figure 3.20

The Type Tool dialog box

Painting and Drawing Tools

Of all the good reasons to brush up—excuse the pun—on using Photoshop's painting and drawing tools, the best one is that these tools are the most fun to use. You'll find many of these same tools in art creation software marketed to the children's market, like Kid Pix. Those programs also have paint buckets, pencils, and a zillion paintbrushes in wacky shapes.

Does this mean your kids (if you have them) will paint circles around you if they ever get their grubby little hands on Photoshop? Well, maybe...but here, we're going to look at some non-obvious tips for using these paint and drawing tools that'll take you worlds away from finger painting or casual scribbling.

Let's look at the tools in this section in the order in which they appear on the Toolbox.

Paint Bucket Tips

This one's easy to use: click on your image (with either a selection or no selection in place) to fill a contiguous area of similarly colored pixels with the foreground color or a selected pattern.

Figure 3.21

The Paint Bucket tool's Option palette

Just like the Magic Wand, the Paint Bucket has tolerance settings for how many pixels it'll reach out and touch. The Paint Bucket works a lot like the Magic Wand. If you selected an area of pixels with the Magic Wand tool and then filled that selection with a certain color, that's basically what you could've accomplished with the Paint Bucket tool in one less step. Figure 3.21 shows the Paint Bucket tool's Option palette.

Mode and Opacity Settings

As you begin to experiment with the Photoshop, you should try exploring different settings in the Mode pop-up menu in the Options palette. This menu appears not only in the Paint Bucket tool's options but in all the other painting and editing tools, too. The various settings shown in Figure 3.22 affect how you apply color to your image. For example, if you apply a yellow color to an image in Lighten mode, only the underlying pixels in the image that are darker than yellow with be lightened with your color. If you paint in Darken mode, only those pixels lighter than your yellow will be painted over by the yellow. The specific effects of each of these mode settings are described in fuller detail in Chapter 4, "Color Essentials."

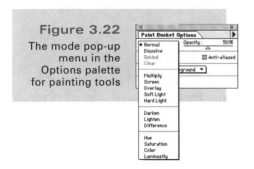

Figure 3.22

The mode pop-up menu in the Options palette for painting tools

Adjusting the Opacity slider on the Options palette affects how transparent your painting effects will be. The lower the Opacity setting you choose, the lighter the amount of color applied will be.

 note

The slider in the Options palette also changes depending on which tool is currently selected. For the Paint Bucket, Gradient, Line, Pencil, Paintbrush, and Rubber Stamp tools, the slider controls opacity. On the Airbrush, Smudge, and Blur/Sharpen tools, the slider controls the applied pressure. With the Dodge/Burn/Smudge tool, the slider sets exposure.

Gradient Tips

The Gradient tool lets you create gradient fills, or blends—these are transitions from the foreground to the background color, or vice versa. You can also choose to create a blend that fades away into transparency, with the right settings from the Gradient tool's Options palette. It's most useful for creating 3-D kinds of effects like adding depth to objects.

There are two types of gradients you can create:

- ❂ Linear fills, which are applied in a straight line from the beginning to the end point you select.

- ❂ Radial fills, which emanate outward.

To create a blend, select the Gradient tool and simply click and drag over part of your image. If an area of the image is currently selected, the blend will only apply to that selection. The first place you click determines where the blend will start, and the point at which you release the mouse after dragging will be the blend's endpoint.

Figure 3.23 shows the Gradient tool's Options palette.

Figure 3.23
The Gradient tool's Options palette

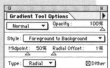

EXERCISE 3.2

Using the Gradient Tool to Create a 3-D Sphere

Photoshop isn't a modeling program that lets you render and manipulate 3-D objects to any great extent, but it can be used to create some realistic-looking 3-D shapes. I usually create spheres and other simple 3-D objects in Photoshop as icons for my Web site. In this exercise, we create a round selection and add a gradient fill to add the 3-D illusion.

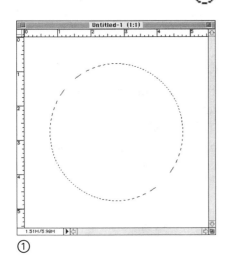

①

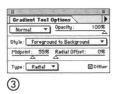

③

1. In a new document, choose the Elliptical Marquee tool. Hold down Shift as you click and drag to form a perfect circle.

2. Make the foreground color a bright color for the finished ball, and set the background color to black.

3. Double-click on the Gradient tool to select it and call up the Options palette. Select a Radial fill and make sure the Style reads Foreground to Background. Set the Opacity to 100 percent, the mode to Normal, and click on OK.

4. Position the cursor inside the selection areas as shown and drag to apply the gradient fill. The first place you click will be where your bright color is most highly concentrated, blending into solid black at the position where you release the cursor.

5. That's it! Your finished sphere should look something like Figure 3.24. You can experiment with different start and end points for clicking your cursor, and with changing the values in the Midpoint Skew and Radial Offset fields in the Gradient tool's Options palette.

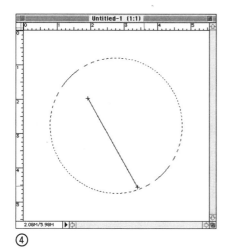

④

Later on we'll look at additional effects like reflections and texturing you can add to objects to enhance their realism. For now though, this exercise should help show you the basics of using the Gradient tool to simulate lighting and shading.

 *tip*

For Print Images, Make Blends in CMYK Mode

In Chapter 2, we talked about how you'll often edit your images in RGB mode (which is optimized for on-screen viewing) and only switch to CMYK mode when you're done. But if you need to add gradient fills, you're better off switching to CMYK mode early on because you can get significant color shifts in blends if you switch from RGB to CMYK after you use the Gradient tool.

Figure 3.24
The Sphere icon:
finished results

Line Tips

A little experimentation will show you how you can use the Line tool to draw lines in any direction or, if you hold down [Shift] as you click and drag your cursor, lines limited to increments of 45°.

You can also draw lines with arrowheads, or lines that contain tints of a color instead of the solid foreground color; these settings are all contained in the Line tool's Options palette, as shown in Figure 3.25.

By entering various widths for your lines and different values in the Arrowhead Shape dialog box, you can create a diverse number of arrows and lines, as shown in Figure 3.26. The values you enter in the Arrowhead Shape dialog box are measured as percentages of the line width. So for example, the default Width of the arrowhead is set to 500 percent, or five times larger than your line width. The default Length of the arrowhead is set to 1000 percent, or ten times larger than your line width. You can also change the concavity setting, which determines the shape of the arrowhead. Setting concavity to zero makes the arrowhead look like a triangle with a flat edge following the point; increasing concavity lengthens the sides of the arrowhead triangle.

• •

 *tip*   **Use the Line Tool as a Measuring Tape**

If you set the width for your Line tool to 0 and display the Info palette (selected from the Window menu), you can use the Line tool as a measuring tape or level. As you click and drag, you can refer to the measurements in the Info palette to track the distance from your line's start and end points, or check to see that an edge measures straight across or down.

• •

Figure 3.25

The Line tool's Options palette and dialog box for adding arrowheads

Line Tool Options

Normal   Opacity: 90%

Line Width: 1   pixels   ☒ Anti-aliased

Arrowheads: ☒ Start ☒ End   [Shape...]

Arrowhead Shape

Width: 500 %

Length: 1000 %

Concavity: 0 %

[OK]   [Cancel]

Figure 3.26
Drawing lines
with arrowheads

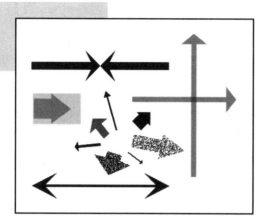

Eyedropper Tips

With the Eyedropper tool, you can sample (that is, pick up) colors from your images to designate as the foreground and background colors. Simply click with the Eyedropper tool on a section of your image to change the foreground color; hold down (Option) on a Mac (or (Alt) for Windows users) when you click to assign the background color. This is a useful tool for touching up image flaws.

By default, the Eyedropper picks up the exact color value of the single pixel you first click. With the Eyedropper's options, you can also change this sample size to the average value of a 3-by-3 pixel area or a 5-by-5 pixel area around the pixel you've clicked.

tip

Shortcut for Selecting the Eyedropper

When you're using one of Photoshop's painting tools—namely, the Paint Bucket, Gradient, Pencil, Line, Paintbrush, or Airbrush—you can quickly switch to the Eyedropper temporarily by pressing (Option) on a Mac ((Alt) under Windows).

Using the Eyedropper with the Scratch Palette

The Scratch palette is an area where you can dab and test strokes of color without affecting your actual image, and it's a natural place to store swabs of colors for reuse—just like a real artist's palette. This is where the Eyedropper tool can come in handy; if you get into the habit of using the Scratch palette, you'll soon find it convenient to take a sample of a color in your image with the Eyedropper and store a smidgen of it in the Scratch palette for safekeeping.

Eraser Tips

As the name implies, the Eraser tool erases pixels, filling them in with the designated background color. Perhaps surprisingly, there are some pretty powerful options in the Eraser tool's Options palette (see Figure 3.27).

First, you'll notice that you can define the eraser's shape to reproduce the effect of an airbrush, pencil, paintbrush, or its default block shape. You can also just click the Erase Image button on the Options palette to erase the entire image, which is the same as choosing Clear from the Edit menu.

The most amazing Eraser effect, though, is one called the Magic Eraser option. Let's say you've made some changes to a saved image. If you change your mind about some of the changes, you can always revert to the saved version, but perhaps you don't want to undo all the work, just a few changes. With the Eraser tool selected and Option pressed (for Mac users; use Alt under Windows), position your cursor over just one part of the image you want to change back. Your cursor will change to the Magic Eraser icon, an eraser with a plain document icon behind it (). As you drag the Magic Eraser over your image, portions of your saved image will reappear. Spooky, huh?

Figure 3.27
The Eraser tool's
Options palette

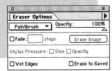

Pencil Tips

As you'll discover with casual doodling, the Pencil lets you color in pixels in either a freeform or straight-line manner. It's most useful for changing the color of single pixels. You can use the Brushes palette in conjunction with the Pencil tool to select a pencil with a coarser or finer drawing surface.

As with so many of the other tools, though, opening up the Options palette is the key to extending its use.

Fading and Stylus Pressure

You can set options for fading and stylus pressure to reproduce the effect of applying pressure on a writing implement while sketching (see Figure 3.28). Fade measures the distance in pixels over which the Pencil's stroke will be applied before fading out; you can choose whether to fade out to the background color or to transparency. With the Stylus Pressure option, you can set the brush stroke's size (a range of thicknesses), color (either the foreground, background, or a median color between the two), and opacity.

Auto Erase

The other neat feature about the Pencil Tool is Auto Erase, an option you can check in the Options palette. With the option checked, you can click and hold to draw a line as usual. After releasing, though, when you click a second time your pencil will draw using the background color. So if you draw one line and then draw another line back over the first one, it will look as though you are erasing over it. This can be useful if you regularly need to toggle between drawing with your foreground and background colors.

Figure 3.28

The Pencil tool's Options palette

Airbrush Tips

The Airbrush puts a diffuse spray of the foreground color on your image, which can produce good effects when coloring grayscale images or just for creating soft gleams of color to touch up objects and images. In Figure 3.29, I used the Airbrush tool to add depth to the square on the left. To create the image on the right, I sprayed a line filled with solid black across the bottom and right sides and a line filled with solid white across the top and left sides.

Like a real airbrush, paint builds up if you hold the cursor in one place for a while. You can use the Brush palette and the Options palette to set Fade and Stylus Pressure options much as you did for the Pencil tool earlier.

Paintbrush Tips

Painting is a very versatile, high-potential activity in Photoshop. Although we've seen that you can use the Brushes palette with several painting tools, the Paintbrush tool is where you can really go wild with them. You can dab on color with brushes that paint fuzzy-edged or

Figure 3.29

Using the Airbrush tool to add shiny highlights to an object

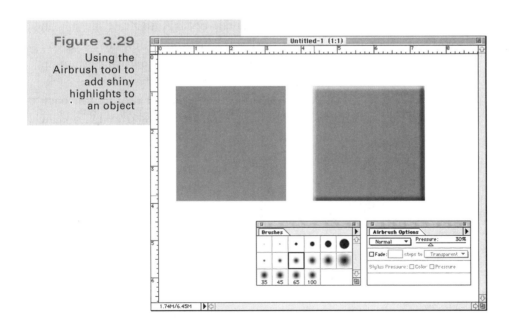

smooth strokes; brushes with fine tips, fat heads, or custom shapes; brushes where the paint is applied continuously or in dotted lines; and even brushes that lighten or darken only selected pixels.

In the Paintbrush tool's Options palette, you can set the same kinds of options for Fade and Stylus Pressure that you had with the Pencil and Airbrush tools. You can also select Wet Edges, which produces the effect of painting with watercolors or felt-tip markers.

tip

Loading Additional Brushes

Photoshop includes several alternative sets of brushes that you can load instead of, or append to, the default set. These brush shapes let you add all sorts of creative effects. Figure 3.30 shows some samples.

Editing Tools

The editing tools primarily retouch the pixels in your document instead of applying paint or some other new content to the image. There are exceptions here, depending on how you use the tools—for example, the Rubber Stamp can be used for painting as much as for editing, and the Smudge tool's Fingerpaint option can get pretty messy.

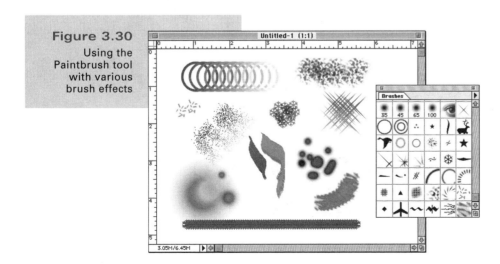

Figure 3.30

Using the Paintbrush tool with various brush effects

As we look at each of these in turn, the emphasis will be on how using them judiciously can lead to dramatic improvements in your images.

Rubber Stamp Tips

With the Rubber Stamp tool, you can copy portions of an image to another part of the same or a different document. You can add leaves to a picture of a tree that's looking a little sparse after a cold snap, or use flesh-toned selections to remove a pair of glasses from a subject's face. We're going to use the Rubber Stamp tool extensively in Chapter 10, "Retouching Essentials."

Smudge Tips

The cursor for the Smudge tool is very cute: you use a little finger to smudge a color as if you've stirred a drop of water into some paint or smeared a charcoal stroke. In portraits, it's often useful to use the Smudge tool to soften wrinkles and to enhance eyelashes—it's like instant mascara! You can use it to smooth out blemishes, too, but for retouching substantial parts of an image it can produce an artificial-looking effect; if this happens, you're better off trying out the Rubber Stamp tool.

As Figure 3.32 shows, its options include Finger Painting; if you check this box, your smudging will now begin with the foreground color smearing into the image's colors. For Mac users, pressing and holding Option (or for Windows users, Alt) will automatically activate the Finger Painting option as you work with the Smudge tool.

Figure 3.31
The Rubber Stamp tool in action

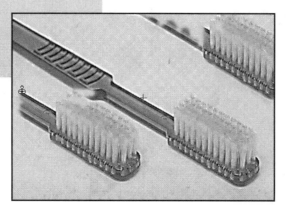

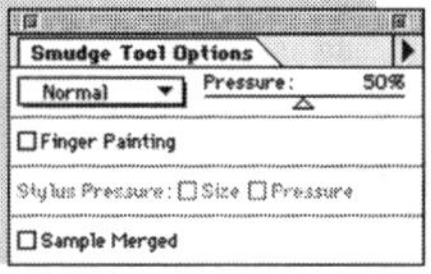

Figure 3.32
The Smudge
tool's Options
palette

Smudge Tool Options
Normal ▼ Pressure: 50%
☐ Finger Painting
Stylus Pressure: ☐ Size ☐ Pressure
☐ Sample Merged

Sharpen/Blur Tips

The Blur and Sharpen tools share a spot on Photoshop's toolbox; they are called Photoshop's focus tools because they affect the color contrast between neighboring pixels. Apply the Blur tool to lessen the contrast, and you'll start to think your glasses are fogging over; use the Sharpen tool to make specific parts of an image come into closer focus.

Both tools have counterparts under the Filter menu; their tools simply allow for a more hands-on and concentrated kind of control over this effect.

Dodge/Burn/Sponge

This three-in-one tool builds on traditional film exposure techniques. It lets you tone an image by lightening or darkening portions of it (using Dodge and Burn, respectively), or by adding or removing saturation and contrast (via Sponge).

To me, the Dodge icon looks like a little pushpin, but it's really supposed to represent a small paddle that a photographer might use to cover a image to diffuse the amount of light that reaches a piece of film as it exposes, thereby lightening the finished print. The Burn icon looks like a little hand cupped in a circle and is also an allusion to a traditional photography technique for concentrating light on an image, thereby darkening it. The Sponge tool, which was only added to the Toolbox in version 3, lets you selectively affect the contrast levels in portions of your image.

Figure 3.33 shows the effects of applying each of Photoshop's editing tools. I used the Dodge tool to lighten the head overall. The features looked a little washed-out then, so I used the Sponge tool to draw out the contrast on the face. I used the Burn tool to darken the shadow on the right cheek just a touch.

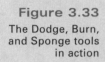

Figure 3.33
The Dodge, Burn, and Sponge tools in action

Table 3.1 Photoshop's Tools, with Icons and Keyboard Commands

ICON	TOOL NAME	KEYBOARD COMMAND
Image Navigation		
🖐	Hand	H
🔍	Zoom	Z
Selection		
⬚	Rectangular/	M
⬭	Elliptical Marquee	
⌇	Lasso	L
✳	Magic Wand	W
✛	Move	V
⌇	Cropping	C

Table 3.1 (continued)

Icon	Tool Name	Keyboard Command
Type		
T	Type	Y
Painting and Drawing		
	Paint Bucket	K
	Gradient	G
	Line	N
	Eyedropper	I
	Eraser	E
	Pencil	P
	Airbrush	A
	Paintbrush	B
Editing Tools		
	Rubber Stamp	S
	Smudge	U
	Sharpen/Blur	R
	Dodge/Burn/Sponge	O

Table 3.1 (continued)

ICON	TOOL NAME	KEYBOARD COMMAND
Additional Toolbox Controls		
	Foreground/Background colors	
	Default Colors	D
	Switch Colors	X
	Quick Mask mode	Q
	Screen display mode	F

Summary

By now you've learned a great many need-to-know techniques for using Photoshop's tools efficiently and effectively. In this chapter you got a chance to try out some of these tools individually; in later chapters, you'll use them in conjunction and with Photoshop's layers and masks for even cooler effects.

Table 3.1 offers an at-a-glance reference to matching tool names with their icons and their gotta-know-'em keyboard shortcuts.

Next up in Chapter 4 is an in-depth look at using color in Photoshop.

4 Color Essentials

IN THIS CHAPTER

Photoshop's Color Modes

Ⓔ

The Color Picker

Ⓔ

Using Color Palettes

Ⓔ

Color Options

Predictability—it's a bad thing for a movie plot but something you really want to strive for in terms of making your color images onscreen match your final print output. Matching colors onscreen with those in your print output is a big concern for any Photoshop designer, because our eyes perceive color on a computer monitor different from how they perceive it on paper.

You're bound to face additional print costs (and lost time on press) for corrections if your colors don't turn out right in the first place. Likewise, you may face color-matching dilemmas when you're working with images for the Web or multimedia productions; your images look vivid and well-coordinated on your Mac, so why do they sometimes look so lousy when viewed under Windows?

To transmit the colors in your mind's eye to your monitor's screen and then faithfully reproduce them in their final form, you need to know the basics of what influences color in your Photoshop documents. This chapter provides an overview of how to predict good results when producing full-color print pieces and on-screen graphics. It also aims to fill in any gaps in your knowledge of color theory—that is, what colors mix and match well. Some specific topics addressed here include:

- 👁 The basics of the RGB, CMYK, HSB, and Lab color models

- 👁 How to use Photoshop's Color Picker dialog box and Picker, Swatches, and Scratch palettes

- 👁 Commercial color systems such as Pantone and Trumatch

- 👁 How to use color look-up tables (CLUTs), especially for Web graphics

- 👁 How Photoshop's painting and editing modes affect color in your images

Precision, Precision: Photoshop's Color Modes

The way we perceive colors can be very subjective. They say the number one reason why mail-order customers return merchandise is over dissatisfaction with the color. Now it could be that mail-order customers are a very picky bunch, but I think it's more likely that something gets lost in translation pretty often between product photo shoots and the final images in print catalogues.

There are several models for translating subjective color terms to precise values that reproduce consistently. When you're choosing colors in your Photoshop work, at various times you may use its different color models: RGB, CMYK, HSB, and Lab. You can specify values in any of these four models in the Color Picker dialog box (see Figure 4.1).

In the *RGB* (red, green, blue) model, a monitor displays color formed by a mixture of red, green, and blue dots emitting beams of light. The dots are so tiny and tightly concentrated that you see the color formed by the mixture of light rather than individual dots. Full-color printing uses the *CMYK* model, which combines four inks (cyan, magenta, yellow, black) to produce a wide spectrum of color. The *HSB* (hue, saturation, brightness) model is a viewing option that describes color components as they relate to the properties of light, or how people perceive color subjectively. The *Lab* model helps produce device-independent color, that is, colors that will remain the same no matter what monitor or printer you use to render them.

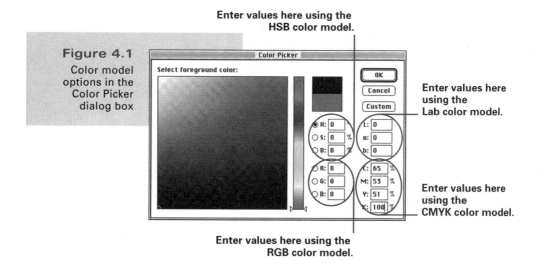

Figure 4.1
Color model options in the Color Picker dialog box

Enter values here using the HSB color model.

Enter values here using the Lab color model.

Enter values here using the CMYK color model.

Enter values here using the RGB color model.

A fuller description of each of these four color models (also called color spaces, or color gamuts) follows, along with suggestions on when you'd want to use them.

RGB

The human eye sees color as wavelengths of red, green, and blue. These three *primary colors* combine in varying levels to form all other colors. This is an example of *additive color reproduction,* where colors become lighter as you add more red, green, and blue light. Combining the highest levels of red, green, and blue forms white (see Figure 4.2). Any device that mixes, transmits, or filters light uses the additive color model—your TV and computer monitor, for example, as well as things like movie projectors and theater spotlights.

In Photoshop's RGB Color mode, each of the three primary colors has 256 levels of intensity; they take values in the range of 0 to 255. Setting all three to 0 will produce solid black (since you're adding no light); upping all three to 255 will produce solid white (as described in the previous paragraph).

Why are there 256 levels in RGB mode, and why do the numbers run from 0 to 255? With RGB, you have access to the full range of the 24-bit

Figure 4.2
The RGB
color model

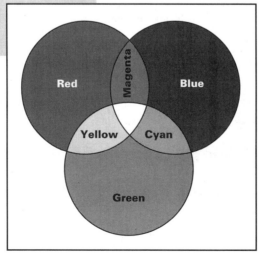

color spectrum. Think back to Chapter 2, which described how 24-bit graphics assign one byte of memory each for red, green, and blue values. One byte is equal to 8 bits, and a bit can have one of two possible values (on and off). Thus, a byte can have 2^8 (or 256) possible values. In *binary notation,* a bit-numbering scheme standard on most computers, a byte can range in value from 0 (with every bit turned off) to 255 (with every bit turned on). This makes RGB an ideal color mode for image editing and for saving images designed for on-screen viewing.

CMYK

If you've worked on full-color print publications, you may be most comfortable with the CMYK model, which is the basis for *four-color process* printing.

The CMYK model uses *subtractive color reproduction*—that is, subtracting light instead of adding it. Unlike a computer screen that emits light (in the RGB model), a printed page absorbs light and reflects some of it. The light that's reflected is the color we actually see. When you look at a picture of a frog, you see the color green because the paper has absorbed everything that's not green inside the outline of the frog. A solid white surface will reflect all wavelengths of light; a solid black surface will absorb all wavelengths and reflect no light at all.

Cyan, magenta, and yellow are the *secondary* colors; they come from the highest concentrations of two of the three primary colors (with no amount of the third color at all). Here's how the primary colors combine to form the secondary colors:

> Blue + Green = Cyan
>
> Red + Green = Yellow
>
> Red + Blue = Magenta

Conversely, two secondary colors combined will produce a primary color:

> Magenta + Yellow = Red
>
> Cyan + Yellow = Green
>
> Cyan + Magenta = Blue

Figure 4.3

The primary and secondary colors

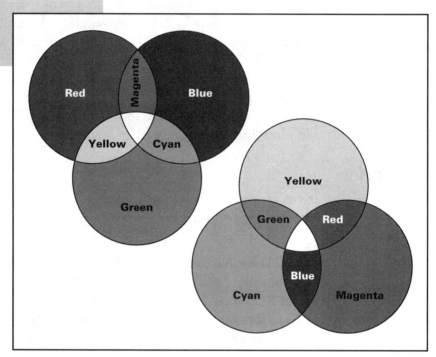

These relationships also point out how each of the primary colors is the direct opposite of a secondary color. For example, cyan is the opposite of red, because all the red is absorbed and the blue and green are reflected. Opposite color pairs (like cyan and red) are called *complementary colors*. Figure 4.3 shows the primary and secondary colors, and their respective complementary colors.

In theory, printing solid concentrations of cyan, yellow, and magenta inks should produce black, but printing with ink is an imperfect process. Printing with the highest combination of cyan, yellow, and magenta tends to produce only muddy browns, so the system calls for black ink to make up for the problem. Black is the K part of CMYK; the letter K is used instead of B because B could potentially be mistaken for blue. Photoshop's CMYK mode measures values for the colors in percentages.

HSB

As nice as RGB and CMYK are for defining colors in fairly precise terms, neither model is really intuitive for differentiating colors the way the human eye does. The HSB model is based on how people perceive color and lends itself well to many subjective terms used to describe color. *Hue* depends on the wavelength of the reflected light; it's described in terms of the names we generally give to colors, such as purple, reddish-yellow, or what's on the label of any crayon from a box of Crayolas. *Saturation,* which is also called *chroma,* defines a color's purity, that is, how little gray is mixed in; zero saturation results in gray, while full saturation results in the purest (or strongest) version of a hue. *Brightness* measures a color's intensity—how light or dark it is.

Hue is measured in a 360° circle, a literal color wheel. Saturation and brightness are both measured in percentages. When you set both saturation and brightness to 100 percent, you'll get the fullest, most vivid representation of any hue. See Figure 4.4 for a representation of how the HSB color model works.

Lab

The Lab mode is the diplomat of Photoshop's color modes; it attempts to transcend color differences between monitors and print devices and produce *device-independent color*. It's based on a mathematical model of all colors visible to the human eye developed by a French standards committee, the *Commission Internationale d'Eclairage (CIE).*

Figure 4.4
The HSB
color model

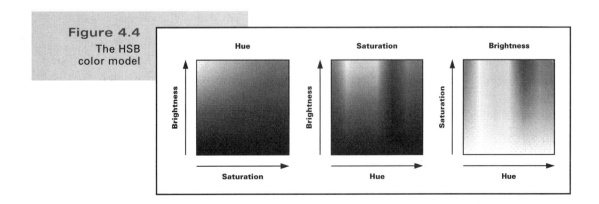

When Photoshop converts between RGB and CMYK, it first internally converts to Lab mode. It then uses the settings in Monitor Setup and Printing Inks Setup in the Preferences submenu under the File command to complete the conversion. (This is another reason why it's important for you to calibrate your monitor—your Monitor Setup preferences will be optimized for your monitor type and you'll have more accurate RGB-to-CMYK conversions.)

Lab measures color across three axes; it essentially does the work of RGB in only two channels, with a third channel thrown in for controlling brightness. Its name is actually an acronym for its three axes. L stands for *luminosity*, which is similar to brightness in the HSB model, and is measured in percentages. The other two stand for imaginary color ranges, known by the initials *a* and *b*. Based on the expansive CIE color wheel, the *a* axis traces a wide span of colors in the green-to-red range; the *b* axis traces a wide blue-to-yellow range. Calling up the Picker palette for the Lab color mode is the best way to see how these other two axes work, as shown in Figure 4.5. You can enter values ranging from 0 to 100 for the L channel, and values from -120 to 120 for the other two.

You might want to use Lab if you're most concerned with changing the lightness (not the colors) of an image, or if you edit Photo CD images frequently. The proprietary color model Kodak uses in its Photo CD format is virtually identical to Lab. If you print using several different output devices—for example, a Canon Color Laser Copier and a QMS Colorscript 100 model—but need to match the color printouts from all of them, you'd do well to save in Lab and create custom Printing Inks Setup settings for each device.

The Color Picker

Now that you've had an introduction to each of Photoshop's color models, you'll have a better grasp on how to choose the precise colors

Figure 4.5
Lab color in the
Picker palette

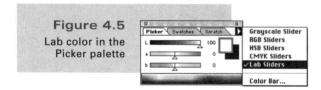

you want. You're ready to call up the Color Picker dialog box, which appears when you click on either the foreground or background colors icon in the Toolbox.

Figure 4.6 shows what you see when you click on either the foreground or background color icons:

Look over Figure 4.6 to see the various parts of the Color Picker. Here's a brief rundown of how you can use each part in your color selections:

👁 The *color field* takes up most of the Color Picker's left side. You can click on and reposition the circular marker in the color field to select different color values. This is a straightforward, grunt-and-point method for color selection—no messing with exact color values necessary!

👁 The *color slider* that appears just to the right of the color field has a pair of *slider triangles* you can drag to select and display different sections of the available color spectrum. For example, with the R radio button clicked, dragging the slider triangles lets you change red RGB values. Dragging the slider triangles all the way to the top will maximize red to its highest possible value (255), and dragging them to the bottom will lower it to its lowest possible value (0). Moving the circular marker vertically and horizontally will vary

Figure 4.6
The Color Picker
dialog box

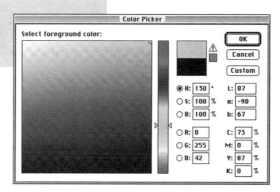

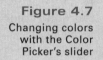

Figure 4.7

Changing colors
with the Color
Picker's slider

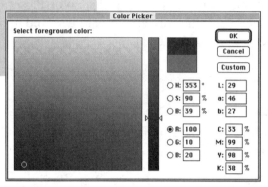

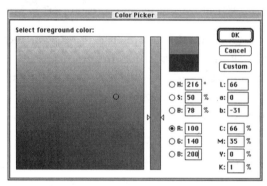

the Green(G) and Blue (B) settings, respectively, while Red (R) remains constant (see Figure 4.7).

tip

Using Arrow Keys with the Color Picker's Slider

Holding down the arrow keys in the color picker will increment or decrement the value of the color component whose radio button you've clicked in the Color Picker. The longer you hold down the up or down arrow key, the more you'll see the slider triangles rise or fall.

◉ When you select a *new color,* it will display in the top half of the small box to the right of the color slider. Your previously chosen color appears in the bottom half of the box.

◉ Since the RGB color gamut (over 16.7 million colors) is wider than CMYK's, at times you may select and work with colors in

RGB mode that can't be printed in CMYK. When you select one of these *out-of-gamut* colors, Photoshop displays an Alert symbol (which looks like an exclamation point inside a triangle) as a warning to you. When this happens, you can click on the Alert symbol itself to compel Photoshop to select the nearest printable color instead. If you plan to use your images only for multimedia formats or other on-screen uses, you don't have to worry about colors that are out-of-gamut for commercial printing.

The *Custom button* lets you choose from a number of third-party custom color inks supported by Photoshop. Most of these custom-mixed inks let you print in a consistent way colors that are hard or impossible to reproduce with CMYK colors. After you click the Custom colors button, you can choose the color family you want from the Book pop-up menu (see Figure 4.8). If you have a swatch book from the third-party manufacturer, it's useful for you to consider the colors you want ahead of time and just type in the swatch's key number to select them. Pantone and Trumatch are probably the best-known color systems on this list, which also includes ANPA (now NAA, which stands for Newspaper Association of America), DIC, Focoltone, and Toyo. This is the option I use in two-color print jobs, where I can select a *spot color* and create duotones. When you select a custom color, the closest corresponding CMYK values for that color are also displayed.

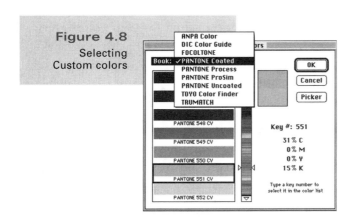

Figure 4.8
Selecting
Custom colors

note Here's a really interesting way to choose and evaluate colors—if you or your company can afford it. Light Source makes a color management system called Colortron that uses a hand-held device to capture a color sample from almost any source—printed material, a piece of fabric, or paint on a wall. ColorTron's software then identifies the closest Pantone match to that sample, as well as the equivalent values using the CMYK, RGB, Lab or other color models. The software can also let you compare or mix color samples against various backgrounds. The system runs about $1,300; check the vendor listings in Appendix B.

For more detail on custom colors, see the section "Third-Party Commercial Inks" later in this chapter.

Using the Color Palettes

Photoshop lets you choose colors in a number of ways. You can use the Eyedropper tool to sample existing colors from an image, or you can use the Color Picker as detailed a while back. Below are some brief descriptions of Photoshop's color palettes—called the Picker, Scratch, and Swatches palettes—which offer a couple of other ways to choose colors in Photoshop. You may have overlooked using these palettes to date, but exploring them here will give you a chance to see if they can help make your Photoshop work easier. If you spend much time searching for and toying with new colors, they'll probably help.

The Picker Palette

Unless you're used to entering numerical values for your colors every time, it's usually more efficient to go to the Picker palette and click-and-choose there instead of displaying the Color Picker dialog box. With the Picker palette, you'll be able to view more of the available color spectrum at once.

You can access the Picker palette by selecting Palettes under the Window menu, then choosing Show Picker from the Palettes submenu (see Figure 4.9). To change the current foreground and background colors, you can click on one of the two large, overlapping boxes on the right side of the palette. A pop-up menu at the right of the palette lets you

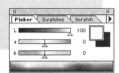

Figure 4.9
The Picker palette

select a color model (grayscale, RGB, HSB, CMYK, or Lab) and to specify the spectrum for the color bar at the bottom of the palette. In the RGB model, for example, you then set values for the red, green, and blue components by dragging the triangles under each of three color sliders.

tip

Switching Color Bars in the Picker Palette

The Color Bar... menu item in the Picker palette's pop-up menu offers a dialog box with four color spectrums from which you can browse: RGB Spectrum, CMYK Spectrum, Grayscale Ramp, and Foreground to Background. A shortcut for reaching these choices is to [Shift]-click on the color itself; this will display the next spectrum choice on the pop-up menu. [Shift]-clicking four times will return you to your original spectrum choice.

The Swatches Palette

The Swatches palette is handy for keeping together combinations of colors you use together frequently. The pop-up menu on this palette has options for loading, saving, and appending custom swatch sets.

tip

Editing Your Swatches Palette

No matter what tool you have selected, your cursor will turn into a paint bucket when you move it over an empty swatch on the Swatches palette.

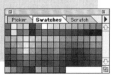

Figure 4.10
The Swatches
palette

Figure 4.11

Creating a
Swatches palette
out of a custom
ink set

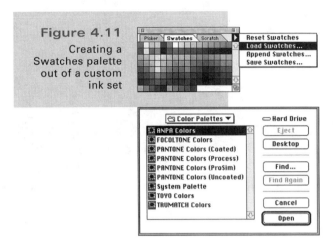

Clicking on an empty swatch will then add your currently selected fore-ground color to the Swatches palette—a quick way to put it aside for future use if you want to select a different color right away. By the same token, you can delete colors on the Swatches palette by ⌘-clicking them (for Mac users) or Ctrl-clicking (for Windows users); your cursor will turn into a scissors icon. You can replace any color on the Swatches palette with your foreground color by Shift-clicking the swatch you want to lose. If the order of your swatches is important, you can insert a new color between two others instead of adding it to the end of the list. On Mac OS-based computers, Shift-Option-click will do the job; on Windows machines, Shift-Alt-click to place your new swatch in its custom position.

The premixed commercial colors that you can access via the Custom button in the Color Picker are all available as custom color palettes that you can load in the Swatches palette. Just click the pop-up menu in the Swatches palette and choose Load Swatches. The Color Palettes folder in your main Photoshop folder (or directory, if you're using Windows 3.1) contains the palettes for the Pantone, Trumatch, and other custom commercial sets (see Figure 4.11).

The Scratch Palette

With the Scratch palette, you can blend colors together and then use them to set new foreground and background colors (see Figure 4.12).

Figure 4.12
The Scratch palette

You can also define custom brushes and shapes in this palette, and try out blends and cloning exercises with the Rubber Stamp tool. The Scratch palette includes a pop-up menu with options for copying, pasting, locking, and resetting the palette, as well as saving and restoring other Scratch palettes.

If you need more space to doodle, you can clear out the Scratch palette by setting your background color to white, then selecting Clear from the palette's pop-up menu. You can also clear a new space—instead of deleting the palette with Clear—by setting your background color to white, then using the Move tool to drag the existing contents out of sight.

Predefined and Custom Color Sets

At times you may need to restrict the colors you use in your images to a strictly limited set. Let's say you want to add a special metallic or fluorescent ink; you're not going to be able to whip those up out of process colors—you'll have to use a custom commercial ink as a spot color. Or perhaps you're working on a series of graphics for a Web site, and you're under strict orders from the client to use colors that display equally well for Mac and Windows users who are running the Netscape browser. In that case you can load a custom color lookup table—a CLUT—and save your file in Indexed Color mode.

If neither of these scenarios apply to you, feel free to skip this section; if you're looking to expand on the kinds of design assignments you can handle, though, it will be useful to have this knowledge at your fingertips.

Third-Party Commercial Inks

Photoshop supports a number of commercial inking systems popular both in the United States and abroad. They are essentially computerized versions of the companies' color swatch books used by designers

and printers to match colors for print publications and on press. If you're just beginning to use custom color sets, make sure you check with your printer's customer service rep and find out which color systems it supports.

As mentioned earlier in this chapter, you can access single colors in one of these sets through the Color Picker, or you can load an entire set as a custom Swatch palette. You could also append colors from one of these sets to an existing Swatch palette you have open.

Here's an overview of the custom ink sets bundled with Photoshop:

- **ANPA Color.** Formerly the American Newspaper Publishers' Association, this group is now known as NAA (Newspaper Association of America). The color set developed by this group consists of inks that reproduce best on newsprint stock.

- **DIC.** A color system widely used in Japan, but not a leading standard in the United States.

- **Focoltone.** This color system developed in England includes 763 inks; it's not a leading standard in the United States, though.

- **Pantone Coated, Pantone Process, Pantone ProSim, and Pantone Uncoated.** These components of the Pantone Matching System (PMS), the primary desktop industry standard, cover a range of printing needs. A longtime producer of spot color standards, Pantone also makes available Pantone Process, which is a process-color swatch set with 3,006 CMYK combinations. Pantone ProSim emulates spot colors in process inks. Pantone Coated and Uncoated include Pantone's spot color ranges designed for use on either coated (the inks will appear glossier) or uncoated (the inks will appear somewhat duller) paper stocks.

- **Toyo Color Finder.** This Japanese color system includes 1,050 inks; although widely used in Japan, it is relatively rare in the United States.

- **Trumatch.** Specifically designed for desktop publishers, this set of over 2,000 process colors (all are reproducible in CMYK) is organized according to hue, brightness, and saturation.

The Pantone and Trumatch systems are the most widely supported by other software programs you may be likely to use with Photoshop, including QuarkXpress, Adobe Pagemaker, Macromedia Freehand and Adobe Illustrator.

Using Color Look-Up Tables (CLUTs)

CLUTs limit the colors you can choose for editing a given image. The ever-increasing market for Web graphics has really expanded the opportunities you might have for using CLUTs in Photoshop. Using fewer colors will reduce your files' final sizes and cause them to display more quickly, and that's always helpful for good Web design. Furthermore, if you use the same CLUT for designing all the graphics on your site, you can infuse all your Web pages with an overriding sense of color coordination.

When should you use a CLUT in your Web graphics? It's never a bad idea, and you should especially consider it if you've received complaints about how your graphics display from visitors who're running browsers under a computer platform different from yours. As a designer, you may use a large-screen monitor configured with thousands or millions of colors, so viewing 24-bit JPEGs is no problem for you; however, a significant number of Web visitors use monitors that can show 256 colors at most. Even if you limit yourself to serving up GIFs with 256 colors or less, you should be aware that the Macintosh and Windows systems palettes aren't entirely in sync. Some areas of solid color in your original graphics may *dither* as they display under a different computer platform—they'll have a speckled or *moiré* effect (see Figure 4.13).

In theory, most graphical Web browsers should be able to display the same 24-bit color spectrum available to the RGB color model. Although Netscape's Navigator and Microsoft's Internet Explorer browsers let designers specify some colors by name, you can specify any RGB value by using its hexadecimal equivalent in place of the 0–255 range used for RGB values. Each RGB value (from 0 to 255) can be represented by a 2-digit or 2-letter hexadecimal value; strung together, an RGB value can be represented as a 6-character alphanumeric hexadecimal code. Table 4.1 will make this a bit clearer; it shows some of the RGB colors we've already looked at and their equivalent respective hexadecimal values.

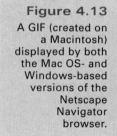

Figure 4.13

A GIF (created on a Macintosh) displayed by both the Mac OS- and Windows-based versions of the Netscape Navigator browser.

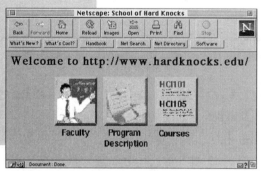

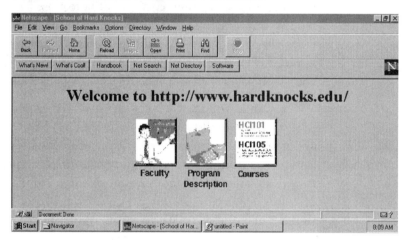

If a user only has a 256-color monitor, however, Netscape will display additional colors by dithering, as we've mentioned earlier. The user's browser will mix some pixels of one color with some of another for an effect that may look OK from a distance but has a speckled appearance when viewed up close—which is how your visitors, sitting in front of their computers, are going to see them.

It's possible for you to create graphics that won't dither under the Netscape browser—you just need to use the Netscape 216-color palette. Netscape has shown that Windows only has a 216-color palette available when it's in 8-bit mode—other colors are reserved for system

Table 4.1 Some RGB Colors, with Hexadecimal Equivalents

COLOR	RGB VALUE	HEXADECIMAL VALUE
Red	(255, 0, 0)	FF0000
Green	(0, 0, 255)	0000FF
Blue	(0, 255, 0)	00FF00
Cyan	(0, 255, 255)	00FFFF
Magenta	(255, 0, 255)	FF00FF
Yellow	(255, 255, 0)	FFFF00
Black	(0, 0, 0)	000000
White	(255, 255, 255)	FFFFFF

use—so it's a good idea to restrict yourself to using the same 216 colors to avoid dithering under Windows. This means using any combination of six specific numeric values—which are 0, 51, 102, 153, 204, or 255—in the red, green, and blue channels. Since there are six possible values in each of three channels, this is how you get 6 × 6 × 6 = 216 possibilities altogether. The nondithering RGB values, then, include all those in Table 4.1, or any other combination using these six values: (255, 51, 102) or (153, 0, 204), for example. Table 4.2 shows the hexadecimal values for these six key numbers.

Using Table 4.2, you can see that the hexadecimal values for colors like (255, 51, 102) or (153, 0, 204) are FF3366 and 9900CC, respectively. There are also a number of Web sites that offer on-the-fly conversion from RGB to hexadecimal; see Appendix A for a partial list.

In the following exercise, you'll create a customized palette that includes these 216 nondithering Netscape colors.

EXERCISE 4.1

Creating a Custom Palette for Web Graphics

Earlier, we described the importance of using colors in your Web graphics that display well under both Mac OS-based and Windows systems. Since there's a 216-color subset shared by the Windows and Macintosh systems palette, we'll create a custom palette for your Web graphics by loading your 256-color system palette, saving it under a different name, and editing out the colors not shared between the two platforms.

The example here uses the Macintosh system palette, but the steps are the same for Windows users. The only difference is that the specific values of the 40 colors you're deleting will be unlike those deleted by Mac users.

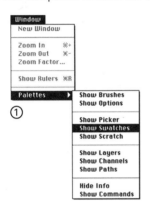

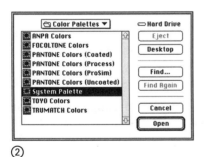

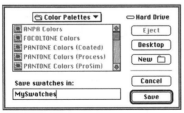

1. Within Photoshop, select Picker from the Window menu, then choose Show Swatches from the Picker submenu.

2. Now you're going to load your default system palette. Click the pop-up menu in the upper right-hand corner of the Swatches palette, and choose Load Swatches. Navigate the folder hierarchy until you load the system palette from your Photoshop application folder.

3. Save this palette under a different name, because we're going to edit it down to a set that you'll just use for saving your Web graphics. Click the pop-up menu in the upper-right-hand corner of the Swatches palette, and choose Save Swatches. Here I've named the new swatch set MySwatches.

4. Resize the window until all the palette's swatches are displayed. There should be 256 values shown; if you counted, you'd see 16 rows with 16 swatch icons each. We're going to remove all 40 swatches that have RGB values that are not 0, 51, 102, 153, 204, or 255. Select Picker from the Window menu, then choose Show Info from the Picker submenu. I've positioned the two palettes side by side, so you can hold your cursor over each swatch and see what its corresponding RGB values are.

5. Locating and removing the 40 rogue (potentially dithering) colors is easier than you might think. On the Macintosh side, all 40 are located near the very bottom of the swatch palette. The very last swatch is a keeper, but the previous 40

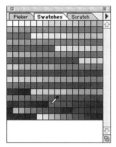
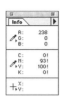

④

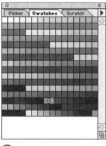

⑤

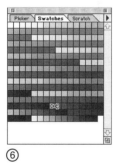

⑥

are the ones that we're deleting. Look for a bright red swatch with the RGB values (238, 0, 0). This is the first one we're going to delete. After we delete it, all the other swatches will move over one space to the left, so you just need to keep your cursor steady.

Hold your cursor over the first swatch to delete. Hold down ⌘ (for Mac users) or Ctrl (for Windows users). As mentioned in the tip a while back, your cursor will change to a scissors icon. Now click the swatch and watch it disappear.

6. The next swatch you should delete will move right into position; you don't even need to move your cursor. Make sure you check its RGB values in the Info palette before you delete it, though, just in case you've inadvertently moved your cursor. On the Mac side, the next swatch to delete will have an RGB value of (221, 0, 0).

7. After you've deleted 40 swatches, you'll wind up with 13 rows of 16 swatches and a half row of 8 swatches (see Figure 4.14). You can now load this Swatches palette every time you save a GIF for a Web site and know that the colors won't dither on Macintosh or Windows monitors. Remember to save your finished palette.

We've looked at how to create and edit custom color palettes in Photoshop, but we haven't yet used them yet in applying such a palette to an image. If you wanted to experiment with editing or creating custom icons, for example, you're best off loading and using your system palette.

Figure 4.14

The custom MySwatches palette, a perfect CLUT for Web graphics

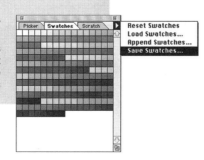

EXERCISE 4.2

Converting an Image to a Custom CLUT Palette

In this exercise, we'll load a 24-bit image and then index it using the MySwatches color palette. This will give us an image that that can be served up on the Web without fear of dithering.

①

②

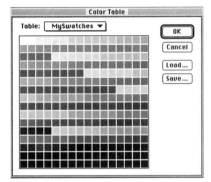

③

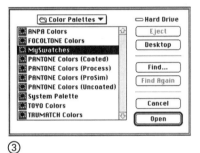

③

1. Open an existing detailed image from your hard drive. If you don't have a graphic of your own that you want to play with, use one of the samples from Photoshop's Tutorial folder. Make sure the Info palette is also displayed. Move your cursor over the image and note the diversity of RGB values that appear.

2. Select Indexed Color from the Mode menu. In the Indexed Color dialog box, click on the Custom option under Palette. This is where we're going to specify using the MySwatches palette.

3. Click on the Load… button from the resulting Color Table dialog box. Navigate the directory structure until you highlight the MySwatches file. Click on OK.

4. Your image now uses only colors specified in the MySwatches palette. Depending on the quality of your original image, you may or may not see any appreciable difference between your original and the remapped image. Move your cursor over the image and notice how all the pixels have RGB values that use one of the numbers specified in the MySwatches palette—either 0, 51, 102, 153, 204, or 255. Save the new image if you want to use it again.

Figure 4.15
Mapping a 24-bit image to the MySwatches palette

Table 4.2 Nondithering Netscape RGB Values	
RGB VALUE	**HEXADECIMAL VALUE**
0	00
51	33
102	66
153	99
204	CC
255	FF

Alternative Options for Limiting Colors in Web Graphics

Maybe you're in a hurry and don't want to spare the time or the mental bandwidth to worry about loading and using a custom lookup table. Or you may already be using the nondithering MySwatches palette, but you know your graphics don't need to use that many colors. You can use the Indexed Color mode to reduce down the number of colors in your image as much as possible.

Select Indexed Color from the Mode menu, then select Adaptive in the Palette section and Diffusion as the Dither method. Experiment with reducing the number of colors (your changes will preview in your image behind the Indexed Color dialog box). If you can get your work down to 32 or 64 colors instead of 256 without reducing its quality too much, your images will be smaller—and load faster to boot.

If you go outside of Photoshop, you can also use a Web graphics utility like Debabelizer to remap Macintosh graphics to the standard Windows color palette.

Color Options in Painting and Editing Modes

Chapter 3 touched very briefly on how the Options palette for Photoshop's painting and editing tools offered Mode settings that could change colors drastically and create a number of special effects. I held off on describing these painting and editing modes until this chapter, however, because they largely deal with color. You're going to want to understand how each setting figures out which colors it will affect; otherwise, using these modes can largely consist of trial and error. Here is a brief explanation of each setting:

👁 **Normal**   With Opacity set to 100 percent, this option lets you paint or edit fully with the foreground color in the effect you're applying, knocking out all underlying colors. If the Opacity is set to a lower number, the value of the color you're applying is averaged in with the color value of the underlying pixels, so the underlying color will show through the effect you're applying.

👁 **Dissolve**   The color you're painting with will replace random pixels that you paint or edit over. The collective effect is that of your image dissolving into the color you're painting with. It works with all the painting tools but not the editing tools. You can get some dramatic effects using this mode with the Airbrush or the Paint tool set with a large-sized brush in the Brushes palette.

👁 **Behind**   This mode only works in images with multiple layers and transparent backgrounds, covered in Chapter 5. It lets you edit transparent parts of a layer—where no other color has been placed—but not the independent images or objects previously placed on that layer.

👁 **Multiply**   This mode combines your foreground color with the underlying pixel colors, effectively deepening the color values the way you'd get deeper colors by coloring with felt tip markers on top of one another. The more you use a tool in Multiply mode, the darker the affected pixels will get.

Screen   This mode creates the opposite effect of Multiply mode by whitening affected pixels. The effect is something like using an ink eraser on a colored drawing. The more you use a tool in Screen mode, the lighter the affected pixels will get.

Overlay   This is a combination of the Multiply and Screen modes that can be used to produce really visually pleasing effects—it enhances contrast and enriches color saturation.

Soft Light   This mode is designed to produce a muted spotlight effect on the areas you're painting or editing.

Hard Light   This mode is designed to produce a rather harsh lighting effect on the areas you're painting or editing.

Darken   Pixels that are lighter than the color you're applying get filled with the new color; darker pixels remain untouched.

Lighten   Pixels that are darker than the color you're applying get filled with the new color; darker pixels remain untouched.

Difference   This mode inverts the colors in your image to the difference between your foreground color and the color of the underlying pixels.

Hue   Painting and editing in this mode will affect only the hue—the pure color—of each pixel you touch, not the saturation or luminosity. Any solid black or solid white pixels will be unaffected.

Saturation   Painting and editing in this mode will affect only the saturation—how much gray is mixed in each pixel you touch; the hue and luminosity are untouched. Any solid black or solid white pixels will be unaffected.

Color   This mode is a combination of painting with the Hue and Saturation modes; both hue and saturation are affected, but not luminosity (brightness). The most useful application for this editing mode is in colorizing grayscale images.

👁 **Luminosity**   This mode is effectively the opposite of the Color mode; it influences the luminosity—or brightness—of the pixels you edit, but not the hue or saturation.

Summary

The information covered in this chapter will serve as a good grounding for the discussions later in the book about how to color-correct images and anticipate other color issues in print production. Learning how to work with custom color palettes will help you create images for applications and systems that have their own internal color models. Gaining an awareness of Web color issues will help you develop coordinated image sets and explore other avenues for improving your graphics' display time and appearance.

Up ahead in Chapter 5, we cover Photoshop's layers feature. It's the biggest change that was added to version 3, and an innovation that will give you unprecedented flexibility in your image editing.

You can create geometric shapes with the Rectangular or Elliptical Marquee tool, then add gradient blends using the Gradient tool. For the shaded sphere, I applied a radial blend across the center of the circle to fade the color from orange to black. For the square bullet, I created two squares with diagonal linear blends; later, I pasted the smaller square on top of the larger one.

Carved or recessed text looks best against a rocky or stucco-textured background. The shadows within the type outlines were created using the Offset filter.

With layers and the Emboss filter, you can create the illusion of raised type on a textured background.

Adding beveled edges to geometric shapes is a good way to create three-dimensional buttons suitable for Web graphics. You can use the Airbrush tool to create soft beveled edges; there are also several plug-ins that make it easy to add beveled edges.

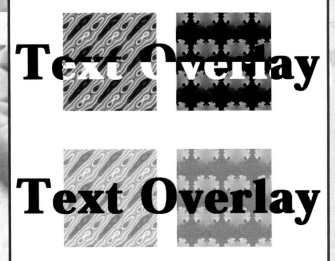

Background textures should be seamless—so the image's borders are not readily apparent—and in good contrast to overlaid type. While you can knock out type in white or another color, as in the top image, it's a strain on the viewer's eyes if there's a lot of text to read. Lowering the opacity of a bright pattern is usually a good solution.

To create drop shadows in this image, I entered the type on its own layer, separate from the background texture. I duplicated the layer, moved it behind the type layer. Next, I filled the letters with black, applied the Gaussian Blur filter, and reduced the opacity.

When you place objects on different layers in a Photoshop image, you have the luxury of editing one part without affecting others. Here, I've reduced the opacity of the background image to make the overlaid type (on a separate layer) stand out more.

To create this spiraling border effect, I used the Paths palette to turn my type selection into a path. I then applied a stroke to the path, using a magenta foreground color and a custom brush from the Brushes palette. As a last step, I pasted a copy of the original text selection on top to aid readability.

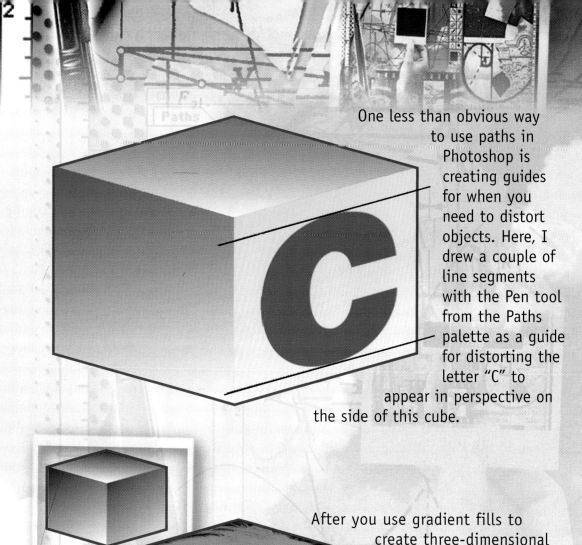

One less than obvious way to use paths in Photoshop is creating guides for when you need to distort objects. Here, I drew a couple of line segments with the Pen tool from the Paths palette as a guide for distorting the letter "C" to appear in perspective on the side of this cube.

After you use gradient fills to create three-dimensional shapes, you can map images onto them using layers with Overlay or Multiply mode settings. Here, I mapped three different images onto this 3-D cube to create a photo cube.

With the Lighting Effects filter, you can create all kinds of realistic-looking textured backgrounds and raised text. Here,

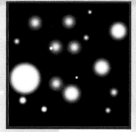

I created an alpha channel (above) and designated it as the texture channel in the Lighting Effects dialog box. This helped produce a bumpy textured surface (right); I saved my light settings so I could add other objects (far right) with the same light source.

Besides drop shadows, the Gaussian Blur filter is great for creating glowing effects behind images.

You can create the custom mezzotint effect shown here by splitting channels in an image, temporarily converting each separated grayscale channel to Bitmap mode, and applying the grayscale conversion technique (shown in the example at the top of the next page) to individual channels. Afterwards, you convert each channel back to the Grayscale mode and merge channels into one document again.

You can use Photoshop's export filter for creating a transparent GIF—like the toothbrush image shown here—to make Web graphics that seem to float on top of background images.

The Good Dental Hygiene Page

Welcome to our little corner of the Web. Step right into our virtual waiting room; we've tried to recreate the atmosphere of the real thing by providing hyperlinks to back issues of online magazines dating back nine to twelve months ago.

More importantly, we hope to provide a resource for answering those little questions that come up between your dental visits.

Everyday Tips

- Visit your dentist twice a year. Don't just schedule an appointment and cancel at the last minute!
- Brush your teeth after meals.
- Floss, floss, floss like there's no tomorrow!
- Avoid sugary snacks.

Other Resources

When you convert a grayscale image to black and white art, you can generate interesting effects by applying a custom Postscript pattern.

For this image, I wanted to let the type in a page layout program run over the shadow but not the hammer itself. I saved the hammer and its shadow in separate files. I added a clipping path to the hammer so its background would be treated as transparent by the page layout program.

Let's say you had a hammer. You might want to consider whether there were better times of day to hammer than others. For example, would you hammer in the morning? Or would you choose instead to hammer in the evening? Location is also very important. For example, your evening hammering might be interrupted—or at least objected to—if your next-door neighbors are light sleepers. We may be assuming too much on this front; it may be the case that you don't live in an apartment building and therefore don't have neighbors who are in such close proximity to your quarters. These are but a few of the kinds of questions you could ask

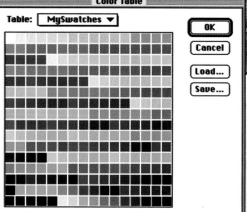

Color Table

Table: MySwatches ▼

OK
Cancel
Load...
Save...

By creating and applying indexed color palettes, you can limit how many and which colors are used in an image. This image of a farmhouse was mapped to the 216-color palette optimized for Web graphics. Notice that some colors dropped out of the sky area, but the rest of the image is virtually untouched.

Lorem ipsum dolor sit amet, consete tur sadipscing elitr, sed diam nonumy eirmod tempor invidunt ut labore tet dolore magna aliquyam ert, sed diamvluptua. At

You can use the layers feature to create translucent overlays on parts of an image for placing blocks of text. The example here just shows some tinkering with opacity, but you can also fill a translucent selection with a gradient fill. This technique is commonly used for creating opening spreads for magazine layouts.

You can get more mileage out of filters by duplicating an image on another layer, applying your effects, and then compositing the filtered image with the original. Here, I duplicated the Mt. Rushmore image on a new layer, applied the Find Edge filter, and then changed the mode of the filtered layer to Multiply. I selected the sky area separately and applied the Clouds filter there.

This composite image was made by silhouetting the close-up view of the eagle on its own layer, then overlaying it (in Darken mode) over an image of the eagle in flight.

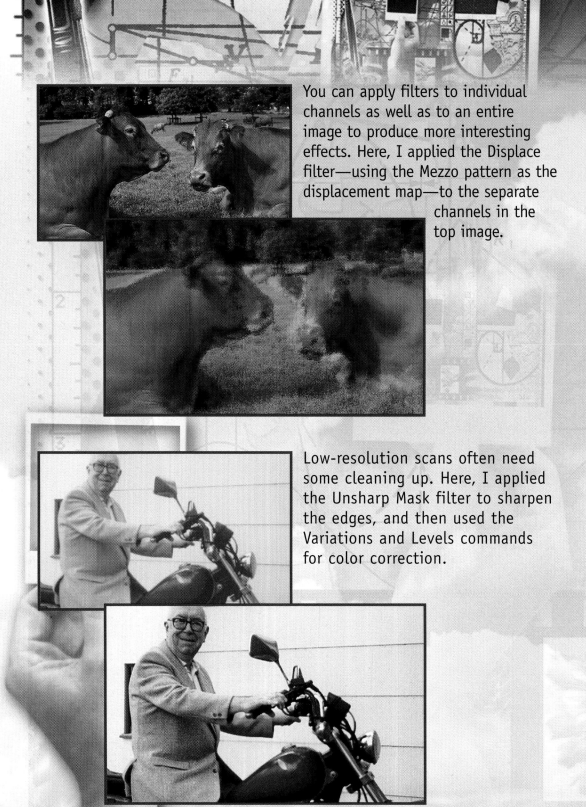

You can apply filters to individual channels as well as to an entire image to produce more interesting effects. Here, I applied the Displace filter—using the Mezzo pattern as the displacement map—to the separate channels in the top image.

Low-resolution scans often need some cleaning up. Here, I applied the Unsharp Mask filter to sharpen the edges, and then used the Variations and Levels commands for color correction.

Clip art images on Kodak Photo CDs often look better after you apply the Unsharp filter, as shown here.

You can colorize grayscale photographs by applying a color fill to a new layer set to Overlay mode. Here, I created a sepia-toned version of the original image by filling the entire image with an orange-brown hue.

You can use the Curves dialog box to increase contrast (above) or reverse the curves to invert the image (below). The latter effect is the same as choosing Invert from the Map menu.

You can add feathery-edged vignettes to any image by choosing the Marquee tool, entering a Feather value in the tool's Options dialog box, designating your selection area on the original image, inverting it, and then deleting the inverted selection. You can also accomplish this effect with the Quick Mask feature.

With masks, you can fill any selected shape with another image or repeating pattern. I used two different masks in this image—one for the repeating pattern in the type outline, and one to fill the oval shape with the dessert image.

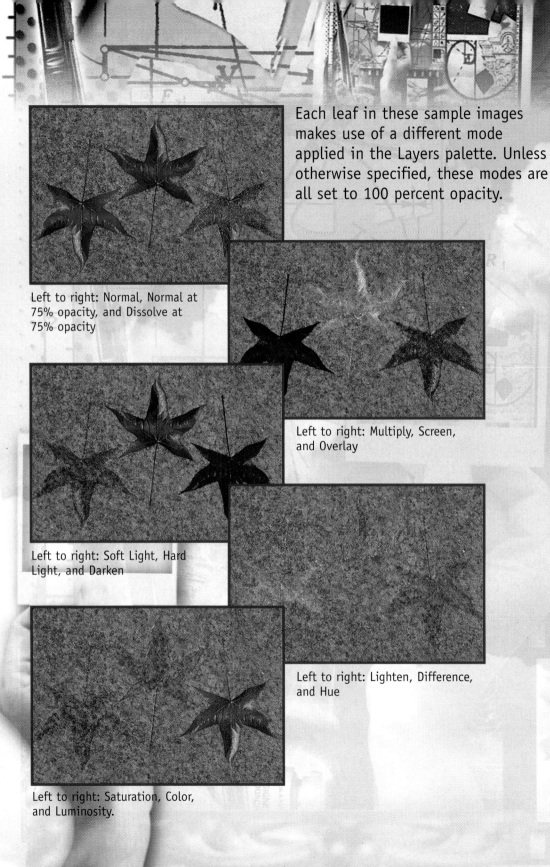

Each leaf in these sample images makes use of a different mode applied in the Layers palette. Unless otherwise specified, these modes are all set to 100 percent opacity.

Left to right: Normal, Normal at 75% opacity, and Dissolve at 75% opacity

Left to right: Multiply, Screen, and Overlay

Left to right: Soft Light, Hard Light, and Darken

Left to right: Lighten, Difference, and Hue

Left to right: Saturation, Color, and Luminosity.

Here's an example of an image that looks great for a background pattern—except that it doesn't tile seamlessly. As you can see in the tiled image at right, it's apparent where the image ends and starts to repeat.

Transforming this jellybean background into a seamless tile is a two-part process. First, you'll need to use the Offset filter to move the image over half its width, and down half its length.

Compare the image at the right with the original above; your offset image will now have a seam running across its middle. Next, you can use the Rubber Stamp tool to smooth over the seam with other parts of the patterned image. When your edited image tiles now, it should repeat smoothly without the disruptive edging you saw earlier.

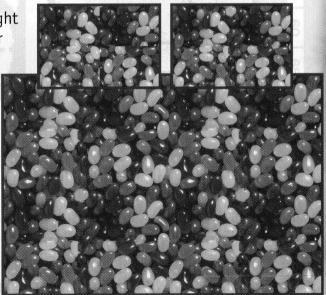

When you're color-tinting grayscale images like the one at left for a two-color print job, you can achieve different effects with overlaying the second color in a separate layer (below left) and specifying a duotone (below right).

5
Layering Essentials

IN THIS CHAPTER

Creating New Layers

Deleting, Manipulating,
and Combining Layers

Translucent Overlays

Special Effects

Using Photoshop's layers feature is analogous to overlaying several sheets of acetate on a presentation board, where you can see through the transparent part to images and text on other layers. Or if you're a Toys R Us kid, it's a little like playing with Colorforms; you can see the composite effect, but still rearrange parts at any time if you want to. The layers feature was a powerful addition to Photoshop 3, giving the program some of the functionality of a vector-based illustration program, where objects can manipulated independently of the remainder of the image. It provides an extremely versatile way to combine images and preview the resulting photocompositions before committing to the changes.

Some of the most breathtaking Photoshop effects come from the judicious use of layers. You can import rendered images from another software package in one layer, add shadows in another layer, and manipulate a background texture in a third. With layers, it's easy to create mask effects—letter or object outlines through which you can see another image. These techniques enable you to create many popular photo effects used on book covers and in advertising and magazine graphics.

Adding layers can require a whopping amount of additional memory, though, so it's important to understand when and how to use layers to create additional effects and retain flexibility in image editing. The major topics to be covered in this chapter include:

- The basics of manipulating layers: creating, deleting, and editing layers

- Moving layers between documents

- Using layers to create masked fills

- Experimenting with layers and special effects

- Blending layers together and creating layer masks

Creating New Layers

The Layers palette controls the arrangement of layers in your documents. Here's where you specify when you want to create a new layer, target a single layer so as to edit its contents, merge two together, and delete a layer altogether.

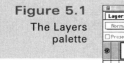

Figure 5.1

The Layers
palette

You can display the Layers palette by selecting Palettes from the Window menu, then choosing Show Layers from the Palettes submenu (see Figure 5.1).

The first time you choose the Layers palette, you'll see its folder-like display partnered with two other palettes, the Paths palette and the Channels palette. These two palettes are discussed in much greater detail in the two chapters that follow this one. For now, just note that you can click on one of these other palettes to bring them to the forefront, then click the Layers palette's tab to restore the Layers palette to the front. You can also click and drag the Layers palette's tab to reposition it anywhere on screen you like.

When you create a new file, the document contains a single layer that's named Background if you clicked the White or Background Color radio button in the Contents section of the New dialog box. However, as Figure 5.2 shows, if you click the Transparent radio button for Contents, then your base layer is just labeled Layer 1.

note

You might think that if you create a single-layer image with a Transparent background you can import it into a page layout program and retain the transparency. This isn't the case, however. If you want to drop out the background in a Photoshop document, you have to outline an object in the document with a *clipping path*, which is covered in Chapter 6.

Floating Selections

If you paste a selection from another document into your new one, or if you use the Type tool to add some type, your new addition will

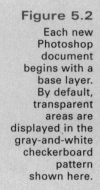

Figure 5.2
Each new Photoshop document begins with a base layer. By default, transparent areas are displayed in the gray-and-white checkerboard pattern shown here.

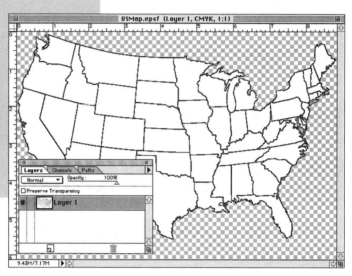

appear as a *floating selection* outlined by marching ants. It will be labeled Floating Selection in the Layers palette as well.

Figure 5.3 shows how your Layers palette changes when you place a floating selection in a Photoshop document. The Background row in

Figure 5.3
The Layers palette adds a Floating Selection layer when you paste a still-selected element in your document.

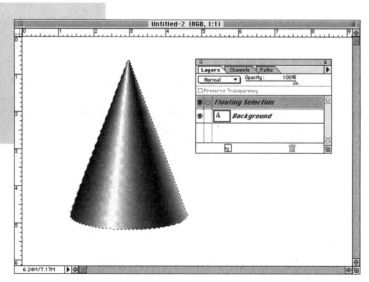

the Layers palette is highlighted in gray, showing that this is the layer you're currently working in; it's also known as your *target layer*. The eye icon (🕸) that appears on both rows shows that both the Background and Floating Selection layers are visible in your document.

After you place a floating selection in your document, you have a couple of choices. You could paste it directly into your background layer, where it becomes an integral part of that layer. If you paste it in and then reselect and move it, it will leave behind a hole that will fill with the background color. Alternatively, you could place your floating selection on its own layer, which will let you reposition it without affecting the elements of any other layer (see Figure 5.4).

To create a new layer just for placing a floating selection, double-click the row in the Layers palette that reads Floating Selection or drag that row to the New Layer icon. This will call up the Make Layer dialog box (Figure 5.5). I'll skip the detail here, as it's very similar to the New Layer dialog box described in the next section.

New Layer Options

There are several ways to create a new layer. You can choose New Layer from the pop-up menu on the Layers palette, or click the New Layer icon at the bottom of the Layers palette (see Figure 5.6).

Either of these actions will cause the New Layer dialog box to appear (see Figure 5.7). The resulting dialog box offers options for the opacity and mode for the new layer, plus whether or not it should be grouped with other layers. When you create a new layer, it becomes your current target layer.

tip

• •

Automatically Creating a New Layer

You can bypass the New Layer dialog box when you create a new layer by holding down Option (for Mac users) or Alt (for Windows users) as you press the New Layer icon (▨) on the Layers palette.

• •

Figure 5.4
Moving an object on its own layer will not affect any other part of your image.

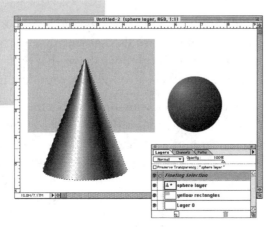

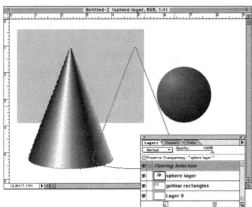

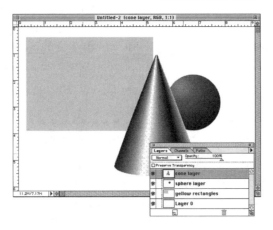

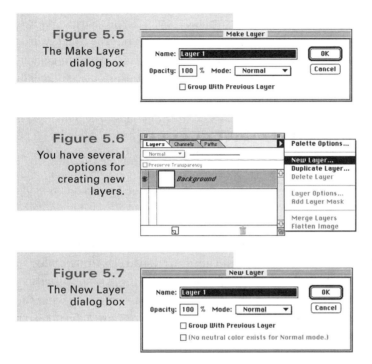

Figure 5.5
The Make Layer dialog box

Figure 5.6
You have several options for creating new layers.

Figure 5.7
The New Layer dialog box

If you change your mind about what to name your new layer, you can rename it at any time by choosing the Layer Options command from the Layer palette's pop-up menu.

note

Once you start adding multiple layers in a Photoshop document, you'll only be able to save it in native Photoshop format. When you're all done editing individual layers and want to save your file in another format, you should choose Flatten Image from the Layers palette's pop-up menu before choosing Save or Save As. See the "Merging Layers" section later in this chapter.

Establishing What Layer to Work On

If you were editing a composite image made up of several images on transparent acetate and wanted to reposition a certain object, you might have to flip through several sheets to find the right one you wanted. Photoshop's layers feature works the same way; if you wanted to edit a black oval on Layer 3, you'd have to make Layer 3 your target layer before you could select the black oval—you wouldn't be able to select it from another layer. This section covers both how to find the right layer when you want to edit part of your image, and how to tell what layer you're in at any given time.

Using the Layer Thumbnails

One way to keep track of what's on each layer is to look at the thumbnail sketch of each layer that appears by default in the Layers palette (see Figure 5.8).

You can also adjust this to view a larger thumbnail sketch or to hide the thumbnail altogether. Click the Layer palette's pop-up menu arrow and choose Palette Options; this will cause the Layer Options dialog box to appear (Figure 5.9). However, the default setting is what usually works best—hiding the thumbnail defeats the purpose of seeing what's on your separate layers, and the larger views take up more screen real estate and take longer to redraw.

Watching the Title Bar

Once you get caught up in manipulating parts of an image you may forget the name of the layer you're working on. With the Layers palette open, you can tell at a glance—that row is highlighted in gray. But you can also tell what layer you're working in even if the Layers palette is closed by looking at your document's title bar. The name of

Figure 5.8

Seeing at a glance what images are contained on each layer

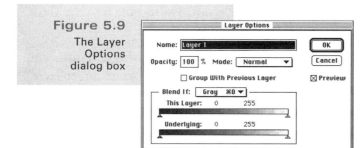

Figure 5.9
The Layer Options dialog box

the layer appears in parentheses after the document title, along with the mode (RGB, CMYK, or whatever) and the current viewing ratio (see Figure 5.10).

Deleting Layers

You've added a funny mustache and devil's horns to that annual report photo of your company's CEO; now you've got to delete that layer and get back to color-correcting his pasty complexion. You need to start by making the about-to-be-cut layer your target layer. Now you can either choose Delete Layer from the Layers palette pop-up menu, or drag the layer's row to the Trash icon in the lower-right corner of the Layers palette, as shown in Figure 5.11.

Figure 5.10
The document's title bar lists the layer you're working in.

Figure 5.11
Options for deleting a layer

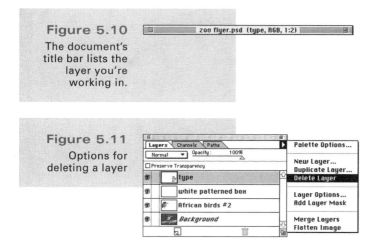

Similarly, you can delete a floating selection by dragging it to the Trash icon in the lower-right corner of the Layers palette.

You can even remove your image's background, leaving a transparent background in place. Make the Background layer your target layer, click on the layer's name in the Layers palette, and drag it to the Trash icon. The Background layer will disappear from the Layers palette and Photoshop's checkerboard pattern that denotes transparency will fill the background parts of your image.

note   **You can always add a Background layer to a Photoshop image, even if you've deleted that layer. Create a new layer using one of the methods described above, then choose Background from the Mode menu in the dialog box, as shown in Figure 5.12.**

Manipulating Layers

This section covers how to move whole layers around at a time, how to link them so that you can move several layers at once, and some quick tips for toggling between layers.

Moving Layers

You can move a whole layer with the Move tool (✛) or edit objects in a single layer with the usual choices you have in your Toolbox. You can

Figure 5.12
Adding a new
Background layer

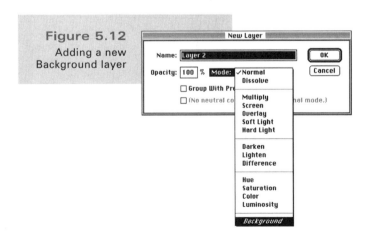

use the directional arrow keys with the Move tool to move a layer in any of the four major directions one pixel at a time; holding down [Shift] will move the layer ten pixels at a time. This is a useful trick for creating shadows: you can select an object in its own layer, duplicate the layer (using the Duplicate Layer feature in the Layer palette's pop-up menu), change the shadow image's color and edges as necessary, then offset it from the original horizontally and vertically by using the directional arrow keys.

Linking Layers Together

It's also possible to link several layers together. You can see how useful this is if you want to reposition an object and its shadow—you wouldn't want to have to move them one at a time and hope to maintain the same spatial relationship using guesswork. To link two layers together, first make sure that one of the two is set as your target layer. Click the empty column to the left of the target layer's thumbnail image in its row in the Layers palette. A link icon (✛) will appear in the column. Next, click the same column in the row for the second layer you want to link to. The link icon will appear in that row, too. When you choose the Move tool and reposition one layer, the second layer will move at the same time.

Viewing and Hiding Layers

As you edit objects on a single layer, you may find it distracting to view the elements on other layers. You can hide the layers other than your target layer by clicking the eye icon (👁) next to their names in each

Figure 5.13

Linking an object in one layer with its shadow in another

row of the Layers palette. You can click the eye column again to make the layer visible once more. You can click and drag your cursor all the way up or down a long list of layers to make them all visible or invisible (Figure 5.14).

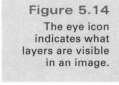

tip   **Hiding and Revealing All Nontarget Layers at Once**

The quick-and-easy way to hide all nontarget layers is to press Option (for Mac users) or Alt (for Windows users) as you click the eye icon for your target layer. Repeating the procedure will reveal all the hidden layers.

Scrolling Through Layers Via Keystrokes

It's also possible to move among layers without ever calling up the Layers palette. Table 5.1 shows the relevant keystrokes you need to know:

If you want to view one layer at a time as you use key commands to jump from layer to layer, just set your target layer to be the only visible layer before you start scrolling from layer to layer.

Copying Layers Between Documents

If you want or need to copy one layer from your image to a different document, Photoshop has a easy built-in way to do so. First, open the file that you want to copy the layer into. Select the layer you want to copy as your target layer, then choose Duplicate Layer from the Layers

Figure 5.14
The eye icon indicates what layers are visible in an image.

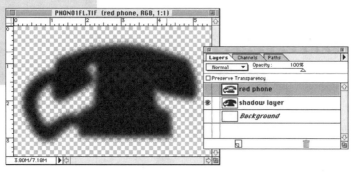

Table 5.1   Key Commands to Move Between Layers

Action	Key command (Mac)	Key command (Windows)
Jump to previous layer	⌘-[	Ctrl-[
Jump to next layer	⌘-]	Ctrl-]
Jump to topmost layer	⌘-Option-[	Ctrl-Alt-[
Jump to bottom layer	⌘-Option-]	Ctrl-Alt-]

palette's pop-up menu. You'll then see a dialog box that lets you select the open (or new) document into which you want to copy the layer.

You can also accomplish this duplicating effect by using the Move tool to drag one whole layer physically to another document's window.

Both of these methods make better sense than just copying and pasting an entire layer—which can really put a strain on Photoshop's memory and slow the program's operations to a crawl.

Copying an image to a new layer in a document is one of the first steps in the next exercise—using layers to create good-looking drop shadows against any kind of background.

Rearranging Your Layers' Order

As in Step 4 of Exercise 5.1, you may sometimes need to rearrange the order of the layers in a Photoshop document. Much like shuffling a deck of cards, you can rearrange the order in which layers in a Photoshop document stack one atop the other.

To bring a layer to the forefront, display the Layers palette and position your cursor over the name of the layer you want to move up. Click and drag the outline of the row (for example, Layer 1 from Exercise 5.1) over and above the name of the layer you want it to overlap (say, the Shadow layer). The line that separates the rows in the Layers palette will turn darker as you move a layer selection over it, which indicates that this is a spot where you can reposition your selection between two other layers (Figure 5.16).

EXERCISE 5.1

Creating a Drop Shadow on a Textured Background

In Chapter 3, you saw an exercise for creating shadows, but that quick-and-dirty method is mostly useful for objects placed on solid-colored backgrounds. If you've got a background image or textured pattern, you're going to need a better method to produce realistic results.

In this exercise, you'll use layers to create an object with a shadow that looks realistic against a textured background. Since the object, the shadow, and the background texture all appear on different layers, you can experiment as much as you want with creating different lighting effects and deeper shadows before committing to a final image.

①

①

1. You'll need two images to start off with: the first should be the object you're going to add the shadow to, and the second will be your background image.

   The image that you want to apply the shadow to should be smaller in size than your background image with the same resolution.

2. Next, you'll need to copy the image you want to apply the drop shadow to into the background texture image. Instead of copying and pasting—the most memory-hogging method—try using the Move tool to drag the object into the background texture image's document window. This will create a floating selection containing your object over the background image. To save the floating selection on its own layer, choose Make Layer command from the Layers palette's pop-up menu. Here, I've just called the layer containing the typewriter Layer 1.

3. Now you've got your object and the background together in one image on separate layers. You'll need to duplicate the object's layer to create the shadow layer.

   Make sure your object layer is selected as the target layer; its row in the Layers palette will appear with a gray background behind it. Now choose Duplicate Layer command from the Layers palette's pop-up menu. Give the shadow layer a new name in the As field of the Duplicate Layer dialog box, and choose the current document as the destination for that layer.

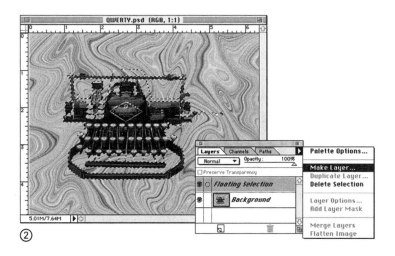

②

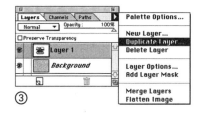

③

③

Here's an alternative way to duplicate the layer: Drag its row from the Layers palette down to the New Layer icon. This will automatically create a new layer with the same name as your object's layer followed by the word "copy" but you can rename this layer by double-clicking its row in the Layers palette. Double-clicking a layer's row will call up the Layer Options dialog box, where you can enter a new name in the Name field.

4. No matter which method you use to create the duplicate layer, you'll discover one glitch: the duplicate Shadow layer is atop Layer 1. You can rearrange the order of the layers by clicking and dragging the appropriate row in the Layers palette to a different position; the only exception is that any layer named Background must remain the bottom layer. More detailed steps for switching the order of your document's layers are included in the "Rearranging Your Layers' Order" section immediately following this exercise.

You should now have three layers in your document: your object layer (called Layer 1 here), a shadow layer (called Shadow here, although so far it's just a duplicate of Layer 1), and your background layer. Here's the order in which you should see these three layers in your Layers palette.

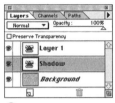

The name of the target layer appears in the document's title bar.

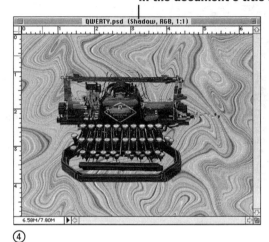

④

④

Note that when you're working in a Photoshop document with more than one layer, the name of the target layer appears in the title bar at the top of the document.

5. With the Shadow layer as your target layer, you can now offset the image slightly from your original object to create the illusion of a shadow. Use the directional arrow tools to move the shadow horizontally and vertically, or just use the Move tool to offset the image.

6. Next, you'll need to edit the shadow image to make it look more realistic. Let's focus on just this layer by hiding the other layers; click the eye icons on the other two layers to make them temporarily disappear from view.

7. Now that the other layers are hidden, you can darken the shadow object by filling in its shape with a dark color.

To apply the dark fill to just the shadow object and not the whole layer, click the Preserve Transparency check box in the Layers palette. Now click the foreground color icon and fill it with a dark color you'd like to use for your shadow. After you've chosen a color and clicked OK, choose Fill from the Edit menu. In the Fill dialog box, make sure that the Use pop-up menu is set to Foreground Color and the Mode pop-

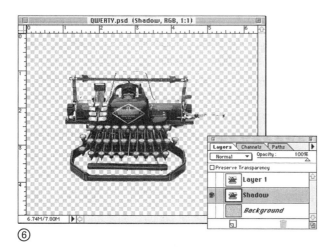

⑥

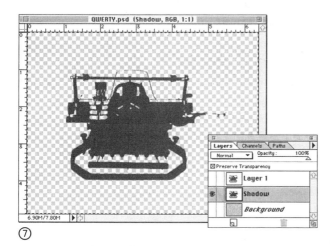

⑦

up menu is set to Normal. You can leave Opacity at 100 percent, but you can also make it a little lower (80 or 90 percent) if you want a hint of the textured background to show through.

8. Next, let's blur the shadow's edges to make it look more realistic. Choose Blur from the Filter menu, then choose Gaussian Blur from the Blur submenu. Enter 5 in the Radius field; you can enter a higher number for a more pronounced blur or a lower number for a less dramatic blur.

9. Let's bring the other layers back into view so you can eyeball the whole effect (Figure 5.15). Click the eye icons next to the other layers. If you'd like, you can still move the shadow image closer or further from the original object by repositioning the Shadow layer. Experiment with moving the object and its shadow together by linking the two layers: click the link column (next to the eye column) in both layers. Use the Move tool to move either the object or its shadow, and you'll see the other layer move too.

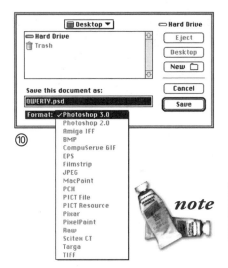

10. Save your file if you want to retain it for future use. Note that the only file format option available to you is native Photoshop format because your file contains multiple Photoshop layers, and those aren't supported by other graphics formats.

note

Chapter 8, "Filter Essentials," discusses Gaussian Blur and the other blur filters in great detail.

Figure 5.15

The completed drop shadow effect, accomplished with Layers

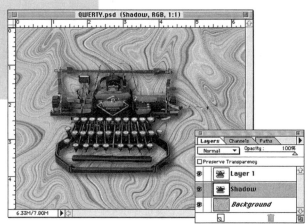

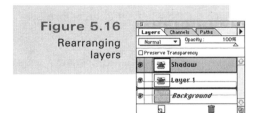

Figure 5.16
Rearranging
layers

The order of the layers in the Layers palette reflects the top-to-bottom order of the layers in your Photoshop document. The Background layer is the only one that you cannot reposition elsewhere in your document—by virtue of its name—but you can easily work around this restriction by giving the layer a different name.

Creating Translucent Overlays

Remember the Opacity setting in the New Layer and Make Layer dialog boxes? Here's where we'll get into what it's really useful for: blending together several layers to produce the effect of a shaded overlay on an image.

Let's say you want to lower the opacity of a rectangular selection (shown behind the text area) on its own layer in the image shown in Figure 5.17. Here, I made the layer with the rectangular selection my target

Figure 5.17
Lowering the
opacity of the
rectangular
selection behind
the text is
accomplished by
using the Opacity
slider in the
Layers palette.

layer, then lowered the Opacity slider to create a lighter colored box so the overlying text would be more readable.

A translucent effect is used frequently in magazines or on book covers to set apart a section of an image where you want to apply type. It helps to draw attention to the type and make that whole area of the image stand out more.

Changing Mode Settings to Create Special Effects

In Chapter 4, we looked at the Mode settings that appear in the Options palette for most of the painting and editing tools—including Multiply, Screen, Overlay, Soft Light, Hard Light, and others. These same Mode settings show up when you define the characteristics of a new layer, and are pretty versatile here too. When you use these modes as you create and stack layers, the colors of the target layer and the layers beneath them are affected.

note The only Mode setting from the painting and editing tools that's missing here is the Behind mode—that setting for painting in just the transparent parts of a layer just doesn't have an equivalent here.

Here's a brief description of how each of these Mode settings can be used in adding layers to an image:

Normal. With Opacity set to 100 percent, here's where the Colorforms analogy for describing layers works best; objects on your target layer overlap pixels on underlying layers and knock them out. As you lower the opacity, more of the pixels in underlying layers show through.

👁 **Dissolve.** Random pixels in your target layer drop out to reveal the underlying layers. As you reduce the target layer's opacity, more and more of the underlying layers will show through.

👁 **Multiply.** Adding a layer with this mode has the effect of creating a darker composite of the image in your target layer with the underlying layers, much as if you were covering an image with felt-tip markings.

👁 **Screen.** Just like the painting and editing tools' version of Screen, this mode is the opposite of Multiply mode; the pixels in underlying layers beneath objects in your target layers are bleached to a lighter composite of the two color values.

👁 **Overlay.** This mode lets you see the highlights and shadows of the underlying layer, but uses the color values in the target layer.

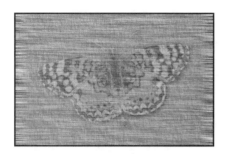

◉ **Soft Light.** This mode adds a softening lighting effect over the underlying layers; the effect is often very subtle.

◉ **Hard Light.** This mode adds a much stronger lighting effect than Soft Light.

◉ **Darken.** Pixels in underlying layers that are lighter than the corresponding colors in your target layer are replaced; pixels in underlying layers that are darker than the corresponding colors in your target layer remain untouched.

◉ **Lighten.** Pixels in underlying layers that are darker than the corresponding colors in your target layer are replaced; pixels in underlying layers that are lighter than the corresponding colors in your target layer remain untouched.

👁 **Difference.** With this mode, you subtract the color values in your target layer from the underlying colors and change colors to their RGB complements.

👁 **Hue.** This layer mode creates a blend of your target layer's color values with the underlying layers' saturation and luminosity. To showcase the mode better, I placed the butterfly image on a layer in Hue mode over a yellow background (left) and a dark maroon background (right).

👁 **Saturation.** This layer mode creates a blend of your target layer's levels of grays with the underlying layers' hue and luminosity. To showcase the mode's effect here, I placed the butterfly image on a layer in Saturation mode over a yellow background (left) and a dark maroon background (right).

 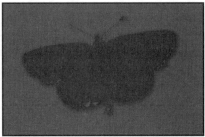

👁 **Color.** This mode blends the Hue and Saturation values of pixels in your target layer with those in underlying layers; Luminosity values remain untouched, so the underlying layers are colorized but remain just as bright as they were before you added your current target layer. The sample image here once again shows the butterfly image atop two brightly colored backgrounds.

👁 **Luminosity.** This layer mode creates a blend of your target layer's brightness with the underlying layers' hue and saturation.

Combining Layers

Now that you've seen how a layer's Mode settings can influence a composite effect, let's look at a couple of the ways you can enact your own version of the movie *The Fly* and blend together two disparate images on different layers.

Clipping Groups

You can use layers to create *clipping groups*—layers that are grouped together in such a way that the outline of an object in one layer is filled with an image or texture from another image. The easiest way to create a clipping group is through the Layers palette. (Option)-click (for Mac users) or [Alt]-click (for Windows users) on the horizontal line between

Figure 5.18
Masking an image with an outlined shape can be accomplished with clipping groups.

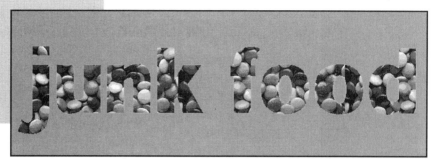

two adjacent layers shown on the Layers palette; this will turn an object on the lower layer into a mask containing the image in the upper layer (see Figure 5.18).

You can also create a clipping group by checking the Group With Previous Layer option in the Layer Options dialog box; it's usually more intuitive, however, to group the two layers from the Layers palette where you can see both thumbnails at once.

Editing More Than One Layer at Once: The Sample Merged Option

You can apply some of Photoshop's tools to work on just one layer, or to affect the pixels in all underlying layers too. The Magic Wand, Paint Bucket, Rubber Stamp, Smudge, and Dodge/Burn/Sponge tools all function this way. This produces the kind of color effects you'd get if all your objects were on a single layer. This way, you retain control over whether or not your Background layer (or other layers) feels the effects of editing you apply in your target layer.

Blending Options

When you double-click any layer besides the Background layer, you'll see that you have options for mixing colors in your target layer with those in underlying layers (Figure 5.20).

note   **In versions of Photoshop prior to 3, these options came under the heading of Composite Controls.**

EXERCISE 5.2

Containing an Image Within Another Object's Outline

In this exercise, you'll learn how to create the kind of masking effect shown in Figure 5.18 by creating a clipping group.

①

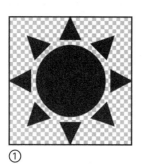

①

①

1. You'll first need to identify an object with well-defined edges to use for creating the outline, and another image or texture pattern to use as the image with which you'll fill the outline. I refer to these below as your outline image and your fill image. I'm also going to suggest creating a separate background layer filled with a solid color to further dramatize the masking effect.

2. Just as you did in Exercise 5.1, use the Move tool or the Duplicate Layer command from the Layers palette to move the outline image and the fill image into their own layers atop your background color. Name the three layers "Fill," "Outline," and "Background." Your fill image needs to appear on the layer on top of the outline image.

3. At this point, your fill image obscures everything on the underlying layers. Hold your cursor over the horizontal line that separates the Fill layer from the Outline layer in your Layers palette, and hold down Option (for Mac users) or Alt (for Windows users). Your cursor should change to a little clipping group icon; click on the line separating the two rows in the Layers palette. You should see an immediate change in your image: you'll see the outline of your Outline object, but it will now surround the image or pattern from your Fill layer.

4. You can undo this effect by Option-clicking (for Mac users) or Alt-clicking (for Windows users) again on the horizontal line between the two layers, or by double-clicking the Fill layer and unchecking the Group With Previous Layer check box. (Note that "previous layer" refers to the next underlying layer.)

②

5. Save your file if you want to retain it for future use. Once again, the only file format option available to you is native Photoshop format because your file contains multiple Photoshop layers, and those aren't supported by other graphics formats.

note **You can also create a clipping group with more than two layers. Experimenting with the Layers palette is the best way to get a sense of what effects you can get with putting multiple layers in clipping groups.**

tip **Creating a Masked Effect with the Paste Into Command**

I have to admit, there is an easier way to create the kind of masked effect you just created in Exercise 5.2. First, select the whole graphic you want to use for the fill image and choose Copy from the Edit menu. Now you can make any other selection in Photoshop and use the Paste Into command from the Edit menu. After you paste your fill image into the other selection but before you deselect it, be sure to save the image to its own layer; that way, you're free to reposition it however you want.

From a design perspective, filling type with an image works best if the image has easily discernible details. If you're filling type with a pattern, make sure it shows stuff that's easy to see—like the junk food in the words "junk food" in Figure 5.18. For a more unified effect, use a bold, sans-serif typeface, and enter 0 for Spacing in the Type Tool dialog box.

Figure 5.19
Your completed effect: a masked image

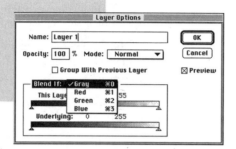

Figure 5.20

Options for blending layers in the Layer Options dialog box

The Blend If section of the Layer Options dialog box lets you set options for how colors in your target layer and underlying layer will blend together.

With the sliders for your target and underlying layer, you can determine how the pixels of your target layer will be pasted onto the underlying background (Figure 5.21). Both layers' slider controls let you select color values in individual RGB channels or overall values (Gray). Both layers' sliders range from 0 to 255, covering the gamut of possible RGB values.

If you look at the slider controls carefully, you'll see that both layers have a white and black slider. These sliders let you exclude ranges of color from each layer when you blend them together. In the This Layer settings, for example, the more you drag each slider to the opposite side, the more colors you exclude from the composite image. All pixel color values that fall in the range between the two sliders will be included in the composite image. In the Underlying Layer settings, the more you drag each slider to the opposite side, the more areas of the underlying image will be forced to appear in the composite image.

Blending together two layers in this way can sometimes force some harsh composite effects. You can create smoother composites by splitting up the two-part black and white sliders. The pixel values that fall in

Figure 5.21

The sliders in the Layer Options dialog box

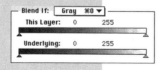

each split range will only be partially colored in the composite image. Gaining mastery of this feature will require a lot of experimenting on your part.

Creating Layer Masks

For each layer you create in Photoshop, you have the opportunity to add a *layer mask,* which lets you vary the transparency of objects in your target layer. This mask only affects a preview of your target layer, so you can experiment without actually committing your changes to the pixels in your target layer. When you're done working with a Layer Mask, you can either put your changes into effect or discard the mask entirely.

To add a layer mask, select the layer you want and then choose Add Layer Mask from the Layer palette's pop-up menu. A second thumbnail sketch, which represents the layer mask, will show up next to the thumbnail sketch of your layer in its row on the Layers palette (see Figure 5.22).

When you have a layer mask active, you can double-click its thumbnail preview to launch the Layer Mask Options dialog box; here you can choose whether the color you paint with will hide or reveal the layer underneath the mask. You'll find it's much like editing a channel, which you'll do in Chapter 7, "Advanced Filter Essentials." You can paint with black to make pixels transparent; painting with white will make them opaque.

Merging Layers

Once you've decided you're finished with editing individual layers, you can collapse all your separate visible layers into a single, composite layer by choosing Merge Layers from the Layers palette's pop-up menu. Any hidden layers will still remain separate, though. Objects in previously transparent layers will still retain their old transparency settings. You'll still only be able to save this file in native Photoshop format.

If you want to create a single-layer image and discard any hidden layers at the same time, you can choose Flatten Image from the Layers palette's

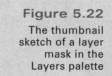

Figure 5.22
The thumbnail sketch of a layer mask in the Layers palette

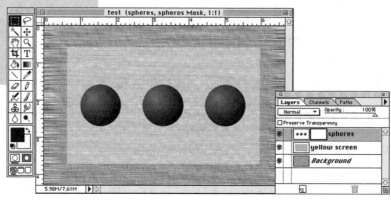

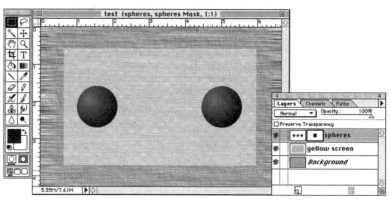

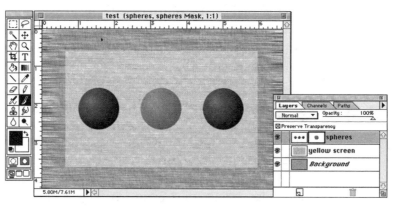

pop-up menu. This will get rid of the image's transparent background, too, if it had one. You should choose this setting if you need to save your image in a file format other than native Photoshop.

Both these methods will reduce your file's size, since maintaining separate layers really adds to file size and memory requirements for Photoshop images.

Summary

With layers, you've got an enormous range of opportunities for combining and blending images. We've touched on some of their most versatile features, but you'll have an even better understanding of their potential after you gain some familiarity with paths—up ahead in Chapter 6—and channels and masks in Chapter 7.

6 Path Essentials

In This Chapter

Path Fundamentals

Pen Tool

Saving and Deleting Paths

Importing and Exporting Paths

Making Silhouettes

In the last chapter you saw that although Photoshop is a pixel-based program for working with bitmapped images, its layers feature—which lets you move objects in an image independently of one another—extends to you some of the versatility of a drawing program. This chapter focuses on another Photoshop feature called paths, which supports even more drawing program capabilities.

The paths feature lets you create selections made up of precise lines and curves, just like those you might draw in Adobe Illustrator or Macromedia Freehand. With the Paths palette (and the Pen tool it contains), you can have much more control over your image editing than you probably thought you could. For example, if you want to export a silhouetted Photoshop image to a page layout program and have text run around its outline—which is no problem for an Illustrator graphic but doesn't happen automatically with Photoshop images imported into a page layout program—you have to use the Paths palette to create what's called a clipping path.

Paths can be a big help in creating composite images; you can make precise selections with the Pen tool to add a crisp, clean edge with smooth curves and sharp angles. You can also copy and paste paths between Photoshop and Illustrator, so if you're an Illustrator whiz (or have a lot of Illustrator clip art) you can import paths from Illustrator when you've finished working in that program.

In this chapter, you'll learn how to use the Paths palette—and the Pen tool it contains—to do the following tasks:

- Draw, save, load, and delete paths.

- Import and export paths between Illustrator and Photoshop.

- Convert paths to and from active selections.

- Fill and stroke paths using other Photoshop tools.

- Add to, subtract from, and intersect paths.

- Add a clipping path to a Photoshop image saved in EPS format.

Path Fundamentals

A path is an incredible tool for making selections, but in a sense that's really all it is—it's not part of your image itself. It's a geometric representation of a shape that floats above your bitmapped image, as if on its own layer—although you can only see this layer showing up in the Paths palette, not the Layers palette. You must turn a path into a selection to capture the underlying pixels. You can also can save a path with an image as long as you save in native Photoshop format. This lets you recapture a given selection area at any time, even if you save and reopen the file.

To display the Paths palette, select Palettes… from the Window menu and then choose Show Paths from the Palettes submenu, as shown in Figure 6.1.

If you're familiar with Illustrator or Freehand, you'll be able to relate well to the paths interface with its pen-based tools for creating lines and Bézier (pronounced "bay-zee-ay") curves, and editing their points and segments. Don't worry if object-oriented drawing is new to you; it can take a while to get the hang of drawing with the Pen tool, but it'll get easier with practice.

Figure 6.2 shows an example of an object created in Illustrator and a path that traces the same shape in Photoshop; note that both have similar interface features, with points and handles that determine the shape of the path segments.

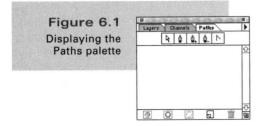

Figure 6.1
Displaying the Paths palette

Figure 6.2

Anchor points, lines, and curves in an Illustrator path and a Photoshop path

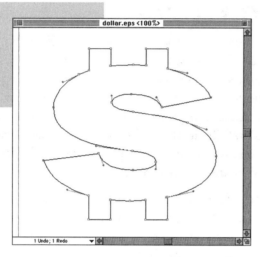

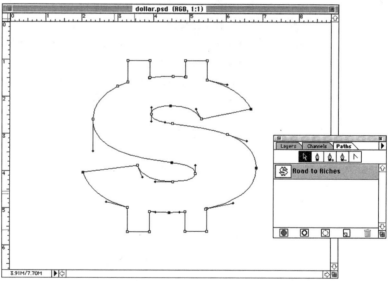

Path Tools

When you display the Paths palette, you'll see five tool icons across the top of the Paths palette (Figure 6.3).

You'll mainly use the Pen tool to create points for your paths, and use the other tools to modify the paths afterward. Here's a brief description of all five:

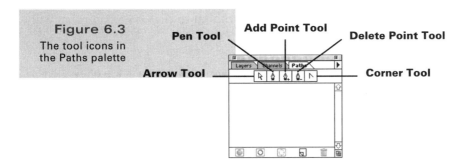

Figure 6.3
The tool icons in
the Paths palette

Pen Tool Add Point Tool Delete Point Tool

Arrow Tool Corner Tool

Pen tool Click with this tool to create *anchor points* connected by straight lines. If you drag your cursor after clicking, your current line segment will start to create a curved path depending on which way you move the cursor.

Arrow tool With this tool, you can select one or more individual points on a path, or path segments.

Add Point tool Clicking over a path segment with this tool adds an anchor point. Holding your cursor over an existing anchor point will change your cursor to the Arrow tool, so clicking and dragging will move that point.

Delete Point tool Clicking an anchor point with this tool will remove it and redefine your path accordingly. Holding your cursor over any part of a path that's not an anchor point will change your cursor to the Arrow tool, so clicking and dragging will move that segment.

Corner tool As you add points to a path, you're creating corners—sharp ones if you click from point to point; curved ones if you drag the cursor after you click. You can use the Corner Point tool to convert your sharp corners to rounded ones and vice versa. By clicking and dragging with this tool on a sharply angled corner point, you can add direction handles that you can use to manipulate the new curve point.

You create a *closed path* by linking your path segments back to your original anchor point; your Pen cursor changes to include a tiny circle

in the lower right corner when you're about to click on a point that will close a path.

• •

Using Key Commands with the Arrow Tool

The following key commands used in conjunction with the Arrow tool can let you manipulate a path more easily:

👁 You can toggle between the Pen tool and the Arrow tool by pressing ⊤.

👁 Hold down Option (for Mac users) or Alt (for Windows users) as you click with the Arrow tool to select all points in the path at once. If, after holding down Option (or Alt), you click and drag, you'll move a copy of the path instead of the path itself.

• •

Additional Path Palette Options

The rest of the Path options appear in the pop-up menu that appears when you click the black triangle in the Path palette's upper right corner, as shown in Figure 6.4.

I'd be getting ahead of myself if I described each of these menu items here; they show up in the later sections of this chapter. At this point, you should just note the single option that comes up in the Palette Options dialog box (Figure 6.5).

Here you can set the size of the thumbnail sketch that will appear in the Paths palette to preview your path's shape. Just as in the Layers palette, you also have the option to turn off the thumbnail preview. It's most useful, though, to leave the thumbnail settings at the default, which makes the sketch visible at the smallest size option.

Figure 6.4

Menu items in the Paths palette's pop-up menu

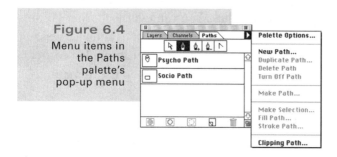

Figure 6.5
Paths Palette
Options
dialog box

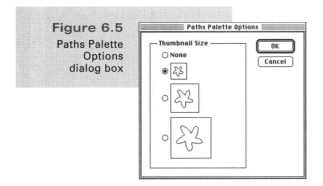

Additional Icons in the Paths Palette

Some of the options in the Path palette's pop-up menu are also in easy reach as icons located along the bottom of the Paths palette (Figure 6.6).

The Fill, Stroke, and Make Selection icons all have dialog boxes that automatically appear if you select these options from the Paths palette's pop-up menu, but won't show up if you click on or drag a path's row to their icons. To make them appear while using the icons on the bottom of the Paths palette, Option-click (for Mac users) or Alt-click (for Windows users) the icons instead of just plain clicking.

Strangely enough, the New Path icon works just the opposite way. Its corresponding dialog box appears if you just click the icon. Option-clicking (for Mac users) or Alt-clicking (for Windows users) will create

Figure 6.6
The icons along
the bottom of the
Paths palette

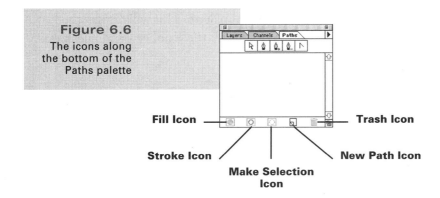

Fill Icon

Stroke Icon

Make Selection
Icon

Trash Icon

New Path Icon

a new path layer without displaying the New Path dialog box, so you won't automatically have an opportunity to name the new path layer.

Drawing with the Pen Tool

Let's move on to trying out the Pen tool. If you're already an accomplished Illustrator or Freehand artist, you should mostly just skim this material for the details of Photoshop's paths interface and move right on ahead—this stuff mainly covers the basic mechanics of drawing lines and Bézier curves. Take a look at the first subsection though; "Taking the Guesswork Out of Drawing Paths" gives useful starter material for everyone, and includes the most helpful tips I've found for controlling the paths you draw.

Taking the Guesswork Out of Drawing Paths

You can always edit a path after you've created it, but there are a couple of good ways to ensure that you draw the exact path you want in the first place.

The Pen Tool's Rubber Band Option

The Pen tool has a really great option—called Rubber Band—that lets you preview what a path segment will look like before you click to place an anchor point. This helps you see what the segment will look like, so you can correct your positioning of an anchor point accordingly before you place it instead of clicking first and then going to lengths to get it right afterward. To turn on the Rubber Band option, double-click the Pen icon in the Paths palette. This will display the Pen Tool Options palette (Figure 6.7). Click the Rubber Band check box to turn on that option.

Figure 6.7

The Rubber Band check box in the Pen Tool Options palette

Pen Tool Options	▶
☒ Rubber Band	

Using the Info Palette

Another very useful way to position your anchor points exactly where you want them is to use the Info palette to track the location of your cursor. Display the Info palette by choosing Palettes from the Window menu, then choosing Show Info from the Palettes submenu.

Among other information, the Info palette lets you see at a glance the horizontal and vertical (x-y) coordinates of your cursor's location. If you need to create complex geometric paths in Photoshop, it can help to think of your Photoshop document in terms of the Cartesian plane, with your x-coordinate measuring the cursor's horizontal position and your y-coordinate measuring the cursor's vertical position. Make sure you have Show Rulers selected in the Window palette. By default, Photoshop places the point of origin (0, 0) in the upper left corner of your document, although you can change this by repositioning the crosshairs in that corner to anywhere else in your document.

If you don't think you'll ever have to be this precise about creating paths, don't worry about measuring where you place your anchor points. If you want to keep track in a general way—say, knowing when you've drawn a line that's two inches long—you can refer to the Info palette.

note   **You can change the unit of measurement for tracking your cursor's coordinates from inches to pixels, centimeters, points, or picas. Just click the pop-up menu on the Info palette and make the changes in the resulting Info Options dialog box.**

Straight Lines

Click the Pen icon to select that tool. The first shape you'll draw with the Pen tool will be a triangle. Click in your document window to set your first anchor point, then release the cursor. Click a second time some distance away; a straight line will appear between your two points (Figure 6.8).

Notice how your new anchor point shows up as a dark, filled-in square; that means it's a currently selected point. At the same time, the first point you created will change to a white square, meaning that it's no longer selected. Release the cursor.

Figure 6.8
Drawing a line
with the Pen tool

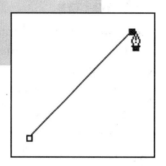

tip

● ●

Constraining Lines in a Path

By pressing and holding (Shift), you can constrain the angle at which you place new points to 45° or 90° at a time. Accordingly, this will constrain the angles of lines you draw to multiples of 45° or 90°. This can be helpful when you need to create classic geometric shapes.

● ●

Now click and release the cursor to add a third point, which will create the second line in your triangle (Figure 6.9). You'll click back on your original anchor point to close the path, creating a triangle shape. As you hold the Pen tool over your first anchor point the cursor will change, with a small circle appearing in the lower right corner of the Pen icon (Figure 6.10). This cursor change takes place whenever you click a point that will close a path.

Figure 6.9
Adding a second
line to the path

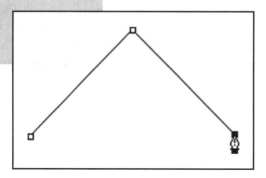

Figure 6.10
The Pen tool's icon changes when you're about to close a path.

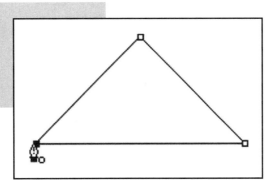

After you've drawn a line or a closed path, you can still edit it as much as you like. You just need to select the point or points you want to position with the Arrow tool. You can either click on the point itself, or—if it's too much work to click so precisely—draw a marquee with the Arrow tool around the area that contains the point you want to select. Any points that fall within that marquee area will be selected, so make sure you don't select more of your path than you wanted. Once you've selected the point or points you want to move, you can either drag them with the Arrow tool or use the directional keys on your keyboard to move them up, down, left, or right a pixel at a time. This is useful when the path you drew is just slightly off from the one you wanted, and you want to nudge the path back into line.

Bézier Curves

Sure, drawing lines is intuitive—but drawing curves is where most people get bogged down in object-oriented drawing. Let's take some basic maneuvers one step at a time.

Click once in your document window with the Pen tool to create an anchor point. Continue to hold the mouse button down after you've clicked, and drag the cursor. When you start to drag the cursor, the Pen icon will change to an arrow. Two *direction handles* will emerge from your point as you drag; their length and angle determine the height and slope of your curve. Observe that there's a *direction point* at the end of each handle (Figure 6.11); at any time while you're drawing a curve,

Figure 6.11
The beginning
of a curve. Note
the curve
handles and
direction points.

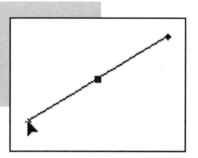

you can switch to the Arrow tool and reposition these direction points to change the height and angle of a certain part of the curve.

Reposition the Pen tool some distance from your first point, then click and drag a second time. You'll see a curved line form between the two points you drew (Figure 6.12).

While you still have the mouse button held down, you can drag the mouse and the curve will slope in the same direction you're dragging the mouse. This is crucial to understanding how Bézier curves work.

Figure 6.12
Adding a second
point draws your
first curved line.

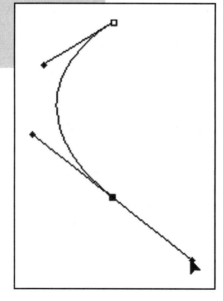

Figure 6.13 shows how dragging the directional handles up, down, and at various angles produces different kinds of curves.

The following mini-exercises—on drawing a sine wave, curves with corner points, and creating jigsaw puzzle piece outlines—will help demonstrate how dragging the directional handles affects your curves' shapes.

Drawing a Sine Wave

You can create a series of curves—like those in a sine wave—by alternately dragging up and down as you place a series of anchor points in a horizontal row.

With the Pen tool selected, click to place a new anchor point and drag straight upward. Next, move your cursor to the right and click to place a second anchor point some distance from your first point; note the size and shape of the resulting curve. Continue to hold down the mouse

Figure 6.13

Dragging the directional handles in different directions changes the slope of your curve segment.

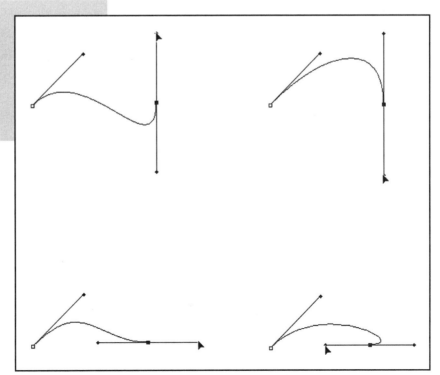

button after you click, then drag straight downward. This should produce the kind of curved arc shown here:

Continue by adding a third anchor point to the right and dragging straight upward once you've placed it. Note that the direction handles on the first points you created disappear after they're deselected; you can always see them again if you switch to the Arrow tool and reselect those points.

After you've created a series of anchor points in a row, alternatively dragging upward and downward with each new point, you should have produced a wavy path like this one:

You can experiment with changing the height of an arc by clicking the Arrow tool on an individual curve segment and dragging upward or downward. This will select the nearest anchor points and directional handles; you can then move them up or down to accentuate or reduce the arc's depth.

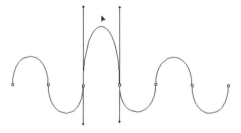

Adjusting the direction points themselves will give you optimal control over the final shape of your curve. Try experimenting with drawing a couple of curved lines, then using the Arrow tool to reposition the direction points to see how the shape of the curve changes.

● ●

Constraining Lines in a Curve

In the same way you can use (Shift) to constrain the angle of lines, you can constrain the angle of your curves' handles to increments of 45° or 90° when you hold down (Shift).

● ●

Drawing Curves with Corner Points

The previous mini-exercise showed how to draw a series of curves in alternating directions. The points in that kind of path are called *smooth points*. Next up is an explanation of how to draw a number of curves connected with *corner points*. The net result is a series of curves that all arc in the same direction, like this:

Create your first two points the way you did in the previous mini-exercise: select the Pen tool, click to create an anchor point, then drag upward. Position your cursor to the right and click to create a second anchor point. Drag downward after you click the second time to create the first curve. Release the mouse button. Here's where you'll do something different—you'll need to turn the second anchor point into a corner point.

Hold down (Option) (for Mac users) or (Alt) (for Windows users). Position the cursor over the second anchor point, the one you just drew. Click the second anchor point, and hold down the mouse button while you drag upward; this will remove the downward direction handle, and change the direction of the next curve. Stop clicking and release (Option).

Now move your cursor to the right to create a third anchor point. Click when you're ready to position the point, and drag downward. You should now have two curves side by side, looking something like the McDonald's arches.

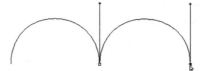

If you like, you can repeat these steps—holding down (Option) and reselecting the last anchor point you created, dragging upward to establish the corner point and change the curve's direction, and so on—to add to your series of curves with corner points.

Combining Lines and Curves

Now let's look at creating paths that contain both straight lines and curves. You'll need to create corner points where the path turns from a line into a curve, and vice versa. You'll create corner points where necessary the way you did in the previous exercise.

First, create a straight line made up of two anchor points; click a third anchor point to the right of the other two and drag downward. This will create a curve following the straight line, as shown here:

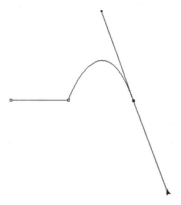

Next, you'll need to make this third anchor point a corner point. As you did earlier, (Option)-click (for Mac users) or (Alt)-click (for Windows users) the third anchor point to convert it to a corner point. Don't hold down the mouse button, though; the next segment you're going to create is a line, not a curve. Now position your cursor further to the right and click to create a fourth anchor point. Your path should now consist of a line, one arching curve, and another line.

tip   **Adjusting an Anchor Point without Leaving the Pen Tool**

While drawing your path with the Pen tool, you can access the pointer tool quickly by pressing and holding down the Command key (for Mac users) or the Control key (for Windows users). Your Pen tool cursor will change to the pointer, allowing you to make adjustments to your path's anchor points or Bézier curves. Your cursor will change back to the Pen tool when you release.

You should feel free to continue to doodle, create abstract shapes, or practice creating other path outlines. This is a good time to experiment with the Add Point (![icon]), Delete Point (![icon]), and Corner (![icon]) icons. You can add an anchor point anywhere on one of your lines or curves by selecting the Add Point tool and clicking on the path itself. To remove an anchor point, use the Delete Point tool and click on an anchor point. You'll get some interesting results from clicking the Corner Point tool on one of your finished paths.

tip   **Cutting Path Segments in Two**

Unlike Illustrator or Freehand, Photoshop has no equivalent for the Scissors tool that can cut a path segment in two, adding two new anchor points. You can, however, reasonably duplicate this feature by using the Add Point tool to add three new points very close together at the point where you'd like to break the path. Next, select the middle point with the Arrow tool and cut it by pressing ⌘-X (for Mac users) or Ctrl-X (for Windows users).

Another good way to gain some practice using the Pen tool is to trace some letterforms. Create some text in a large point size in a new document, then use the Pen tool to trace the edges. With practice, you'll gain control over the Pen tool's functions as you learn to replicate exactly the letters' elegant curves, lines, and sharp angles—and perhaps gain a deeper appreciation of typography at the same time!

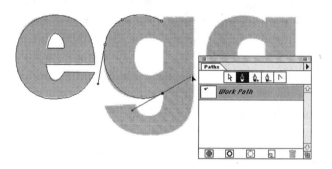

Saving and Deleting Paths

You need to save a path by name when you're making clipping paths (discussed at length later in this chapter) or if you have to interrupt your path work but want to return to it later. As you probably saw when you practiced creating different paths in the mini-exercises so far, you can have as many distinct paths and path segments as you like on one path layer; they will simply all be saved under the same path name. You can, however, create different path layers with their own names.

When you choose the Pen tool and start creating a new path, your work takes place on a plane called Work Path in the Paths palette. To give this path layer its own name, you can just double-click its row in the Paths palette. The Save Path dialog box will appear. If you create more path segments after you save a new path by name, Photoshop automatically adds them to that path layer; you don't have to save the path again.

You can create a new path by choosing New Path from the Paths palette's pop-up menu or clicking the New Path icon ( ) along the bottom of the Paths Palette. The New Path dialog box will appear.

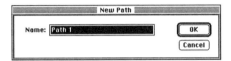

Double-clicking the name of a saved path in the Paths palette will cause the Rename Path dialog box to appear.

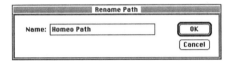

Dragging a path's row down to the New Path icon will create a duplicate of your path layer; there's also a menu item in the Paths palette's pop-up menu for duplicating a path layer. Just as in the Layers palette, you can click on a path's name in the Paths palette to work on a different path layer. However, other path layers are hidden from view whenever you're working on a given path layer.

If you want to delete a path layer, you can just choose Delete Path from the Paths palette's pop-up menu, or drag that path's row in the Paths palette down to the Trash icon.

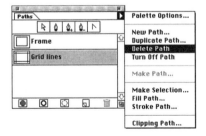

Importing and Exporting Paths

You may sometimes want to export your path shapes to another graphics program to add certain special effects that you can't achieve with paths in Photoshop. For example, Photoshop doesn't let you scale, rotate, or

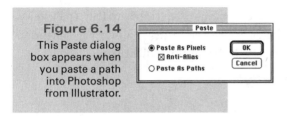

Figure 6.14
This Paste dialog box appears when you paste a path into Photoshop from Illustrator.

skew paths. Luckily, though, it's easy to work around these limitations in Photoshop if you also have a copy of an illustration program. You can export a Photoshop path to Illustrator or Freehand, effect the change you want, then import it back into Photoshop.

To do this, you first need to select the whole path in Photoshop and copy it. Switch to your illustration program and paste the selection into a new document. Now you can impose the changes you wanted, from rotating to resizing the path. Note that you can also add all sorts of additional effects to this path, but to bring those into Photoshop you'd have to rasterize the path, converting everything to pixels.

Figure 6.14 shows the Paste dialog box you'll see in Photoshop when you begin to paste a path from Illustrator. Note that you have a choice to paste the selection in as a path or in pixelated form—which will let you retain all blends, stroking, and any other effects you added in Illustrator, at the price of losing the ability to select the path itself.

Converting Paths to Selections and Back Again

Paths are one of Photoshop's more elegant features, but they're most useful after you turn them into selections. Once you've converted a path to a selection, you have access to all of Photoshop's tools, filters, and other effects.

Converting Paths to Selections

There are several ways to turn a Photoshop path into a selection. You can choose Make Selection from the Paths palette's pop-up menu, which

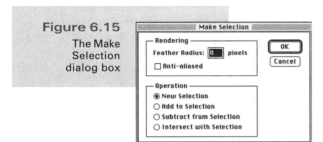

Figure 6.15

The Make Selection dialog box

will cause the Make Selection dialog box (shown in Figure 6.15) to appear. You can also click the Make Selection icon ([◯]) on the Paths palette, or drag the path's row down to the icon. Neither of these last two methods will automatically display the Make Selection dialog box. However, you can make it do so by holding down [Option] (for Mac users) or [Alt] (for Windows users) when you click on or drag a path's row on top of the Make Selection icon.

One of the best reasons to use paths to make a selection is if you need to add to—or subtract from—a selection you've already made, and want to be able to do so precisely without taking chances on accidentally deselecting or altering your existing selection. You can leave your selection as is, create a new path and outline the new addition, then call up the Make Selection dialog box to add, subtract, and intersect your path with your previous selection, as shown in Figure 6.16. After choosing a Make Selection Option, choose Turn Off Path from the Paths palette's pop-up menu to see the kinds of results shown in Figure 6.16.

You can also launch the Make Selection dialog box to add feathering and toggle anti-aliasing on or off when you make a selection. By default, you get anti-aliasing but no feathering.

Converting Selections to Paths

You needn't draw all your path shapes from scratch with the Pen tool; you can convert any active selection into a path with the Make Path... command from the Paths palette's pop-up menu. You should experiment, though, because a Photoshop-generated path may not be as close a fit as one you draw yourself. Any selection you make in

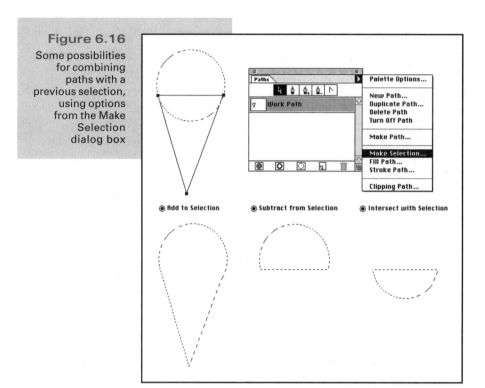

Figure 6.16
Some possibilities for combining paths with a previous selection, using options from the Make Selection dialog box

Photoshop appears with a marching ants border around it; when you convert this to a path, the program has to use a little guesswork in placing anchor points and generating the curves or lines to connect them. Photoshop uses a setting called *tolerance* in deciding where to place these anchor points.

Deciding what tolerance setting to use can be a tricky call. The higher you make the tolerance setting, the looser the path and the more ill-defined your selection area will be. Lower tolerance settings, however, can create overly complex paths. Using a tolerance setting of .5 (the lowest possible value) to 2 pixels will work for most situations; you can specify any tolerance setting in .5-pixel increments. The highest possible tolerance setting is 10; a path created with a tolerance of 10 will probably bear little resemblance to your original selection (see Figure 6.18, far right).

Figure 6.17
Some different tolerance settings. From left to right, the letter G selection is saved to a path using a tolerance level of .5 pixel, 2 pixels, 5 pixels, and 10 pixels

G G G G

Filling and Stroking Paths

As I've mentioned already, the editing effects that you can apply to your paths from within the Paths palette are limited, but the two main ones—filling and stroking—can produce some very colorful effects.

Filling

Choosing Fill Path from the Paths palette's pop-up menu will cause the Fill dialog box to appear (Figure 6.18). The Fill Path menu item has an icon counterpart that appears at the bottom of the Paths palette (⬛). Dragging a path's row over the Fill Path icon will fill the path with the current settings in the Fill dialog box; the default setting for clicking the Fill Path icon is 100 percent of the foreground color in Normal mode. Option-click (for Mac users) or Alt-click (for Windows users) the Fill Path icon to display the Fill dialog box.

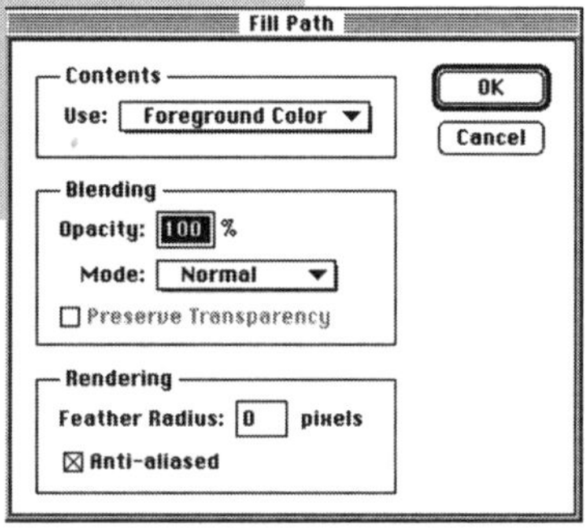

Figure 6.18
The Fill dialog box for the Paths palette

```
┌─────────────── Fill Path ───────────────┐
│  ┌─ Contents ──────────┐   ┌─────────┐  │
│  │ Use: [Foreground Color ▼] │   │   OK    │  │
│  └──────────────────────┘   ├─────────┤  │
│                              │ Cancel  │  │
│  ┌─ Blending ──────────────┐ └─────────┘  │
│  │ Opacity: [100] %        │              │
│  │ Mode: [ Normal    ▼]    │              │
│  │ ☐ Preserve Transparency │              │
│  └─────────────────────────┘              │
│  ┌─ Rendering ─────────────┐              │
│  │ Feather Radius: [0] pixels │           │
│  │ ☒ Anti-aliased          │              │
│  └─────────────────────────┘              │
└──────────────────────────────────────────┘
```

Your fill options here are basically the same as those available when filling selections using Fill from the Edit menu. You can fill in your path with various colors or a saved pattern, use a variety of blending modes (just as in the Layers palette), and even feather or anti-alias your path's edges.

If you have several discrete paths on a path layer, you can choose between applying a fill to just one path segment or to every path on the layer. Deselect all points if you want to apply the fill to all paths; otherwise, you should select individual path segments—in which case, the menu item available to you in the Paths palette's pop-up menu will read Fill Subpath.

Stroking

I have to admit, I never tire of playing around with the Stroke effects available via the Paths palette because there are so many cool effects to create. When you click Stroke Path from the Path palette's pop-up menu, the Stroke Path dialog box that appears gives you a choice of Photoshop tools to use in applying your stroke effects (see Figure 6.19).

Like the Fill Path option, the Stroke Path menu item also appears as an icon at the bottom of the Paths palette (⬤). Dragging a path's row over the Stroke Path icon will fill the path with the current settings in the Stroke Path dialog box; the default setting for the Stroke Path icon is the Pencil tool (ho hum). Option-click (for Mac users) or Alt-click (for Windows users) the Stroke Path icon to display its dialog box.

You can create some very psychedelic effects by stroking with the Paintbrush tool with one of more unusual brushes selected in the Brushes palette. Exercise 6.1 will walk you through creating one such example.

Figure 6.19
The Stroke Path
dialog box

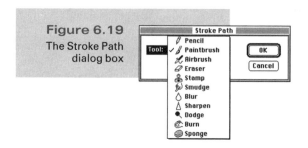

EXERCISE 6.1

Creating Elaborate Borders by Stroking a Path

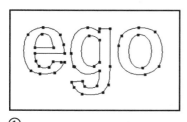

1. You'll need to choose or create a path to use for this exercise. Here, I entered some text with the Type tool, then chose Make Path from the Paths palette's pop-up menu.

2. Now you'll need to choose a foreground color to use for your stroking effect. The color should be appropriate to the desired end effect—for example, use a bright color for a gaudy effect. If your foreground color is too dark, you won't be able to see the effects of the stroke.

3. Display the Stroke Path dialog box by choosing Stroke Path from the Paths palette's pop-up menu. Click the Tool pop-up menu; you'll see you can choose from a number of Photoshop tools.

   You can do a lot of experimenting here, but for this exercise we're going to use the Paintbrush tool. Don't click OK at this point, though—before you choose the Paintbrush for the effect, you have an opportunity to modify its settings and choose a custom brush. Click Cancel to make the dialog box disappear.

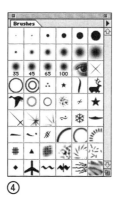

4. I want to set the Paintbrush's opacity to 80 percent, so I've double-clicked the Paintbrush icon to display its Options palette. Click the Opacity slider down to 80%. Now, let's choose a good custom brush for stroking. Choose Palettes from the Window menu, then Show Brushes from the Palettes submenu.

If you don't see as wide a selection as you'd like, remember you can choose Load Brushes or Append Brushes from the Brushes palette's pop-up menu and select the additional brushes supplied with Photoshop.

5. Now that you've chosen the tool you want, go back and choose Stroke Path again from the Paths palette's pop-up menu. Choose Paintbrush from the Tool pop-up menu and click OK.

6. If you want to get rid of your path at this point, you could either rasterize it into a selection or delete it by choosing Make Selection or Turn Off Path, respectively, from the Paths palette's pop-up menu.

Figure 6.20
End results of stroking with the Paintbrush tool

Making Silhouettes with Clipping Paths

In the last chapter, you learned about using layers to mask out parts of an image. However, a transparent background created in Photoshop won't stay transparent if you import that image into QuarkXpress or PageMaker.

In this situation, what you need is a clipping path, that is, a shape or path that creates a silhouette to mask out the background or other parts of your image when combined with other elements—like wrap-around text, shaded backgrounds, or other images—in a page layout or illustration program.

A clipping path will also ensure that the text on the page will run around your outlined image correctly. You'll also need to save your Photoshop image in EPS format for a clipping path to take effect when you import it into another program.

Once you've named a path to use as a clipping path, you can choose Clipping Path from the Paths palette's pop-up menu to display its dialog box (Figure 6.21). Click the pop-up menu in the Clipping Path dialog box to select which path to use.

Figure 6.21

The Clipping path
dialog box

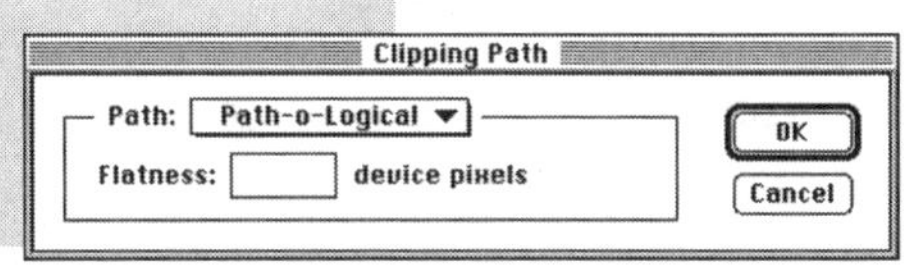

The only other option you can set in this dialog box is the path's *flatness*. Flatness determines how exact your printer or imagesetter will be in creating the segments of your path. Lower settings mean greater fineness, and print time will rise accordingly. As the flatness settings increase, curved parts of your outline's shape will start to transform into straight line segments. Unless your service bureau tells you to enter a certain value, though, you can leave this blank—the printer or imagesetter will substitute its own settings. If the image generates a PostScript error when your page layout program attempts to print it, though, you'll need to go back and save a flatness setting with the clipping path. The possible values for setting flatness range from .2 to 200 device pixels.

Exercise 6.2 will walk you through each step in creating a clipping path.

EXERCISE 6.2

Adding a Clipping Path to an Image

①

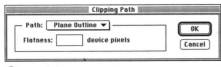

③

1. You'll first need to pick an image that you want to silhouette and import into a page layout program.

2. Use the Pen tool to create a new path outlining the part of the image you want to include in the clipping path. Make sure you save the path by selecting Save Path from the Paths palette's pop-up menu, or by double-clicking its row in the Paths palette and giving it a name.

3. Select Clipping Path from the Paths palette's pop-up menu. Choose the name of your saved path. As mentioned earlier, you don't need to enter a specific flatness setting unless your service bureau tells you to do so. Click OK.

4. Notice that the name of your path now has an outline in the Paths palette, although the screen image doesn't change. You'll only see the clipped effect after you import the image into another program.

   Before you save this document as an EPS file, make sure it's in the right color mode for your final output—for example, CMYK instead of RGB.

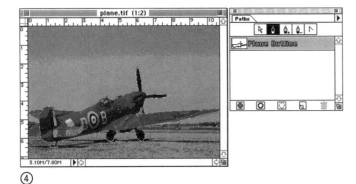

④

5. Now you can choose Save or Save As from the File menu to save your image in EPS format. The EPS Format dialog box will appear, and you can double-check to make sure that the right path name shows up as the clipping path to be used.

6. Launch your page layout program and import the image into a document. Here, I've imported the image into QuarkXpress. Observe how various page elements affect your silhouetted image differently from images with no clipping paths.

Pat yourself on the back—creating a clipping path can be a tricky business, and you've just added a very advanced technique to your Photoshop repertoire. Make sure you run a print test with a sample silhouetted image with your service bureau, and ask them to let you know if there are any additional steps you should take to ensure your silhouetted images will output well on their equipment.

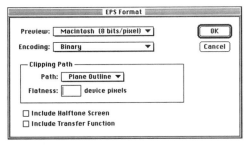

⑤

Figure 6.22
A silhouetted image with a clipping path, imported into QuarkXpress

Summary

Besides the Magic Wand tool, using the Paths palette is one of the best ways to make selections in Photoshop. As you've seen, though, it can take a while to get the hang of using the Pen tool. You should be very proud of yourself; there are many designers who've used Photoshop for years without putting the Paths palette to use the way you have in this chapter. Look how far you've come—and so fast!—with this very difficult Photoshop concept.

Next up is coverage of Photoshop's channels and masking features, including what kinds of effects can you create with alpha channels and Quick Masks.

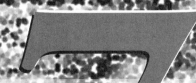

Channel and Mask Essentials

By now, you've had some experience with making selections in Photoshop using the Marquee and Magic Wand tools. Another way to think of a Photoshop selection is as a *mask*, or kind of like a stencil. If you've ever used stenciled lettering to create a poster or a sign ("Post No Bills"), you've seen how a mask works. It lets you create an effect by blocking out (masking) all the parts you don't want changed. Even if you're kind of sloppy, or if you sneeze while you're painting, you won't mess up the part that's covered by the stencil—it's completely protected.

You can save a mask by name in what Photoshop calls an *alpha channel,* so you can retrieve your mask and use it again at any time. This eliminates frustrating situations where you've painstakingly marked out a complicated selection area with the Lasso or Marquee tools, only to click inadvertently off to the side and lose the selection. It's also really useful if you need to return to a selected area at a later point in your image editing. You can even use multiple alpha channels to toggle between different selection areas in your document with ease.

Add channels and masks to the list of Photoshop features—like layers and paths—that are extremely powerful but not at all intuitive. I found it easier to understand channels once I learned about *color channels.* To refresh your memory of Chapter 2, when you're working with images in RGB or CMYK mode, each of the colors represented by those acronyms has its own channel in Photoshop. These color channels function the same way that alpha channels do. In other words, you can selectively adjust the Red channel in an RGB image separately from Green and Blue. By fooling around with individual color channels, you can experiment with dramatic color changes in ordinary images for a silkscreened or Andy Warhol painting effect.

Understanding how and when to use masks and color channels will lead you to the upper echelons of Photoshop society. These features are among the most difficult concepts to grasp, but with judicious use you can create the most sophisticated photocompositions and special effects—and let's not forget maintaining impeccable color control.

In this chapter you'll learn how to:

👁 View and edit an image's individual color channels.

👁 Create, load, and delete alpha channels.

👁 Use Photoshop's Quick Mask mode to create temporary alpha channels.

👁 Use alpha channels to create special effects.

Introduction to Channels

If you create a selection using the Marquee or Lasso tool, the boundaries of your selection show up with the border of marching ants you've seen several times by now. Masks are another way of making selections, but they look rather different. Masks are similar to stencils; they trace a silhouette around your selection to show what's covered up and what isn't.

When you create a channel to hold a mask, you see your selection boundaries in black and white. Typically, everything within the area you've defined as selected appears in white, while the masked-out part shows up as solid black, as shown in Figure 7.1. Any anti-aliased or feathered edges appear in various levels of gray. If you like, you can reverse the colors so the masked-out part is white instead of black; I'll explain how to do this a little later, in the description of the Channel Options dialog box.

Creating a channel in Photoshop to hold a selection mask is functionally the same as using the Marquee tool to make a selection with the same dimensions—it's just that the two selections will look different and you can reselect a masked area at a later time. Figure 7.2 shows how drawing a selection with the Marquee tool still keeps your full

Figure 7.1

A mask in an alpha channel

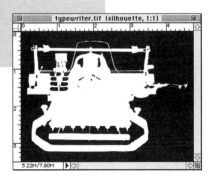

Figure 7.2

A selection drawn with the Marquee tool functions the same as a mask created in a channel—the selection methods just look different onscreen.

image onscreen, while creating a mask delineates the selected area (in white) from the covered-up area (in black) and hides the image itself.

Viewing an Image's Color Channels

Before you get started looking at color channels in a document and creating new alpha channels to hold selection masks, you should open a sample image and display the Channels palette.

Select Palettes from the Window menu, then choose Show Channels from the Palettes submenu (Figure 7.3).

Figure 7.3

The Show Channels menu item

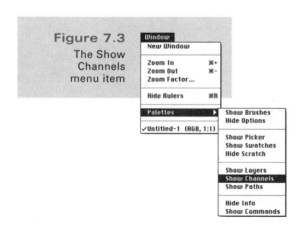

Figure 7.4
The Channels palette

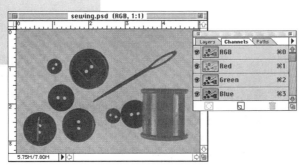

You'll see the Channels palette appear on your screen, looking like Figure 7.4. Before exploring the options available via this palette for manipulating and adding new channels, let's look at the color channels that already exist for your image.

If necessary, convert your sample image to RGB or CMYK color mode. You'll find that an RGB document has three single-color channels—one each for red, green, and blue—and a CMYK document has four single-color channels, one each for cyan, magenta, yellow, and black. RGB and CMYK documents also both have a composite channel showing your whole image with all channels displayed and combined.

It's less interesting to look at the default channels for a Grayscale image—there's only one, called Black—or for a graphic in Indexed color mode, which only has one channel called Index. Figure 7.5 demonstrates how images in different color modes give you different kinds of color channels.

Looking at Individual Channels

You'll need to know how to view and edit a single channel at a time to control each color precisely without affecting the other color channels, and—as you'll see a little later in this chapter—to edit a mask in an alpha channel.

Notice how each of the channels shown in your Channels palette has a little eye icon (👁) next to it. Just as you saw in the earlier chapters in descriptions of the Layers and Path palettes, you can click each of these eye icons in the Channels palette to hide or display a channel.

Figure 7.5

The color channels you have in your images depend on what color mode they use.

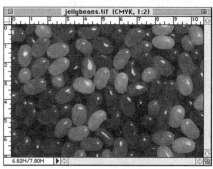

With an RGB image open on your screen, try clicking the eye icon by the Green channel's row in the Channels palette to hide that channel from view. When you hide a single color channel in an RGB or CMYK mode, you'll see that the eye icon by the composite view also disappears. That makes sense, because if you're only looking at the red and blue channels in an image, you're not seeing what the whole graphic looks like any more (Figure 7.6).

Although you've hidden the Green color channel from view, it's still selected and can be edited. Notice how the backgrounds of all the channel rows in the Channels palette appear in gray—that means they're still selected and editable. Click the RGB composite channel to restore the eye icon to all rows and bring all channels back to view.

Now you're going to select a single color channel to view and edit alone. Each channel has an automatically assigned key combination for displaying it individually. These key combinations appear at the right of

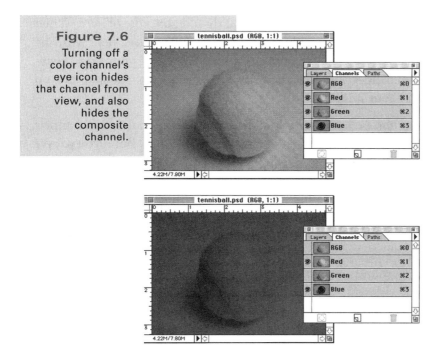

Figure 7.6
Turning off a color channel's eye icon hides that channel from view, and also hides the composite channel.

each channel's row in the Channels palette. Try pressing ⌘-3 (for Mac users) or Ctrl-3 (for PC users) to display just the Blue channel in your document. Notice how the backgrounds change in the Channels palette: now only the Blue channel has a gray background and the others appear as white. The eye icon also appears only next to the Blue channel, not by any of the others (Figure 7.7).

Figure 7.7
Using key combinations to select and view a single channel at a time

There are a couple of other things you should take note of here. When you've selected a single channel to edit, as you've done here with the Blue channel, you're now working with what's called your *target channel*—all changes you effect are targeted to just this channel and no others in your image.

You may also be surprised to see that the colors in individual channels show up in grayscale, instead of in their actual colors. But if you've ever seen CMYK film separations for graphics or a book cover, for example, you'll see it's the same concept at work—the darker the black part of the color channel, the higher the concentration of that single color. White areas in an individual color channel are like the transparent parts in a piece of film—white means that the color is entirely absent. When you use Photoshop's tools to edit a channel, you should use black as your foreground color to add more of that channel's color to an image. Painting with white will remove that channel's color from areas of your image—or, looking at it another way, you'll effectively paint with that channel's complete opposite, or its complementary color. You can also paint with shades of gray to blend in some amount of a channel's color to your image instead of saturating the area with a solid color.

Displaying individual color channels in grayscale is Photoshop's default setting, but if you like you can view individual color channels with the actual colors in place. From the File menu, choose Preferences and then General. Check the box that reads "Color Channels in Color" and click OK (Figure 7.8).

Figure 7.8

Changing the appearance of colors in individual color channels from grayscale to the actual colors themselves

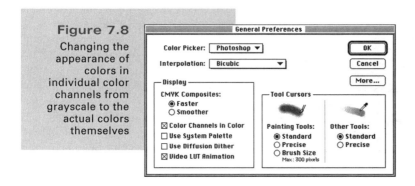

Using Color Channels to Capture Hard-to-Select Areas

If you ever have an inordinately hard time selecting the right part of an image—too many uneven edges to use the Marquee or Lasso tools, and not enough color contrast to use the Magic Wand, let's say—you might have an easier time finding color contrast if you look at the image's individual color channels. Very often, at least one channel has greater color contrast than the composite image. After you've made your selection, you can return to your composite image or save your selection to an alpha channel (Figure 7.9).

Figure 7.9

Using individual color channels lets you select part of an image more easily.

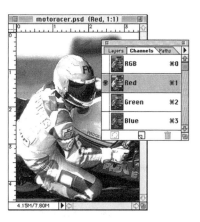
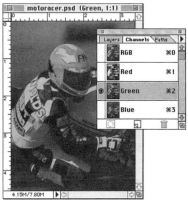
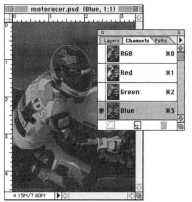

Editing Combinations of Channels

Just as you can view and edit two or more layers together (see Chapter 5), you can view and edit two or more channels together—independently of other channels. I'm going to return now to the tennis ball graphic shown in Figure 7.7, where only the Blue channel is displayed. You should follow the same steps with an image on your screen.

With the Blue channel still selected as your target channel, hold down (Shift) and click the Red channel's row in the Channels palette. Now you'll see that both the Blue and Red channel rows have gray backgrounds and eye icons appearing in the Channels palette (Figure 7.10). Any editing or painting you do here will affect just these two channels; it won't touch the Green channel at all.

note   If your image has multiple layers, you'll need to target the background layer in the Layers palette if you want to edit two or more channels together.

To see your image's composite view again, displaying all channels, press (⌘)-(0) (for Mac users) or (Ctrl)-(0) (for Windows users).

Alpha Channels

Now that you've explored the color channels Photoshop provides, it's time you experimented with adding your own channels to an image. Next I'll show you two ways to place an additional channel in a document. First, you'll make a selection with the Marquee tool and save it

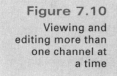

Figure 7.10
Viewing and editing more than one channel at a time

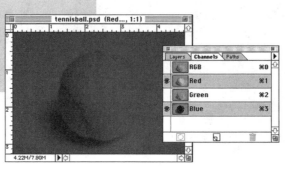

as a mask in a channel; then you'll try defining the channel first and carving out a selection area to put in it.

Saving a Selection in a New Channel

You'll need a sample image—use either the one you already have open or another graphic that's at your disposal. Use one of the selection tools—like the Rectangular or Elliptical Marquee, Lasso, or Magic Wand—to choose just a portion of your image. Choose Save Selection from the Select menu. This will cause the Save Selection dialog box to appear (Figure 7.11).

The Destination pull-down menu shows your document's name, but you could also save this new selection as a channel in another open document or in a new document altogether. Here, we'll use the defaults as shown to create a new channel in this document. Click OK to create the new channel.

• •

Using a Shortcut to Create a New Channel

After you've selected a portion of your image, you can just click the Selection icon at the bottom of the Channels palette to convert your selection to a mask in its own channel.

• •

Look in the Channels palette and you'll see that a new row has been added for your new channel (Figure 7.12). If your document is in RGB color mode, the new channel is called #4; if it's in CMYK mode, the

Figure 7.11
The Save
Selection
dialog box

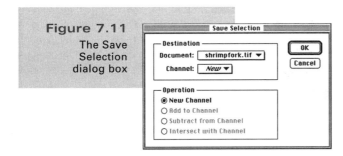

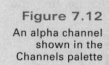

Figure 7.12

An alpha channel
shown in the
Channels palette

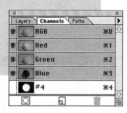

new channel is called #5. Since the image in my example is in RGB mode, the first alpha channel here is called #4.

So far, you've created a new alpha channel but haven't viewed it onscreen yet. Look at the thumbnail image next to the new channel's row in the Channels palette. The thumbnail sketch for the alpha channel should look like a black-and-white stencil—the area you selected appears in white, with the rest of the image masked out with solid black.

Let's view the new alpha channel with the rest of the image and then by itself. Click the eye icon column in the row for #4; you should see your selection area bordered by marching ants, and the rest of the image covered with a red overlay (Figure 7.13). If you paint sweeping strokes with one of the painting tools over your image, only areas inside the selection will be affected.

Now let's look at the new alpha channel by itself; see Figure 7.14. Click the eye icon in the RGB composite channel to hide all other channels.

Figure 7.13

An alpha channel
viewed with the
other channels
in a document.
The red overlay
covering the
other channels
works like
a stencil,
protecting them
from edits made
to the alpha
channel.

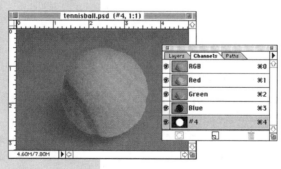

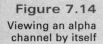

Figure 7.14
Viewing an alpha
channel by itself

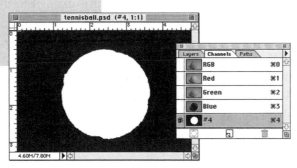

You should see a full-screen view of the black-and-white stencil image you saw in the channel's thumbnail sketch.

You can use the various paint tools here in this alpha channel to modify the shape of your saved selection area—but remember you're not yet affecting your actual image per se. For example, you can use the Airbrush or the Paintbrush with various brushes selected to soften the edges of your selection area.

tip **Setting Marquee Tool Options Before Making Selections**

There's an easy way to blur the edges of a selection area evenly when you first save your selection to an alpha channel. Just click the Feather check box and enter a pixel value in the Marquee Options palette when you make a Marquee selection. After you save the selection to an alpha channel, this will blur the edges of your masked selection just as it does any other selection.

You'll also have better luck creating masks with smooth edges if you check the Anti-aliased check box in the Options palette for the Lasso, Magic Wand, and Elliptical Marquee tools.

By now, you've created a selection and used it to create a new channel. You can also first create an alpha channel and then carve out your masked area from scratch using Photoshop's tools. That's what we'll do here to create a second alpha channel.

Choose New Channel from the Channels palette's fly-out menu, or just click the New Channel icon (⬛) at the bottom of the Channels

palette. You'll see the Channel Options dialog box as shown in Figure 7.15. Here you'll see you can use Photoshop's defaults for using color to represent masked-out areas and white to show selected areas in your channel, or choose to invert this scheme. You can also modify the default color (red) and the opacity of the mask that appears over areas outside your alpha channel when you view your composite image and the alpha channel together onscreen. The half-opaque red mask is reminiscent of *rubylith*—the film graphic designers use to mask out parts of images on hard copy.

You can also use this dialog box to enter a different name for this channel (#5). Click OK when you're done.

note If you'd like to change the name of the channel you created earlier when you saved an existing selection (#4), just double-click its row in the Channels palette. The Channels Options dialog box for this channel will appear.

Next, you'll see for yourself how useful it is to be able to reload selections once you've saved them. Let's return to your RGB composite channel and then load the first saved selection you placed in an alpha channel.

Loading a Selection

Return to the RGB channel by clicking the eye icon next to the RGB channel, or by pressing ⌘-0 (for Mac users) or Ctrl-0 (for Windows users). If either of the alpha channels remains in view, just click the eye icon to hide it.

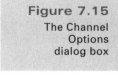

Figure 7.15
The Channel
Options
dialog box

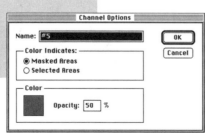

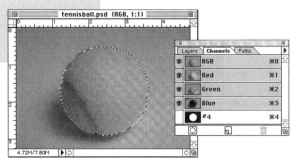

Figure 7.16
Loading a saved
selection

Choose Load Selection from the Select menu. In Figure 7.16, I've chosen the first alpha channel I created earlier, #4. The selection saved in the alpha channel now appears as an active selection.

Shortcuts for Loading Selections

There are a bunch of quicker ways you can load saved selections:

- Option-click (for Mac users) or Alt-click (for Windows users) the channel you want from the Channels palette to load it.

- Here's a keyboard-only shortcut: hold down Option (for Mac users) or Alt (for Windows users) as you type the channel's key combination shown in the Channels palette.

- You can also drag a channel's row down to the Selection icon (⬚) at the bottom of the Channels palette to load it.

Adding to, Subtracting from, and Intersecting Channels

Back in Chapter 3, you saw how helpful it can be to add to or subtract from a selection—for example, if your active selection didn't quite capture the exact area you wanted. Channels also let you add to or subtract from a selection, or intersect two different selections to capture the overlapping part.

When you create a second alpha channel in a document, you'll discover you have more options available in the Channel Options Dialog

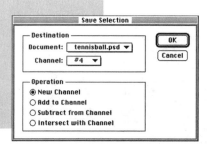

Figure 7.17

Options for adding to, subtracting from, and intersecting channels when saving a selection

box than you did the first time. As Figure 7.17 shows, you can save your selection to an existing channel instead of a new one, and you can choose to add the two selections together, subtract from the first selection any overlapping area from the second, or save only the portion that does overlap, or intersect, between the two.

Similarly, you can load a saved selection and add to, subtract from, or intersect it with a current active selection. When you choose Load Selection from the Select menu, calling up the Load Selection dialog box, you should see the additional options shown in Figure 7.18. As this example shows, you can even turn to another document (shrimpfork.tif) to find and load a selection (highlights).

tip

● ●

Saving Memory When Storing Channels

Storing additional channels in a Photoshop document can really increase file size. If you've created multiple channels in order to add to or inter-

Figure 7.18

The Load Selection dialog box

sect them, make sure you delete the original alpha channels when you know you no longer need them.

You can conserve file size if you save your images with channels in native Photoshop format instead of as TIFF files, for example, because Photoshop's built-in compression techniques compress alpha channels especially well.

The Channels Palette Menu

By now you've used several options in the menu you get when you click the black triangle in the Channels palette's upper right corner, as shown in Figure 7.19. It's time to familiarize yourself with the rest of the available options.

The next section provides brief descriptions of the options in the Channels palette menu.

Palette Options

The Palette Options control the size and appearance of your channels' thumbnail previews in the Channels palette.

You can change the size of the thumbnail sketch shown in the Channels palette, just as you could with the Layers palette. Just choose Palette Options from the Channels palette's pop-up menu, and the Channel Palette Options dialog box will appear. You have your choice of three thumbnail sizes—or none at all. You probably won't have a real need to change the default setting (the smallest size), however.

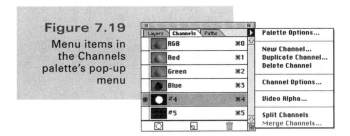

Figure 7.19
Menu items in the Channels palette's pop-up menu

New Channel

As you saw earlier, you can use this menu item to create a new channel without needing to make a selection first. Alternatively, you can just click the New Channel icon (⬛) at the bottom of the Channels palette. Both methods will cause the Channel Options dialog box to appear.

If you want to bypass the Channel Options dialog box when you create a new channel, hold down Option (for Mac users) or Alt (for PC users) when you click the New Channel icon.

Duplicate Channel

You can use the Duplicate Channel option to make a copy of a channel either in the same document you're working in, or export a copy to another open Photoshop document with the same dimensions. When you call up the Duplicate Channel dialog box, you can give the channel copy a new name; you also have the option of creating an inverted copy of your image—like a film negative—by clicking the Invert check box.

You can also just drag a channel's row down to the New Channel icon (⬛) to make a duplicate channel.

Delete Channel

Target a given channel and choose this command to delete it. It's a good idea to delete extra channels whenever it's feasible to do so, because channels hog so much disk space. You can also just drag a channel's row down to the Trash icon (🗑) to get rid of it.

Channel Options

As you saw earlier, Channel Options lets you name a channel, choose either black or white as the color to use in defining selection areas in an alpha channel, and control the color and opacity of the mask overlay that appears when you view your composite image along with your alpha channel.

Video Alpha

You can use this command to make alpha channels that you can use to overlay opening and closing title credits for video files. You'll need to first save your titles and graphics in an ordinary alpha channel, then choose Video Alpha. In the resulting Video Alpha dialog box, you should then click the Channel pop-up menu to choose the channel you want. After you've converted an alpha channel to a video alpha channel, the eye icon next to the channel's row in the Channels palette will change to a little television icon (📺). You'll see this command in action in Chapter 14, "Multimedia Essentials."

Split Channels

This command lets you save all of a document's channels to separate Photoshop documents. After splitting a graphic's channels into different files, you can apply various filters, then recombine them into one document—and thus create special effects that would be impossible to achieve otherwise.

After you choose Split Channels from the Channels palette's fly-out menu, you'll see that each channel will appear on your screen in a separate document window and the original document will close.

Merge Channels

This command lets you combine several single-channel documents into one Photoshop document. A typical use would be to restore a document

after you split up its channels (with the Split Channels command) and applied various filters or other effects to the separate documents. You'll have a chance to try this in Exercise 7.1, "Creating Mezzotints with Split and Merge Channels," later in this chapter. But you can also merge channels from different documents, as long as all the channels involved have the same height and width in pixels.

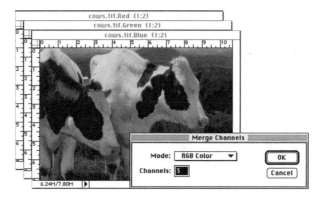

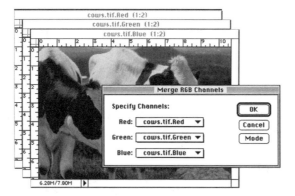

You can merge three single-channel documents into a document with RGB or Lab color mode; you'll need four single-channel documents to merge into one CMYK image.

EXERCISE 7.1

Creating Mezzotints with Split and Merge Channels

You can add an interesting mezzotint effect to an image by splitting channels, converting each separate channel to Bitmap mode and applying a bitmap pattern, then converting back to grayscale and merging channels. It's a roundabout procedure, but it will give you lots more options for the type of mezzotint patterns available with just the Mezzotint filter (see Chapter 8), so your touched-up images will look all the more impressive. This effect is especially nice if your only photo resources are stock photos, and you want to avoid a straightforward cut-and-paste look when using them.

1. Open up an RGB or CMYK image. Make sure the Channels palette is visible.

2. Choose Split Channels from the Channels palette's fly-out menu to separate your image into separate grayscale documents. You'll wind up with three separate grayscale files for an RGB graphic, and four for a CMYK image.

3. Next, we want to convert these new grayscale documents to Bitmapped mode. You'll have several pattern options for converting grayscale images to bitmapped ones when you choose Bitmap from the Mode menu. For our purposes here, though, we want to apply a custom pattern—using one that comes packaged with Photoshop—so we need to define the pattern first. The Custom Pattern option is grayed out in the Bitmap dialog box that appears when you choose Bitmap from the Mode menu unless you define a pattern first. If the Bitmap dialog box is open on your screen, click Cancel to make it disappear.

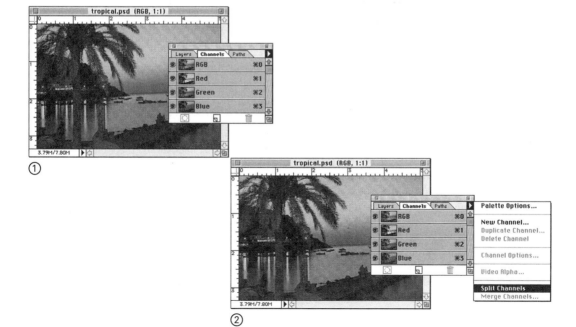

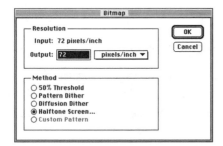

③

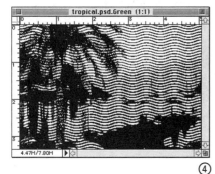

③

④

Here, I'm going to open up an Illustrator file with a wave-like pattern. For Mac users, look in the Goodies folder in your Adobe Photoshop folder In a folder called Brushes & Patterns (for Windows users, the folder is just called brushes), open the Postscript Patterns folder and choose the document called Waves. (You can let the Adobe Illustrator file rasterize when you open it.) Select the whole image (⌘-A for Mac users; Ctrl-A for Windows users), then choose Define Pattern from the Edit menu.

Great! Now you're ready to go back to your grayscale files.

4. For each of these grayscale files, you'll need to convert the mode to Bitmap. Beginning with the first document, choose Bitmap from the Mode menu. Note the various options shown in the Bitmap dialog box. Here, we'll click the Custom Pattern radio button. Notice how your grayscale document turns into a black-and-white image with your pattern running through it. Repeat for the other grayscale images from your original file.

5. Now that you've applied the custom pattern to all three files (or four, if your original was a CMYK document), we're going to take the steps needed to merge these separate channels back together again. Convert the mode for the currently selected bitmapped image to Grayscale mode; repeat for the other bitmapped images.

6. Within any of your grayscale documents, click the black triangle in the upper right corner of the Channels palette and choose Merge Channels. You'll see one more dialog box giving you the option to select other documents besides the ones you started out with to merge together. Click OK to accept the default files.

7. Check out your finished effect in Figure 7.20. How about trying this with another pattern—or using the pattern in only one channel? You can also experiment with applying various filters from the Filter menu—covered in detail in Chapter 8—to your separated grayscale documents before merging the channels back into a single document.

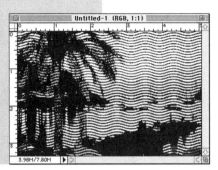

Figure 7.20
By using Split Channels to apply patterns to separate color channels, followed by Merge Channels, you can achieve many unique effects.

Effects with Type Masks

Whenever you enter type in a Photoshop document using the Type tool, your characters appear as an active selection when you're done. It's easy then to choose Save Selection from the Select menu and turn your type selections into their own channels. In this section, you'll gain some practice using type selections to create special effects—both because it's easy to make type selections and because there are so many real-world applications for snazzy type effects. You can use channels to create effects like embossed text, recessed text, and shadowed text.

note

You can achieve many type effects by using layers as well as channels; this gives you the flexibility to reposition the shadows at a later time if you want—say, by lengthening or shortening them. But it's also possible to create these final effects with channels alone—you don't *have* to create separate layers for the different shadow effects. Before version 3, after all, Photoshop designers only had channels at their disposal for creating these kinds of effects.

In the next exercise, you use channels to create recessed text against a textured background. This is useful for making type that looks like it's carved in stone, traced in sand, or dug into any other kind of substance. You'll save your text selection to a channel, then use that channel to create and offset the shadows that will add depth to the type.

EXERCISE 7.2

Creating Recessed Text

①

③

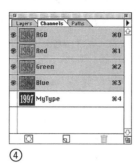

④

1. Begin by opening the image you're going to use for the background inside your recessed text. Texture backgrounds work well for this kind of effect—they let you make your recessed text look like it's been carved or etched, not computer-generated. Light-to-medium-colored textures work best because you'll be able to see the texture details clearly in the recessed text when you're done.

2. Next, make sure that the Layers palette is showing; we'll get to the Channels palette in a minute. If necessary, choose Palettes from the Window menu and then pick Show Layers.

3. Now you're ready to add your type to the image. Make sure you have a dark color selected for the foreground color. Select the Type tool and click on the image. The Type Tool dialog box will appear. Enter the text you want to add to the image and click OK.

4. The type you just entered shows up as an active selection. If you want to reposition the selection to a better spot, go right ahead.

   Now you're ready to turn your type selection into a channel and put it aside for later use. Display the Channels palette. Choose Save Selection from the Select menu and give your type selection a name. After you create the new alpha channel, you can double-click it to name the channel. Here I've called it My Type.

5. Save this type selection in its own layer—that'll help keep your options open if you want to reposition your type at any time. Make sure the Layers palette is visible. Drag the row called Floating Selection down to the New Section icon. When the Make Layer dialog box appears, give the new layer a name. Here I've named the new layer Lettering.

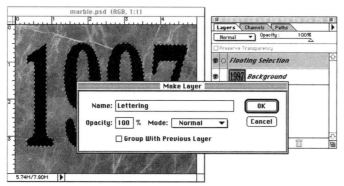

⑤

⑥

⑥

6. Next, you're going to lower the opacity for your type on the Lettering Layer so the textured background shows through. Drag the Opacity slider in the Layers palette to a value between 30 percent and 40 percent.

7. Next, we'll create a layer for the shadows in the image. Create another layer, like the one I've called Shadows here. Load the lettering from your type channel into the layer called Shadows by choosing Load Selection from the Select menu. Since my type is in a channel called MyType, that's the name of the selection I'm loading here.

8. Select the inverse of your type selection by choosing Inverse from the Select menu. Fill the selection area with 100 percent black. Your shadow layer should now look like the following picture:

9. In this step you'll blur the edges of this type outline and offset the layer—that's how we're producing the effect of a shadow inside the type outlines. Choose Gaussian Blur from the Filter menu (you'll get the full discussion of filters in Chapter 8) and enter a low value, between 5 and 10. The higher the value you enter, the more indistinct the type outline will look. Now choose Other… from the Filter menu and select Offset. The values you enter here determine the direction the shadow will fall. Here, I offset the shadow three pixels to the right and three pixels down.

⑦

10. Now load the type selection again by choosing Load Selection from the Select menu, or remember the shortcut of Option-clicking (for Mac users) or Alt-clicking (for Windows users) on the channel's name in the Channels palette. Choose Inverse from the Select menu and press Delete to crop only what's inside the letter outlines.

   Your image should look pretty good by now—you've got that cool recessed shadow you created in the Shadows layer atop the somewhat opaque type in the Lettering layer.

11. For a finishing touch, you can load the selection again and add a border. Choose Stroke from the Edit menu to add a one-pixel black border around the letter outlines if you like.

   Save this exercise as you will refer to it in Chapter 11 in Exercise 11.7.

⑧

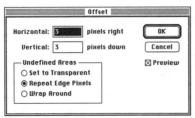

⑧

⑨

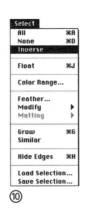

⑩

⑩

Figure 7.21

Your final recessed effect—after you run through these steps once or twice, you'll have committed this technique to memory.

Quick Mask Mode

If you need to make and edit a selection carefully but know that you'll only need to select that area once, then you should use Photoshop's Quick Mask Mode to make a temporary mask instead of creating a new channel. A Quick Mask gives you all the versatility of using Photoshop's painting and editing tools to refine a selection area that you have in a channel, but you won't need to go through the extra steps that go into saving a selection, loading it, targeting that channel, and bringing the composite image back into view before editing the selection.

Quick Masks work well as shortcuts once you've already started working with channels and have gotten used to seeing the red overlays—the ones that look like rubylith—that Photoshop uses to represent masked areas when you bring both a saved channel and your composite image into view. After you select an area of your image, click the Quick Mask icon ( ) to enter Quick Mask mode. When you make a selection and then choose Quick Mask mode, Photoshop automatically puts the red overlay into place (Figure 7.22).

Editing in Quick Mask Mode

Once you're in Quick Mask mode, you can fine-tune your selection using any of Photoshop's painting or editing tools, including the Airbrush and Paintbrush with any brush selected. This lets you make much more refined selections with partially selected pixels. Painting

Figure 7.22
Using Quick
Mask mode

with white as the foreground color will remove the red overlay and add to your selection; painting with black will add more of the overlay and subtract from your selection.

You can reverse the Quick Mask color preferences if you like, so that painting with white will add to your selection and painting with black with subtract from it, just as you can when you're working with a channel selection. Just double-click the Quick Mask icon (⬤) to display the Quick Mask Options dialog box (Figure 7.23); these are the same options you saw earlier in the Channel Options dialog box.

Figure 7.23
The Quick
Mask Options
dialog box

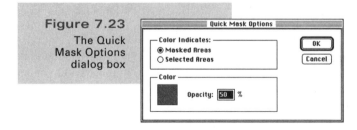

tip **Reversing Quick Mask Color Preferences in a Hurry**

If you regularly decide to paint your selections in color and use the transparent overlay to indicate the masked area, there's a quicker way to setting these options than calling up the Quick Mask Options dialog box. Option-click (for Mac users) or Alt-click (for Windows users) the Quick Mask icon on the toolbar when you're ready to enter Quick Mask mode, and the default color preferences will automatically reverse. Notice that the little Quick Mask icon changes too to reflect your preferences.

Whether you decide painting in color should add to or subtract from your Quick Mask selections, you'll probably want it to coincide with the Channel Options settings you use. Otherwise, you'll likely get mixed up when you're editing your selections if you do some in channels and some in Quick Mask mode.

No More Marching Ants

The other bonus to editing your selection in Quick Mask mode this way is that you won't see the marching ants border around your selection. The hard-edged marching ants border never really represents soft, graduated edges in your selections that well anyway, right? Here, you'll see your partially selected pixels covered with just a lighter shade of the red overlay mask, meaning that those pixels are partially protected and remain partially editable.

Here's an exercise to give you some experience with working in Quick Mask mode. The effect you'll create is one you saw when you first learned about feathering the edges of a marquee selection in Chapter 3—fading an image into a background for a vignette effect.

EXERCISE 7.3

Creating a Vignette Using Quick Mask Mode

①

①

②

1. Open the image you want to use for this exercise.

   You'll use the Gradient tool for this exercise, so you'll need to make sure your settings are in order. Make sure the Opacity is set to 70%, the Radial option is selected, and the Midpoint and Radial Offset are both set to 50%.

2. Click the Quick Mask icon in the toolbox to enter Quick Mask mode. With the Gradient tool selected, position your crosshairs in the center of your image and draw a diagonal line to an outer edge of your image. The Quick Mask red overlay will appear, showing the masked area of your image.

3. Switch to Normal mode by clicking the Normal icon next to the Quick Mask icon in the Toolbox. Set your background color to the color you want to blend your image into.

4. Now press ⟨Delete⟩ (or ⌘-⟨X⟩ for Mac users; ⟨Ctrl⟩-⟨X⟩ for Windows users) to subtract the unmasked portion of the image. Congratulations—you've learned another way of making selections without using channels, as well as a second method for creating vignette effects!

Figure 7.24
A completed vignette effect, accomplished via a Quick Mask.

Summary

Go ahead and heave a great sigh of satisfaction—with this chapter's coverage of channels and masks, you've just learned the last of the basic concepts that round out your Photoshop need-to-know arsenal. As you dip into the second half of this book, you'll see we're turning now to creating more embellished effects—including filtering just ahead in Chapter 8—and learning the situation-specific tips you'll need to optimize your graphics for viewing in print, multimedia, and online applications.

In Chapter 9, you'll see the most complicated—and hopefully, the most arresting—applications for channels, masks, and layers as you learn to create sophisticated composite images. Photocompositing has certainly helped the *Weekly World News*—with its images of space aliens shaking hands with Bill Clinton and Bob Dole—stay in business (at least, I *hope* those are composite images...). There are also plenty of more mundane reasons why you might need a composite image—adding an absent person to a group photo, for example, or improving on a less-than-wonderful product shoot. Up ahead next, though, we'll turn to an in-depth look at how to use filters to dress up your images and alter them dramatically.

8
Filter Essentials

Photoshop's filters give you a fun, fast, one-stop-shopping way to create digital special effects. You can use them to generate the most artistic painting effects, stylized touch-ups, twisted and twirled distortions. Filters offer a no-hassle way to reproduce some of the Photoshop effects you can create manually—like beveled edges or an embossed look—as well as many striking effects you'd be hard-pressed to create otherwise.

There are also filters that can help you with every step of photo retouching and color correction. For example, you can use filters to bring blurry edges in a poorly scanned photo into better focus, get rid of moiré patterns that result when you scan a halftoned page, or add dramatic lighting effects to a ho-hum kind of image.

In this chapter, you'll get a chance to see not only what each filter does but how they specifically differ from one another—for example, the differences between Blur and Gaussian Blur. You'll also discover what kind of effects you can produce with combinations of filters, so that you can get more mileage out of your filters.

You'll also get to see suggested real-world applications for which you might want or need to use a certain kind of filter. This may prove to be the most useful part of the chapter for you—it's fun to fool around with each filter one by one to see what kind of effects you can produce, but you may be under the gun. If you have to come up with a stunning design *right now,* you may not have time to figure out by brute force how to achieve the look you want.

Here's a broad look at the topics covered in this chapter:

- 👁 How filters work, and how to speed up their operation

- 👁 Each of the standard filters included with Photoshop and what you can use it for

- 👁 How to extend the effects of filters by using them in channels and layers

- 👁 The Custom Filter command and Filter Factory plug-in

- 👁 The effects you can create with third-party commercial and freeware filters, and where you can obtain these filters

Putting Filters to Work

The name is an allusion to photographic filters, but in a way a Photoshop filter is a little like a coffee filter or an air filter—it can perform its own specific processing operation to produce an entirely new end product. You can apply filters either to an entire image or to a selected portion of one.

You can apply a filter to any part of an image, such as an area you mark off with one of the Selection tools or an alpha channel you've loaded. If you're working in an image with multiple layers, you can also apply a filter to a single layer at a time without affecting any others. If you haven't made a selection before you apply a filter, it will affect the entire image.

note **Photoshop won't let you apply filters to images in Bitmap or Indexed Color modes, because filters will likely introduce colors outside those modes' ranges. You'll need to convert to Grayscale or RGB mode instead.**

You can select filters in Photoshop by choosing any menu item from the Filter menu. The standard set that comes with Photoshop includes Blur, Distort, Noise, Pixelate, Render, Sharpen, Stylize, Video, and Other filters. (We'll get to what these categories of filters do in a minute.) Some of these filters are built right into your Photoshop application, but you'll find others included as *plug-ins,* a standard component set Adobe devised for creating add-ons to the program. Vendors of other graphics software packages have created filter plug-ins that work with Photoshop as well as with their own programs; these include Kai's Power Tools from MetaTools and the Andromeda series of filters. Appendix B includes information on third-party vendors and their products, including filters.

You can add freeware filters—like those you might find on the Web or on AOL or CompuServe's graphics file libraries or in third-party collections—by placing their files in the Plug-Ins folder inside your Photoshop folder. As you'll see later in this chapter, you can even create your own filters in Photoshop and add them to your Plug-Ins folder.

There's a Filters folder inside your Plug-Ins folder where you can store all your filters for safekeeping, but Photoshop will recognize your filters even if you leave them scattered elsewhere in the Plug-Ins folder. The Filters folder just helps you keep your filters organized by putting them all in one spot, away from other kinds of plug-ins.

 note

If you install filters in Photoshop while the program's still running, you'll have to quit and relaunch Photoshop before you see their options available to you.

Depending on which filter you apply, it may go into effect right away or it may prompt you with a dialog box for supplying specific parameters. When you see a filter dialog box, you'll usually get a chance to preview the results you'll get for the values you enter—as in Figure 8.1.

If you pass your cursor over the dialog box's preview image, it'll turn to a hand icon you can use to click and drag on the image to preview different portions of the image. If it's tedious to click and drag to the right part of the image you want to see, you can just click your cursor on that portion of the image itself, and and the dialog box's preview will show the filter applied to that portion of the image. You can click the Zoom buttons under the preview box to increase or reduce the size of the preview image you see.

Figure 8.1
Using a filter's dialog box to preview the results

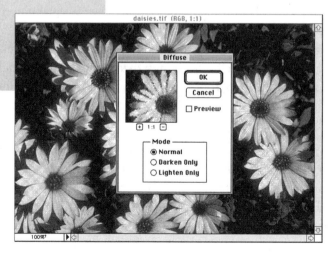

The dialog box for each filter also has a check box marked Preview; if you keep this box checked, you'll get to see the effects of your filter applied to your full image before you click OK to execute the change. This feature can be pretty memory-intensive, though, so if you want to speed up your filtering you can turn off the Preview check box. You'll still be able to check out the effect using the preview image in the filter's dialog box—there's no way to turn that off.

tip

Bring Up a Filter's Dialog Box More Than Once

After you apply a filter, you can reapply it by pressing ⌘-F (for Mac users) or Ctrl-F (for Windows users), but you won't see the filter's dialog box a second time. If you want a chance to see the dialog box again and perhaps change the filter's settings, you should press ⌘-Option-F (for Mac users) or Ctrl-Alt-F (for Windows users) instead.

Applying Filters at Partial Strength

Wouldn't it be nice if the filter dialog boxes had Opacity settings so you could apply a given filter at, say, only 50 percent intensity instead of full strength? Photoshop has a couple of workarounds for accomplishing just that.

First, if you use one of the selection tools or load an alpha channel to make a selection before you apply a filter, you can *float* it by choosing Float from the Select menu. This will turn your selection into a floating selection, placing it on its own temporary layer and enabling you to edit it separately from the rest of your image. If you look at your floating selection's row in the Layers palette, you'll see that you can toy with the Opacity slider control, reducing the floating selection's opacity—and the intensity of your filter—as much as you want when you apply your filter to the selection.

Figure 8.2 shows an example to illustrate this. Applying Crystallize at a level of 10 to the metallic cone at far left overpowers its shine and curves, as shown by the middle cone. After floating the selection first, I applied the same filter at 50 percent to produce the crystallized texture effect in the cone at far right.

Figure 8.2

Selecting the cone at far left and lowering the opacity to 50% before applying the Crystallize filter produces the effect at far right, instead of the overpowering results of applying the plain filter (middle).

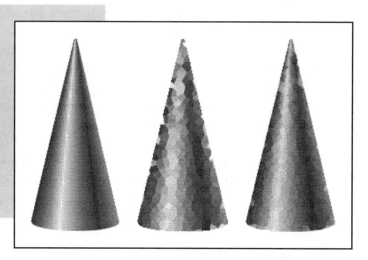

Why Are Filters So Slow?

Some filters function by examining every pixel in an image before transforming them in some way. Other filters sample larger areas of your image to make broader determinations about brightness and hue before effecting their changes. Either way, it can be a time-consuming process.

The proress bar (Figure 8.3) is a partial consolation—it lets you judge how quickly (or slowly) your filter is working. You can always click the Cancel button if you're too impatient. If you're just experimenting with different filters and settings, you can save time by relying on the preview images in your filters' dialog boxes to judge results whenever possible before committing to applying a filter.

Here are a couple of tips for speeding up your filters:

👁 Deselect the Preview check box in a filter's dialog box. This will prevent you from seeing the filter applied to your whole image,

Figure 8.3

A progress bar showing how long it's taking Photoshop to apply a filter

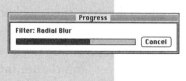

but you'll still get a chance to see a miniature before-and-after view in the dialog box's preview image.

👁 The more RAM and free hard disk space available to your filters, the better. As you may have discovered the hard way, few things are more annoying than watching a filter chug along 90 percent of the way to execution only to run out of memory. Follow the tips in Chapter 1 for optimizing memory and performance on your machine.

Blur Filters

Blur filters reduce the contrast between pixels and their surrounding neighbors, so you can use them to soften hard edges in your images where there's too much contrast.

Blur and Blur More

The Blur filter produces a straightforward blurring effect, as if your glasses had slipped down your nose. If softens contrasting edges and can reduce noise—that is, individual pixels that sharply contrast with surrounding ones. The Blur More filter just produces a more exaggerated Blur effect.

Figure 8.4 shows one really useful application of the Blur filters— namely, blurring background objects so as to highlight objects or figures in the foreground. The top picture in Figure 8.4 shows a nice, picturesque San Francisco skyline. In order to emphasize the row of houses, I first used the Pen tool in the Paths palette to outline the houses. Next, I converted the path to a selection using the Make Selection option in the Paths palette. I loaded the selection to an alpha channel for later use, and then chose Inverse from the Select menu to select everything but the houses. I ran the Blur More filter several times over the background buildings to obscure some detail. In the bottom image, the row of houses is vivid and draws the eye to itself instead of to any of the other buildings.

Figure 8.4
Using Blur filters
to make a
foreground
object stand out

Gaussian Blur

With Gaussian Blur, named for the bell-shaped Gaussian distribution curve, you have greater control over the blurring effect. (The Gaussian distribution curve, by the way, slopes gradually at first, then quite drastically in the middle, before tapering off gradually at the end again.) You enter a value between 0.1 and 250 to effect a certain amount of change between contrasting pixels; higher values indicate more extreme blurring. This is a good filter to use for exaggerating shadows when they're on their own layer.

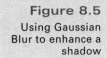

Figure 8.5
Using Gaussian
Blur to enhance a
shadow

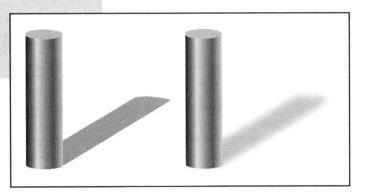

Figure 8.5 demonstrates how Gaussian Blur enhances a shadow effect when you're adding the shadow yourself. In the image on the left, I made a copy of the rod's outline, placed it on its own layer, filled it with gray, and distorted it off to one side to serve as the shadow. In the image on the right, I applied a Gaussian Blur of 6 to the shadow layer and reduced the opacity a little further.

Motion Blur

As the name implies, this filter helps produce the illusion of capturing an object in motion, as shown in the before-and-after pictures in Figure 8.6. The filter dialog box lets you control the angle and intensity of the motion effect.

Figure 8.6
Applying
Motion Blur

Figure 8.7

The two Radial Blur options: spin and zoom

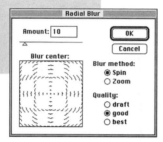
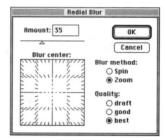

Figure 8.7

The two Radial Blur options: spin and zoom

Radial Blur

There are two kinds of blurring effects you can produce with this filter. The *spin* method whirls the edges of your image with a circular motion; the *zoom* method produces blurred lines from all edges focusing in on the center of your image. The dialog box for Radial Blur includes a wireframe preview instead of an image preview to indicate the intensity of the effect. You can enter values between 1 and 100 or drag the slider control in the dialog box to control the level of the blur (Figure 8.7).

You can also choose one of three quality levels in generating a Radial Blur—called draft, good, and best. Figure 8.8 shows the Radial Blur filter in action.

Figure 8.8

Three Einsteins: The original is on the left. The middle image uses the Radial Blur filter's Spin option at a level of 10. At right, the image uses the Radial Blur filter's Zoom option at a level of 35.

Distortion Filters

These filters produce a variety of real funhouse-mirror effects, reshaping an image rather than altering the colors of pixels. You may have few everyday uses for them, but they're always an option for striking or unusual effects. One notable exception to the general weird-and-warped flavor of most of the distortion filters is Displace, so I've covered that one last, after all the other distortion filters.

Pinch

The Pinch filter distorts an image by squeezing it inward or outward. You can enter values between -100% (which bloats your image in a complete outward pinch) and 100% (for a complete inward pinch). Figure 8.9 below shows an image of a quarter pinched inward in the dialog box's preview image. (I was going to pinch pennies instead, but hey, there's inflation for you.)

Polar Coordinates

The Polar Coordinates filter shapes rectangular objects into circular shapes, and vice versa. Probably the only popular visual representation of this filter in action is the Mercator projection of the globe. I use Polar Coordinates sometimes for generating unusual or hard-to-draw shapes for logos or background patterns. Figure 8.10 shows three images on the left that have been filtered from Rectangular to Polar (center) and, going back to the original images, from Polar to Rectangular (right).

Figure 8.9
The Pinch filter

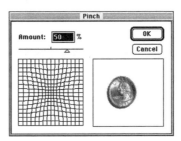

Ripple

This filter creates a rippled, wavelike effect. In the example shown in Figure 8.11, I've applied the Ripple filter to an image used to make a tiling background for a Web page. (You'll see Web graphics covered in more detail in Chapter 13.)

Shear

This filter can create effects that really do look like funhouse-mirror distortions. It twists your image according to a curve that you specify in the Shear dialog box (Figure 8.12). To define the curve, you click on the vertical band that appears in the grid in the Shear dialog box. You can click on the band multiple times, adding a new control point each time for editing the curve. You can click the Reset button to restore the

Figure 8.11
The Ripple filter.

Figure 8.12
The Shear filter
in action

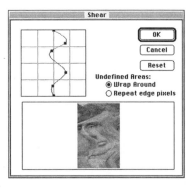

band to its original default settings. You also need to choose one of two settings for distorting pixels in areas undefined by the curve: Wrap Around or Repeat Edge Pixels.

Spherize

This lets you create an easy-to-produce raytracing effect—mapping an image onto a spherical shape. One use for this filter is to make caricatures of people—for some reason (as Figure 8.13 illustrates), it's always funny to mess with the size of someone's head.

Twirl

This whirling effect will make your image look like you dropped it in a blender or washing machine. You can set the angle in the Twirl dialog box. Using higher angles is akin to using the Liquefy setting on your

Figure 8.13
Two spherized
Einsteins, at
100% and -100%
respectively

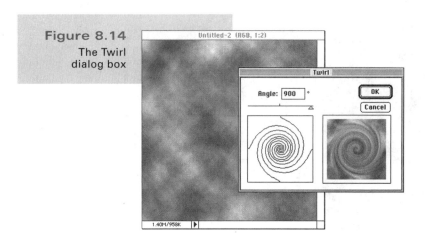

Figure 8.14
The Twirl
dialog box

blender, as opposed to Stir. As Figure 8.14 shows, it's also nice to use the Twirl filter on a gridded pattern because the effect is most clear.

Wave

The Wave filter, like Shear, is good for creating funhouse-mirror effects—but you have much more control with this filter. In the Wave dialog box, you can control how many waves you get, from 1 to 999. You can specify minimum and maximum values for the distance (wavelength) and height (amplitude) of each wave. In addition, you can choose from one of three wave types (Sine, Triangle, and Square) and percentages for horizontal and vertical scaling distortions.

Too many choices? You can always just click the Randomize button in the Wave dialog box to have Photoshop generate its own wave for you. Just as with the Shear filter, you'll need to tell Photoshop what to do with areas of undefined pixels: wrap around the image from one end of the screen to the other with Wrap Around, or tile the image using the Repeat Edge Pixels option.

While you can do all sorts of goofy things to pictures of your friends with the Wave filter or use it to make "flaming" text, the most practical use I have for it is in creating interesting textures or background patterns. It works especially well if the patterns you start off with have horizontal lines running through them.

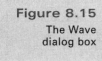

Figure 8.15
The Wave
dialog box

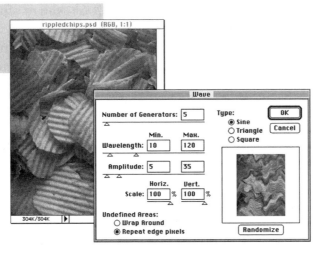

Zigzag

With the Zigzag filter, you'll be able to create all kinds of realistic water splashes and dropping-pebbles-in-a-pond type effects (Figure 8.16). It's a natural filter for framing or enhancing any kind of nautical image.

Displace

The Displace filter is by far the most sophisticated of the distortion filters, offering a unique way to add texture and dimension to an image. You'll really have to put your thinking cap on to use this filter effectively and, over time, intuitively.

Figure 8.16
The Zigzag
dialog box

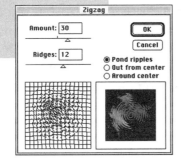

When you apply the filter, Photoshop asks you to supply the direction and distance for the filter to move pixels in the image. The filter could potentially shift each pixel in your image—either horizontally or vertically, to the left or to the right. The directional instructions the Displace filter uses are determined by a second image you specify, called a *displacement map* (also called a *dmap*).

The Displace filter looks at the brightness of each pixel in your displacement map and uses the color value it assigns them to determine which pixels in your original image to affect and how far it should move them. You might want to refer back to the discussion of color and brightness in Chapter 4. The important part to remember is that brightness represents a color's intensity; a brightness value of 0 translates into solid black, and the highest brightness value—100—represents solid white.

Here's how the Displace filter assesses each pixel:

👁 Black pixels have the lowest value. They are displaced down and to the right. Values in between medium gray and black are displaced in the same direction (down, to the right, or both), but to a lesser amount than that specified in the Displace dialog box.

👁 White pixels have the highest value. They are displaced up and to the left. Values in between medium gray and white are displaced in the same direction (up, to the left, or both), but to a lesser amount than that specified in the Displace dialog box.

👁 Neutral or medium gray pixels remain static; they are not displaced at all.

You can use any file saved in native Photoshop format (as long as it's not in Bitmap mode) as a displacement map, but you can get the most predictable results from seamless tiles or plain geometric designs—preferably in Grayscale mode, for reasons I'll go into a little later. A number of displacement map files come packaged with Photoshop; you can also search on the Web or commercial online services for tried-and-true displacement maps that other Photoshop users have created and made available to the public. Figure 8.17 shows a very simple demonstration of the Displace filter at work.

Figure 8.17

The Displace filter moves pixels in an image (top) according to the brightness values in a second image you specify, called a displacement map (center). The results of mapping the original image to the displacement map show up in the bottommost image: the top triangular portion moves down, the bottom triangular portion moves up, and the left and right sides are unmoved.

In the Displace dialog box, you enter values for horizontal and vertical displacement, as shown in Figure 8.18. These values are percentages, actually, not pixel amounts. The highest value you can enter, 100, will displace areas in your image an absolute value of 128 pixels when they correspond to solid black or white areas of the displacement map.

After you use the Displace dialog box to specify an amount to shift pixels horizontally and vertically, Photoshop prompts you to choose a file as your displacement map. As you experiment with dmaps, you'll

Figure 8.18

The Displace dialog box— showing the settings used in Figure 8.17

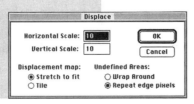

be better able to predict from looking at them what your displaced results will look like. Once you've selected a dmap file, the Displace filter will shift pixels in your image according to the color values of pixels in the dmap.

note

From here I can hear Barbie saying, "Math is hard!" Well, that may be, but I've long contended that graphic designers and Photoshop users in general already know and can understand more math than they give themselves credit for. The best way to get a handle on displacement maps is to roll up your sleeves and try mapping a sample image or two to see what kind of results you can get.

Let me take a question from the back: Does your displacement map have to be the same width and height as your original image? No, it doesn't—for learning purposes it's easier if they are the same size because it'll help you see at a glance how the color values in the dmap influence the distortions in your original image. But they certainly don't have to be the same size, and Photoshop has two ways of handling differences in size between images and their dmaps. You can click the radio button Stretch to Fit in the Displace dialog box, and that will force the dmap to stretch to match the proportions of your original. Alternatively, you can click the radio button marked Tile, which will treat the dmap as a repeating tile pattern. As you can see, that's the option I chose in Figure 8.17. Most of the dmaps included with Photoshop work well as repeating tile patterns—which is good to remember when you're in a rush to whip up some new background patterns.

Here's one last point I feel obliged to make before you turn to the exercise and try using your own displacement map. A lot of the calculations behind the way the dmap works depend on how many channels are in that image. It's simplest to imagine using a Grayscale dmap, which only has one channel. Pixels are displaced according to the x- and y-axes in this channel, as described a little earlier: white (or high) values are displaced upward according to the specified Vertical Scale value, and to the left as defined by the Horizontal scale value. Black (or low) values use the Vertical Scale and Horizontal Scale values to displace pixels down and to the right, respectively. But when a displacement map has two or more color channels—remember, RGB and Lab images have three channels, and CMYK images have four—the filter displaces according to the first two channels. It uses the first channel to set horizontal displacement, and the second channel to determine vertical displacement. As a result, it gets much harder to predict how your image will be displaced when you've got to think about color range differences in individual channels rather than the map as a whole. At first, anyway, better you should stick with grayscale displacement maps!

note If you take a look at the dmaps packaged with Photoshop, you should notice that although they are RGB images, the Blue channel in each is empty. This makes sense, because there's no reason for an RGB displacement map to contain any information in the third channel when the Displacement filter is only going to use the first two channels.

Noise Filters

The filters in this category help you clear up graininess in images—or actively add it. Let's take a look at adding graininess first.

Add Noise

This filter can give your images a gritty look, one that you can almost feel. It's also a useful filter for reducing the problem of *color banding*—an effect that can happen when there are too few steps in the transition from one color to another (Figure 8.19). Because the filter introduces

Figure 8.19

Using the Add Noise filter on color blends can help reduce banding.

EXERCISE 8.1

Using a Displacement Map

①

①

②

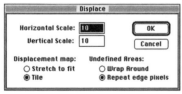

③

1. Open up your image for mapping, and choose the file for the dmap itself. Photoshop includes a number of dmaps in the Plug-ins folder, in a subfolder called Displacement Maps. Here, I'm using a picture of a rose as my base image and a dmap from Adobe called Crumbles.

   You don't actually have to open your dmap file, but I tend to open the one I'm using to remind myself of the effect I'm going after.

2. Make sure your original image is your active document. Select Distort from the Filter menu and then choose Displace from the Distort submenu.

3. In the resulting Displace dialog box, you'll need to make some decisions about how many pixels to displace, how to map the differently sized images to one another, and what to display in undefined areas. Here, I've chosen the Tile option to tile the displacement map, and the Repeat Edge Pixels option to fill any gaps left by the mapping algorithm.

4. Next, you'll get a prompt to select a dmap. Toggle through your directory structure to select the file you want to use. Click OK.

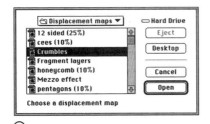

④

5. You've done it! Stand back and assess the results of your displacement mapping.

How about trying out a different dmap and seeing what that one looks like? Or what kind of results can you get if you change the number of pixels to displace? The more you experiment with the Displace filter, the more confident you'll be that you can add any and every kind of texture imaginable to your images.

⑤

randomly colored pixels into an image, it also has a lot of potential for making up textured backgrounds.

You can type a value between 1 and 999 in the Add Noise dialog box (Figure 8.20) or drag the slider control; higher values add more noise. When you specify a value for adding noise—say, 20—Photoshop can then replace each pixel with a color up to 20 values greater or less than your original color. As a result, the greater the amount of noise you use, the more pronounced and colorful effect you'll see in your image. If you click the Monochromatic check box, though, Photoshop will add noise in all channels, so that the filtered effect depends on differences in luminance, not hue—producing gray noise.

In the dialog box, you'll see two radio buttons for distribution method, called Uniform and Gaussian. The Uniform method picks colors at

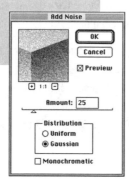

Figure 8.20
The Add Noise
dialog box

random to replace the original pixels, using the range you specified. The Gaussian method for picking colors uses the Gaussian bell curve, so you'll get a much more extreme distribution with many more light and dark pixels.

note   As mentioned earlier, you can float an image selection to further influence the kind of noise that's added. If you use a layer or a selection set to the Lighten or Darken overlay mode, you can compel Photoshop to add either light-pixels-only or dark-pixels-only noise.

Despeckle

This filter under the Noise menu helps reduce noise or blur oversharpened areas. It can also remove imperfections from a dusty scan or interference from video stills.

Unfortunately, Despeckle doesn't have its own dialog box—so there's no way to tweak its controls directly.

Dust & Scratches

This filter targets small areas in an image that contrast strongly with surrounding pixels and helps blend them in for a continuous effect. In the Dust & Scratches dialog box, you can enter a Threshold value between 0 and 255 to tell Photoshop which pixels to change when it analyzes them (Figure 8.21). Photoshop treats the value you enter as a

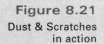

Figure 8.21
Dust & Scratches
in action

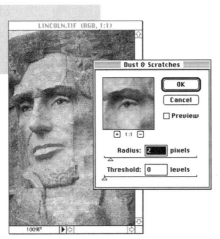

tolerance setting; it will find and change contrasting pixels within an otherwise continuously toned area if those pixels have brightness values that fall outside that tolerance level.

In the Dust & Scratches dialog box you also enter a Radius value (between 1 and 16 pixels) to tell Photoshop how wide an area it should search at a time.

Median

This filter has an interesting approach to reducing noise. After you specify a Radius value (between 1 and 16 pixels) for Photoshop to search, the program determines the median brightness value of all pixels in each area and replaces the center pixel with that value.

One of the single most useful functions for the Median and Dust & Scratches filters—in conjunction one or more of the Blur filters—is to obliterate moiré patterns that appear when you scan an image from a printed copy. You don't notice the dots in a halftone, but your scanner will!

I should say up front that most newer scanners now have plug-ins for fixing this kind of common problem, but not all do. If your scanner doesn't have a descreening plug-in, you should experiment with using combinations of the Median, Dust & Scratches, and Gaussian Blur filters. If the scanned photos are in color, try converting your scanned

image to CMYK color mode and applying these blurring filters on each separate channel to get the best results.

Pixelate Filters

These filters introduce some cool painterly effects, making your images look like they were created from large dabs of color, patterns, or tiles. The only problem is, you may have trouble finding practical uses for them. Let me trot out my Einstein TIFF to help demonstrate some of these options.

Color Halftone

This filter will transform your image to a colorful halftoned jumble, a grid of large halftone dots reminiscent of Roy Lichtenstein's comic-book paintings. The effect is a cute one, although if the dots are too big it can be hard for your viewers to figure out what they're looking at.

Crystallize

Crystallize overlays your image with a grid of polygon-shaped cells, kind of like a honeycomb. You can enter a cell size between 3 and 300 to control how big the polygon shapes will be. The colors of the pixels in your original image influence the colors used to fill the cell shapes, but much of your original image's detail can be lost—more detail disappears the larger the cell size you choose.

Facet

This filter will give your image a hand-painted look. It searches out areas of largely continuously toned color in your image and fills odd pixels out to create broader similarly colored areas. As a result, you can lose a lot of detail from your original image.

Fragment

This filter produces a somewhat blurry effect, as though the image was in motion. It copies the pixels in your image four times, averages them, and lowers their opacity. The effect is more obvious in line art images; you might find some use for it in blurred background layers just to emphasize an object in a foreground layer.

Mezzotint

The Mezzotint filter uses a pattern of lines, dots, or strokes in one of several weights to simulate your image. If you mezzotint a grayscale image, the result is a two-toned, black-and-white reproduction. For color modes—RGB, CMYK, or Lab—the Mezzotint filter will go to work on each channel in the image.

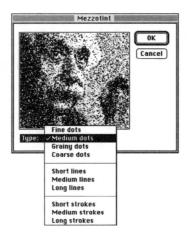

I like the idea of this filter but think its options for patterns are just too limited; I almost always lean toward using the more roundabout, but more controllable method of mezzotinting described in Exercise 7.2, "Creating Mezzotints with Split and Merge."

Mosaic

A little like Crystallize, this filter blends pixels into larger monotone squares. You can specify the size of the squares in the dialog box's Cell Size option box.

Pointillize

If Georges Seurat were alive today, would he just use the Pointillize filter instead of going to all that work in his paintings? This filter is reminiscent of the pointillist style of painting, breaking up the colors in an image into random dots. You can control the size of the dots used by specifying a value between 3 and 300.

Render Filters

The filters in the Render category produce a variety of lighting effects.

Clouds

Apply this filter to create a cloud-filled pattern in your image. It uses random pixel values in the range between your foreground and background colors. Just use a light or bright blue color for your foreground color and white for the background, and voilà—instant sky pattern!

If you hold down (Shift) as you apply the Clouds filter, you'll get fewer in-between shades—so your clouds will appear fluffier and your sky more vivid.

Difference Clouds

Essentially, this filter runs the Clouds filter and then subtracts the returned pixel values from the existing color values in your image, as if you were working in Difference mode. This can produce some pretty ominous storm clouds (Figure 8.22).

Figure 8.22
You can apply the Clouds or Difference Clouds filters to create an instant sky or cloud-filled pattern.

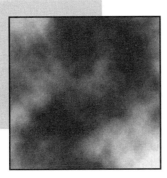

Lens Flare

Most photographers go to great lengths to avoid lens flare effects, but if you want you can use this filter to reproduce the effect of a bright light (like the sun) shining directly into a camera lens, as shown in Figure 8.23. The dialog box asks you to set the type of lens to simulate, and you can also choose a brightness percentage (between 10 and 300) by typing in a value or using the slider control. You'll also need to click in the preview of your image to indicate the center of the bright light source.

Texture Fill

You can use this filter to load an image—grayscale only—into an alpha channel to overlay as a custom texture. In Figure 8.24, for example, I used the Texture Fill filter to replace the plain background behind the tennis ball with a stucco texture. First, I created a grayscale image containing a stucco texture. (Look in the section on the Emboss filter a little further in this chapter for my All-Purpose Stucco recipe.) Next, I created an alpha channel for the background in the tennis ball image. Since the background in this image did not have its own layer already, I created a new layer for my new pattern. I filled the new layer with the color white with an opacity of 1%, so that the selection area wouldn't be empty when I loaded the alpha channel. I loaded the background alpha channel next, and then chose Texture Fill from the Render

Figure 8.23

Applying the Lens Flare filter to the image at top adds to the arid, isolated desert atmosphere (bottom image).

Figure 8.24
Choosing the
Texture Fill filter
produces this
prompt to select
a grayscale
image.

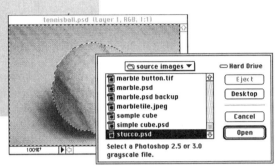

submenu of the Filter menu. Photoshop then prompted me to choose a grayscale image for the texture fill. I chose my stucco texture and lowered the layer's opacity to allow the tennis ball's shadow to show through while making sure the stucco texture was still visible.

The Texture Fill filter is also most useful for loading a texture in conjunction with the Lighting Effects filter, described next.

Lighting Effects

The Lighting Effects filter is a most powerful one. It lets you shine as many as 16 different light sources on your image for a variety of shadowy and reflective effects. It can also serve as a primitive method of raytracing because you can combine these light sources with texture fills as mentioned earlier.

note **The Lighting Effects filter only works with RGB images—but remember that any texture channel you want to load must be a grayscale image.**

Lighting Effects has a very complicated dialog box. Let's run down the list of properties you need to set:

Style

If you've ever done lighting for a school play or amateur production, you're already familiar with the variety of light sources at your disposal here. The rest of us can experiment with the Preview check box clicked.

You can click and move the ellipse (or its handles) on the preview image to reposition the spotlight and the lighting angle. Widen the ellipse to see your image grow brighter. If you click on the white center spot, you can move the whole light around.

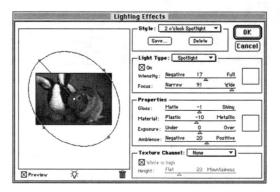

You can create multiple light sources by dragging additional Light Bulb icons ⚬ from beneath the preview image into the preview area. If you change your mind about a light bulb you've added, just drag it to the Trash icon 🗑 to the right of the Light Bulb icon.

Light Type

Here you can click a check box to turn the light on. You can choose one of three light types:

👁 **Spotlight**   Casts the light just like a spotlight on a theater stage or in a circus ring. You can drag the slider controls to adjust the intensity and focus of the spotlight.

👁 **Omni**   Makes the light radiate in all directions from the center point, as if the light is sitting directly above your image. If you drag out one of the handles on this ellipse in the preview image, the light will become more diffuse; dragging the handle inward will make the light more concentrated.

👁 **Directional**   Aims the light in a straight line from the angle you specify. The directional light you see in the Preview will look like a straight line with handles, not an ellipse with handles. As with the other two Light Type settings, dragging the handles toward or away from the center will increase or diffuse the light accordingly.

Properties

For each light source you add, you can set the following properties:

- 👁 **Gloss**   A range of finishes from dull (matte) to shiny (glossy), and percentages thereof.

- 👁 **Material**   The color of the reflected light on your image. Options range from plastic on one extreme to metallic on the other.

- 👁 **Exposure**   The amount of light used.

- 👁 **Ambience**   The other light present in the image. This lets you combine light from the light source with the general lighting. You can also specify a color in the color swatch to the right of the Properties section of the dialog box that you can use for the color of the Ambient light, and use the slider control to specify the amount of Ambient light used.

Texture Channel

Here, you can specify a grayscale image for the Lighting Effects filter to apply as a texture map to the image. You can use this setting to create embossed effects and other surface texture patterns.

To use this setting, you must take a few steps before you even open the Lighting Effects dialog box. You must first create an alpha channel and load your desired texture into it. When you open the Lighting Effects dialog box, you must choose the alpha channel containing that texture from the Texture Channel pop-up menu. You can add an embossed effect to the texture by clicking the White Is High check box. The Height slider controls the bumpiness of your texture; you can drag the slider control to select a value from Flat on the low end to Mountainous on the high end.

Great, great—but what can you use all of this for? In this next exercise I want to show you how you can use these two filters to add 3-D textures and sophisticated lighting to a flat image.

EXERCISE 8.2

Using the Lighting Effects Filter with a Texture Channel

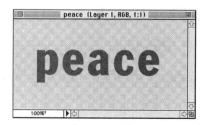

①

②

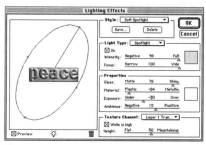

③

1. For this exercise, you'll need to open or create a file with two layers—a colored background layer and a layer with some type on it. In separate steps, we're going to emboss the type—with better results than you can get with the Emboss filter—and then add a rocky surface to the background layer.

2. Now target the type layer, then choose Lighting Effects from the Render submenu of the Filter menu. To highlight the type, we don't even need to create a new alpha channel. Why? Since the type is on its own layer, called Layer 1, we can choose Layer 1 Transparency in the Texture Channel option at the bottom of the Lighting Effects dialog box. I set the light source at about 45°, so that it appears to be coming from the upper right corner of the image. I toyed with the Light Type and Properties settings until I was happy with the embossing effect.

After you've fussed with Lighting Effects settings to your satisfaction, you can click the Save button to keep them for future use. This is a good idea if you're going to create a number of textured effects for the same project, so they can all enjoy the same light source settings. Click OK when you finish.

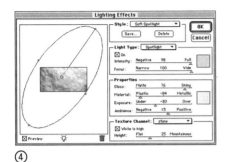

④

⑤

3. Now, on to the background layer; make sure you've got the right layer targeted. Since this isn't a transparent layer, you're definitely going to need to create an alpha channel for adding a texture channel. I created an alpha channel and filled it by applying the Clouds filter a couple of times. Similarly, you could create a texture by using Photoshop filters or by pasting a texture from another file into your new alpha channel. I've named the new channel "stone." (It's true—using the Clouds filter can help you create a stonelike texture. Hang in here and you'll see for yourself.)

4. It's time to choose the Lighting Effects filter again. Here, I used almost exactly the same settings I did for the type layer. I lowered the Height a bit, from 50 to 25. Click OK when you finish.

5. Here's a look at the composite effect. You've now seen how one filter can create two very different kinds of textured effects—and its potential to create a great many more.

Sharpen Filters

Sharpen filters help draw distinct edges out of blurry objects. They're especially useful after you've scaled or distorted images using the Effects submenu from the Image menu.

Sharpen and Sharpen More

The Sharpen Filter increases the contrast between neighboring pixels throughout an image. Sharpen More is just a more intense application of the Sharpen filter.

Sharpen Edges

Like the Sharpen filter, Sharpen Edges increases contrast, but only affects the edges of each object in your image. It doesn't touch continuously toned areas. Any of these first three Sharpen filters are useful to apply after you've scaled an image or a selection to a smaller size, or executed another distortion or skew effect.

Unsharp Mask

As shown in Figure 8.25, this filter emphasizes the sharpness of the edges of each object in your image. The real advantage of this filter over the other Sharpen filters is its dialog box, which lets you specify a percentage (up to 500%) for how much the image should be sharpened. You can also specify in pixels a Radius value for how far the sharpening should extend beyond contrasting edges. The Threshold field is useful if you want to specify sharpening only if the contrast between edges is a significant amount; this lets you selectively sharpen edges only where they'd stand out the most. A good use for applying Unsharp Mask is after you've converted an image's color mode from RGB to CMYK, or made any other conversion involving interpolation.

Stylize Filters

These filters can produce dramatic changes to the color of pixels in an image, often with artistic results.

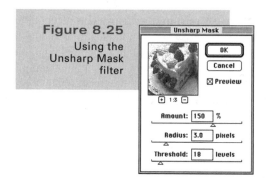

Figure 8.25
Using the
Unsharp Mask
filter

Diffuse

This filter creates a blurred effect as if you were viewing the image through a frosted pane of glass. You can use this filter to add eroded or weathered edges to objects and type. Using the Lighten Only option will make your objects appear to dissolve into nothingness, while the Darken Only option makes it look like the borders are spreading—*bleeding,* in design speak—into surrounding areas.

Emboss

This filter provides an easy way to create all kinds of raised lettering and embossed edge effects. You control the degree of the embossing by entering the angle for the direction of the light source, ranging from 0 to 360°. You could also enter negative values from 0 to -360°, which are automatically converted. You may also specify the depth in pixels of the embossing and a percentage (up to 500%) for applying color.

Extrude

With this filter, you can map your image onto a set of three-dimensional blocks or pyramids that will seem to burst out of the image directly toward you (Figure 8.26). You can set the size of the pyramids or blocks by entering a value (between 2 and 255) in the size field, and the depth of the extruding pyramid or block by entering a value for the Depth field. There is also a Random setting that will generate random depths for the extruding objects.

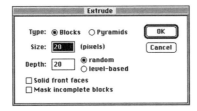

I've used Figure 8.26's "before" image to showcase the rest of the Stylize filters.

EXERCISE 8.3

All-Purpose Stucco

1. Create a new grayscale document for your texture pattern. Choose Add Noise from the Noise submenu of the Filter menu. Set the amount to 999 and click the Gaussian Distribution radio button.

2. Choose Gaussian Blur from the Blur submenu of the Filter menu. Set the radius to a low number, say, between 0.5 and 2. The larger the Gaussian Blur radius setting, the coarser your stucco pattern will be.

3. Now we're going to set an extreme level of contrast using the Brightness/Contrast dialog box. Choose Adjust from the Image menu, then choose Brightness/Contrast from the Adjust submenu. Crank the contrast all the way up to 100.

4. Applying the Emboss filter is the next crucial step. Set the angle at 135° to keep the light source coming from the upper left corner, or at 45° to direct the light source from the upper right corner.

5. If the stucco effect is a little harsh for your taste, use the Blur or Blur More filter to weather the edges of the pattern.

Find Edges

You can use this effect to produce images that look like traced outlines of your originals drawn in charcoal or pencil. The filter works by searching out areas of major color contrast and then enhances the pixels along the contrasting edges.

Figure 8.26
The Extrude filter: before and after

Solarize

This filter reproduces the photographic effect of solarization, in which film is exposed to light partway through the development process. After you apply the Solarize filter, some of the tones in your image will be reversed—as if you had combined the negative of your image with the positive version. The net result is that some of the tones are reversed for an interesting (if less-than-practical) effect.

Tiles

The Tiles filter divides areas of your image into square checks and offsets them slightly from their original positions. From the Tiles dialog box, you specify the minimum number of tiles to appear in each row and column, as well as the maximum percentage each tile can be offset. You can choose to fill the gaps between the tiles with the foreground or background color. Alternatively, you could fill gaps between the tiles with a reverse color image of your original picture by clicking the Inverse Image radio button, or the original image itself by clicking the Unaltered Image radio button. The filter can be useful for creating background patterns.

Trace Contours

This filter produces effects that can be similar to Find Edges. Here, though, you can enter a value between 0 and 255 in the Level field to determine at what level of contrast you want to trace the image's contours. You can also use the Upper and Lower options to specify whether the value you've entered is the point above or below which contours should be traced.

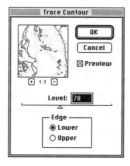

Wind

This filter helps add the effect of motion to an image by adding small horizontal lines to object borders with transitional areas of color in your image. You can choose the intensity of the windblown effect in the Wind dialog box by choosing among the Wind, Blast, and Stagger settings. The dialog box also lets you choose which side—left or right—to simulate the wind's direction.

Video Filters

These filters help you edit images that you get from or plan to output to videotape. Chapter 14 covers video plug-ins for Photoshop at greater length.

De-Interlace

You can use this filter to remove the interlaced scan lines that may accidentally become captured on still video frames.

NTSC Colors

This filter will convert colors in your image to the range used in standard television settings.

Other Filters

This Filter menu item is really an odds-and-ends collection of leftovers. It includes a few general filters for changing contrast, as well as the useful Offset filter and, for the truly inspired, the Custom setting for experimenting with creating your own filters.

High Pass

This filter functions similarly to the sharpening filters by removing gradual tonal changes in your images while preserving highlights. The only option you have in the High Pass dialog box is setting the radius for judging contrast in the image, in a range from 0.1 to 250. The higher the settings you use for High Pass, the more you can distinguish high-contrast from low-contrast areas in your image. Low values, though, tend to strip out the color in your images. You can produce some interesting color-enhancing results with this filter, though, if you apply it to individual color channels only.

Minimum and Maximum Filters

The Minimum and Maximum filters are the digital equivalents of the traditional printing concept of *spreading* and *choking*. The Minimum filter can enhance dark areas in your image, swelling them outward and giving them more oomph. The Maximum filter does exactly the opposite with light areas of your image.

Offset

Buried as it is at the bottom of the Other filters, I wouldn't be surprised if you haven't experimented much with Offset. But it's a wonderfully versatile function for moving your image or portions of your image over a specified number of pixels (Figure 8.27). Photoshop doesn't have a "step and repeat" function, but many Photoshop designers have come

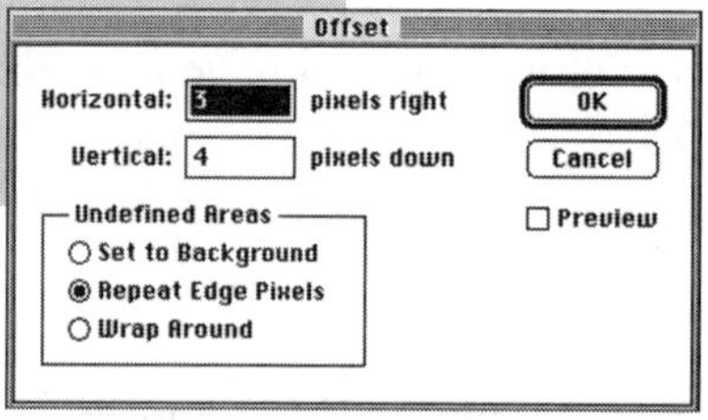

Figure 8.27
The Offset
dialog box

to accomplish such things by ∞eplicating a layer and using the Offset filter to offset the repeated part a certain distance, such as for shadows.

Custom

Do you harbor dreams of becoming the next Kai Krause? It's just a first step, but you'll want to try the Custom setting from the Other submenu under the Filter menu (Figure 8.28). With its controls, you can create algorithms for generating your own sharpening, blurring, and embossing filters.

Keep an eye out for *custom kernels* that Photoshop devotees make available on the commercial online services and on their Web sites for public use; these already-been-tested settings are a nice way to discover new filter variations without a lot of legwork.

Further Filter Adventures

If you're really interested in making your own filters, try playing with the Filter Factory plug-in that comes with Photoshop. The Filter Factory is a Photoshop 3 plug-in that lets you make your own filters and

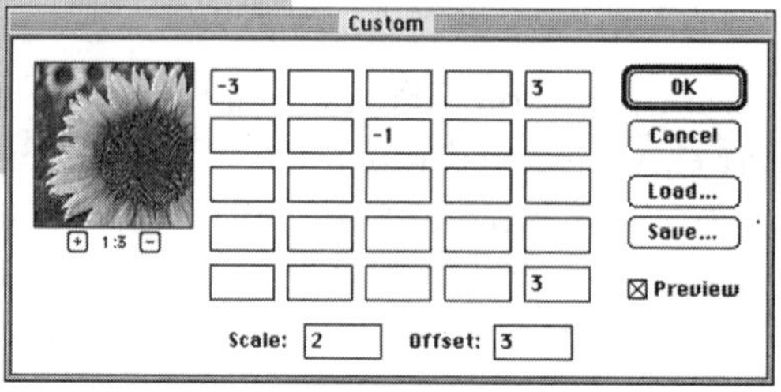

Figure 8.28
The Custom
dialog box

compile them in their own files. Unfortunately, the plug-in can be slow and less than intuitive to use.

tip

Online Resources for Using Filter Factory

👁 Filter Factory Compendium **http://www.fns.net/~almateus/ffc.htm**

👁 Filter Factory Mailing List **http://www.cnu.edu/~ffactory**

👁 Visual Manipulation—FilterFactory **http://www.partysan.de/visual/ MAIN.HTM**

note

Today's extra credit homework: If you've had any programming experience using C—or were ever looking for a reason to learn C—you can obtain the Photoshop Software Developer's Kit (SDK) from Adobe's Web site and create your own filter plug-ins. These will be specific to the platform you're using, but since they're in C you can recompile them to make versions for Photoshop users on other platforms. The URL for information about the SDK at Adobe's Web site is http://www.adobe.com/supportservice/ devrelations/sdks.html.

Plug It In, Plug It In

There are a great many third-party filters available as Photoshop plug-ins. In the two tables that follow, I detail briefly the major commercial filter collections and those created and made publicly available by individuals.

note

I've run across several Web sites with similar listings; no doubt they will continue to have more current listings after this book becomes dated. For example, BoxTop Software maintains a list of Photoshop plug-ins available online at: http://www.aris.com/ boxtop/plugpage/welcome.html **along with a file archive for down-loading. You can download many of the Macintosh filters listed here for free from the Info-Mac archives and mirror sites, in-cluding:** http://hyperarchive.lcs.mit.edu/HyperArchive/Archive/gst/ grf/pshp.

Table 8.1 Commercially Produced Packages of Photoshop Filters

VENDOR	FILTER OR COLLECTION NAME	PLATFORMS
Adobe Systems, Inc.	**Gallery Effects: Classic Art 1**	**Macintosh, Windows**
	Chalk & Charcoal	
	Charcoal	
	Chrome	
	Craquelure	
	Dark Strokes	
	Dry Brush	
	Emboss	
	Film Grain	
	Fresco	
	Graphic Pen	
	Mosaic	
	Poster Edges	
	Ripple	
	Smudge Stick	
	Spatter	
	Watercolor	
Adobe Systems, Inc.	**Gallery Effects: Classic Art 2**	**Macintosh, Windows**
	Accented Edges	
	Angled Strokes	
	Bas Relief	
	Colored Pencil	
	Diffuse Glow	
	Glowing Edges	
	Grain	
	Note Paper	
	Palette Knife	
	Patchwork	
	Photocopy	
	Rough Pastels	
	Sprayed Strokes	
	Stamp	

Table 8.1 (continued)

Vendor	Filter or Collection Name	Platforms
Adobe Systems, Inc.	**Gallery Effects:** **Classic Art 2** (continued)	**Macintosh, Windows**
	Texturizer Underpainting	
Adobe Systems, Inc.	**Gallery Effects:** **Classic Art 3**	**Macintosh, Windows**
	Conte Crayon Crosshatch Cutout Glass Halftone Screen Ink Outlines Neon Glow Paint Daubs Plaster Plastic Wrap Reticulation Sponge Stained Glass Sumi-e Torn Edges Water Paper	
Alien Skin Software	**Black Box 2**	**Macintosh**
	AS Carve AS Cutout AS Drop Shadow AS Glass AS Glow AS HSB Noise AS Inner Bevel AS Motion Trail AS Outer Bevel AS Swirl	

Table 8.1 (continued)

VENDOR	FILTER OR COLLECTION NAME	PLATFORMS
Andromeda Software Inc.	**Andromeda Series 1**	**Macintosh, Windows**
	Designs	
	Diffract	
	Halo	
	Prism	
	Rainbow	
	Reflection	
	sMulti	
	Star	
	Velocity	
Andromeda Software Inc.	**Andromeda Series 2**	**Macintosh, Windows**
	3D Surface Mapping	
	Mezzo Filter	
Human Software	**CD-Q 1.18**	**Macintosh**
	AutoMask	
	Squizz	
Knoll Software	**CyberMesh**	**Macintosh**
MdN Corporation	**Color Correction**	**Macintosh**
	Gray Scale	
	Highlighter	
	Infrared	
	Pop Art	
	Reversal	
	Variable Color	
MetaTools	**Kai's PowerTools 2.1**	**Macintosh, Windows**
	KPT 2.1 3D Stereo Noise	
	KPT 2.1 Cyclone	
	KPT 2.1 Diffuse More	
	KPT 2.1 Fade Contrast	

Table 8.1 (continued)

VENDOR	FILTER OR COLLECTION NAME	PLATFORMS
MetaTools	**Kai's PowerTools 2.1** (continued)	**Macintosh, Windows**

KPT 2.1 Find Edges Charcoal
KPT 2.1 Find Edges Soft
KPT 2.1 Find Edges&Invert
KPT 2.1 Fractal Explorer
KPT 2.1 Gaussian Electrify
KPT 2.1 Gaussian Glow
KPT 2.1 Gaussian Weave
KPT 2.1 Glass Lens Bright
KPT 2.1 Glass Lens Normal
KPT 2.1 Glass Lens Soft
KPT 2.1 Gradient Designer
KPT 2.1 Gradients on Paths
KPT 2.1 Grime Layer
KPT 2.1 H-P Noise Maximum
KPT 2.1 H-P Noise Medium
KPT 2.1 H-P Noise Minimum
KPT 2.1 Page Curl
KPT 2.1 Pixelbreeze
KPT 2.1 Pixelstorm
KPT 2.1 Pixelwind
KPT 2.1 Scatter Horizontal
KPT 2.1 Seamless Welder
KPT 2.1 Selection Info
KPT 2.1 Sharpen Intensity
KPT 2.1 Smudge Dark Left
KPT 2.1 Smudge Dark Right
KPT 2.1 Smudge Lighten Left
KPT 2.1 Smudge Lighten Right
KPT 2.1 Special Blue Noise
KPT 2.1 Special Green Noise
KPT 2.1 Special Red Noise
KPT 2.1 Texture Explorer
KPT 2.1 Vortex Tiling

Table 8.1 (continued)

VENDOR	FILTER OR COLLECTION NAME	PLATFORMS
MetaTools	**Kai's PowerTools 3.0.2**	**Macintosh, Windows**
	KPT3 3D Stereo Noise	
	KPT3 Glass Lens	
	KPT3 Gradient Designer	
	KPT3 Help	
	KPT3 Interform	
	KPT3 Lens f/x	
	KPT3 Page Curl	
	KPT3 Planar Tiling	
	KPT3 Seamless Welder	
	KPT3 Spheroid Designer	
	KPT3 Texture Explorer	
	KPT3 Twirl	
	KPT3 Video Feedback	
	KPT3 Vortex Tiling	
Xaos Tools	**Paint Alchemy**	**Macintosh**
	Terrazzo	
	TypeCaster	
	TubeTime	

Table 8.2 Shareware and Freeware Photoshop Filters

FILTER NAME	DESCRIPTION	CONTACT INFO
Chris' Filters	**An extensive filters collection that includes:**	**Chris Cox** 110 Oakland Circle Madison, AL 35758-8663 *ccox@teleport.com* **http://www.teleport. com/~ccox/** *ChrisCox@aol.com*
	AddRight1 AddRight2 NoCopyVertical NoCopyDiagonal BitPatterns Swirlies Hairy Noise SmudgeRight Average Checkers BitShift Grid Add More Noise Total Noise Fractal Noise Plaid Psycho UnAlias Edge3x3 Erode Dilate Skeleton ColorKey ChromaKey FastKey	
Expression 3	**A filter that can create images that change over time according to a mathematical formula or expression.**	**Jim Bumgardner** *jbum@netcom.com* *jbum@aol.com*

Table 8.2 (continued)

FILTER NAME	DESCRIPTION	CONTACT INFO
Frank's Color Filters	RemoveColor—removes color from a selection	**Frank Owen** *fjo@interaccess.com*
	Colorize—adds color to gray pixels within a selection	
	Change Color—changes the color of all pixels in a selection	
Frosty	A Photoshop filter plug-in that puts a variable frost look on any selected area of an image.	**Neil Schulman** *NWCS@delphi.com*
Photoshop Dither Filters	**The Photoshop Dither Filter package is a set of filters for Adobe Photoshop that dither grayscale images to black and white so that they can be printed on a bilevel device, such as a laser printer.**	**David Hull** *GCA00443@niftyserve.or.jp* **http://pertsserver.cs. uiuc.edu/~hull/ halftone/kawa**
	MidnightTV—creates noise like a TV station off air	
	Inai-Inai-Bar—encrypts and deencrypts graphic files	
	Mr Sa-kan—Creates brick walls	
	MagicalCurtain—Creates gradients similar to KPT's Gradient Designer	
	FrameCurtain—Ditto	

Summary

As you've seen, you can use Photoshop's filters across a wide spectrum of image editing, from subtle changes up to earthquake-level distortions. I want you to leave with an appreciation for the subtler ways to invoke filtering changes—for example, at partial opacity on a layer—as opposed to the sweeping changes you get from just applying a filter from the menu command.

Straight ahead in Chapter 9 is an overview of how to create good-looking scans. If you aren't using a scanner to snag images, feel free to skip on ahead to Chapter 10, "Retouching Essentials."

9
Scanning Essentials

IN THIS CHAPTER

How Scanners Work

Choosing Scanner Material

Finding Scanner Software

Resolution and Halftone Scanning

Adjusting Brightness and Contrast

Just as you'd expect better quality results from high-end cameras (and film) than you would from lower-priced consumer models, you can expect the quality of your scans to vary widely depending on the device you use to digitize your images.

If quality is the most crucial factor in your projects, you're far better off outsourcing your photo and slide scanning work to a professional service bureau for drum scanning or high-end flatbed scanning. Many publishing companies reserve their in-house scanners almost exclusively for *FPO* scans—creating "for position only" images that the service bureau replaces with its own high-res scans just before final film output. But if you have a small-scale production budget, or have more artistic uses for a scanner—such as capturing textures from or reproducing images of real-life objects—then it'll be worth it for you to learn techniques for optimizing your desktop scans for final output.

Many designers are of two minds about desktop scanners. While such scanners are deceptively simple to operate, it can be very difficult to cajole them into producing high-quality scans.

Chapter 1 touched on basic hardware questions about what different kinds of scanners are available and how they work. This chapter will focus on how to get the most from desktop scanners on an everyday basis.

If you're in a shopping mood, "Which scanner should I buy?" is always a popular query on Usenet newsgroups like *comp.graphics.apps.photoshop*—and you'll get a large focus-group sample, and usually covering newer models than any book could profile.

This chapter covers the following topics related to scanning images in Photoshop:

- 👁 Criteria to look for in images to be scanned

- 👁 Basics of using scanner plug-ins with Photoshop

- 👁 Resolution, including special requirements for scanning slides and line art

- 👁 Adjusting brightness and contrast in your scanned images

- 👁 Converting your images to Kodak's Photo CD format

How Scanners Work, in 250 Words or Less

I tried to pack in as much info as I could in this brief section to establish some common ground without getting bogged down in detail. The major differences among scanners have to do with how they register light (or how they produce pixels), how many pixels they can see per inch (resolution), and how they register shadows.

- 👁 **Registering Light**   High-end drum scanners like the ones at service bureaus use *photomultiplier tubes* (PMTs). The flatbed scanner on your desktop uses *charge-coupled devices* (CCDs), which are faster than PMTs but not as sensitive about picking up low levels of light.

- 👁 **Resolution**   The more CCDs across the scanner bed, the greater the resolution; 300-ppi or 600-ppi are common. Most scanners also offer interpolation, which attains higher resolution by making guesses about image data. Photoshop can interpolate data better than most scanners, so if you need to simulate higher levels of resolution than your scanner can accommodate—say, 1200 dpi—you're probably better off with straight scanner output. You'll find tips for Photoshop interpolation later in this chapter.

- 👁 **Dynamic range**   This capability describes the range of density the scanner can see. It's usually coupled with a measure called the maximum density, or *dMax,* which notes the level of the darkest shadow the scanner can see. This is an important setting to look for if you scan many transparencies.

Color scanners work just like grayscale scanners but filter red, green, and blue separately, either in three passes or in a single all-in-one pass.

Choosing Good Scanning Material

Is it too obvious to say that the scans you'll get are only as good as the originals you use? Successful reproduction has much more to do with the quality of your original image than with any tweaking you do later in Photoshop. This is especially important when you're making your own

scans with a low- or midrange desktop scanner, because you'll be limited in terms of what corrections you can make during the scanning process.

Here's a straightforward checklist of good-to-have features in your raw material:

- Use sharp, focused images with good contrast. What constitutes good contrast? Look for easily discerned white and black elements, with a wide range of tones in between.

- Look for detail throughout the image, including highlights, midtones, and shadowed areas.

- For color images, you'll want a good balance without an overcast of a single color. (Even if you plan to use one in your final image, better you should add it yourself later in Photoshop, if possible.)

If you have a choice between very similar images when you're making a scan, look for greater detail in terms of highlights, midtones, and shadows.

note Here's one situation where this whole checklist will matter little—if you're planning to do a great deal of photocompositing and image editing and just need to scan an image to capture an object's outline, it won't matter much if the overall lighting or quality of the image is poor.

Finding Scanner Software

Most scanner manufacturers create plug-in modules that can replace the scanner's stand-alone software and allow scanning from within Photoshop. After you use a Photoshop plug-in to make a scan, a new untitled document containing the scanned image will open in Photoshop.

Like the third-party Photoshop filters you saw in the last chapter, scanner plug-ins can be copied over to the Plug-Ins folder within your Photoshop folder. For organizational purposes, you should keep scanner plug-ins in the Acquire/Export folder within the Plug-Ins folder. After you've installed your scanner's plug-in, it should appear as a menu

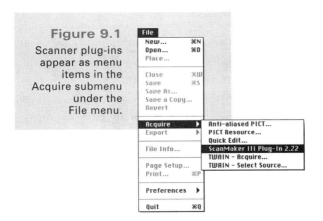

Figure 9.1
Scanner plug-ins appear as menu items in the Acquire submenu under the File menu.

item you can choose from the Acquire submenu under the File menu (Figure 9.1).

If you don't have a Photoshop plug-in for your scanner software, you should check with the manufacturer directly or search file libraries at the manufacturer's Web site, if one exists. When you contact the manufacturer for assistance, make sure you have the model number of your scanner at the ready.

Other scanning software options available to you include third-party commercial packages like Ofoto or OmniPage. Your scanner should also come with a TWAIN (Technology Without An Interesting Name) module. Many applications support the TWAIN standard interface, letting you perform scanning inside other applications just as you can with Photoshop.

Most scanner software packages have settings for correcting brightness, contrast, and color (Figure 9.2). Check the owner's manual for your scanner if you're unfamiliar with any of the options in your scanner software's window; until you know what they do, you'll never use them.

Before you slide your artwork in your scanner and click the Scan button in the software's dialog box, you should know ahead of time how you'll use the final image. This will help you calculate the right resolution to scan at.

Figure 9.2
The interface for a scanner's Photoshop plug-in

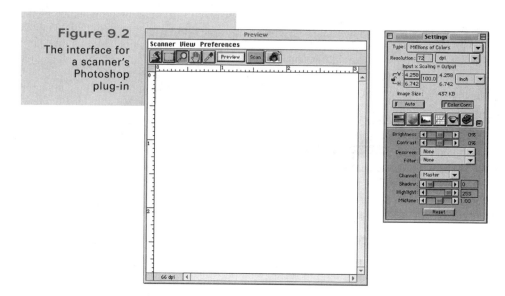

Resolution

Let's step back a sec to consider resolution, which we haven't really discussed since Chapter 2. Back then, I mentioned that image resolution is a measure of how many pixels—that is, how much information—can fit in a given unit of measurement. An image's resolution is commonly measured in pixels per inch (ppi); the more pixels there are per inch in an image, the more detail you'll see. If you scan at too low a resolution, you'll immediately see the results in the scanned image—a blurry or pixelated appearance with not enough detail in the image as a whole.

You might conclude from the previous paragraph that you should always scan at the upper end of your scanner's capabilities, whatever that may be—say, 300 or 600 ppi. But this will lead to a Catch-22 situation—file size is directly tied to your image's resolution, so you could wind up with staggeringly huge file sizes.

So what's the best resolution to use when you're scanning images? If you're scanning images for print production, your scanning resolution should be twice the amount of your printing resolution, or line screen frequency, which is measured in lines per inch (lpi). If you don't know what line screen your job will be printed at, your printer can tell you. Your projects will almost certainly use one of the standard line screen settings, such as 85 lpi for newspaper printing; 120, 133, or 150 lpi for most book and magazine printing; or 200 to 300 lpi for coffee-table-quality books. Once you know your line screen—say, 133 lpi—you can plan to scan all your photos at twice that number—in this case, 266 ppi.

Scanning at more than twice your line screen is overkill, though—you'll increase your images' file size but the extra detail in the files won't come through to the printed page. You'll also tie up the imagesetter for a very long time as it processes all that extraneous data, possibly causing it to crash.

What if you're scanning images for use as Web graphics? Although in this case you may never send your images to print to a service bureau's imagesetter, you should allow it within the realm of possibility. Thus, as a safeguard, you should still begin by scanning at twice the line screen settings you use for your print work and then resize down to your screen resolution using Photoshop. This gives you more flexibility in resizing or editing—not to mention using the image in print if the need ever arises without needing to scan again.

When you resize an image either up or down—also called *resampling* or *interpolating*—you're bound to lose some information because Photoshop has to make guesses about how to fill in missing pixels (if you're enlarging) or which information it can sacrifice (if you're reducing the image). For example, if you reduce an image and then enlarge it to the original size, the final image will not be as good as the one you started with because Photoshop interpolates—it can't just restore the pixels you cut earlier.

Although Photoshop will interpolate as it scales down (or *downsamples*), its best method for doing so will still outgun those in the scanner software. This is another good reason to scan at higher-than-screen-resolution settings. You can always delete information from your image file to reduce its size, but you can't restore the same data easily.

 note Photoshop has several interpolation methods, which you can view and change by choosing Preferences from the File menu, then choosing General. Of the three, Bicubic is the most accurate interpolation method; it analyzes contrast and is the best choice for continuous tone images and just about all other resizing situations in Photoshop. The other two are Nearest Neighbor, which is the fastest but least accurate, and Bilinear, which falls in between Bicubic and Nearest Neighbor in terms of quality.

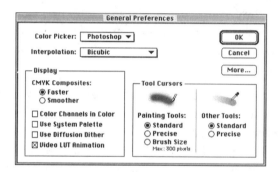

Now that you've heard me recommend scanning at twice your line screen—maxing out around 266 ppi or 300 ppi—for print images and Web graphics, you may be wondering when would you ever need to scan at a higher resolution. Who needs those 600 ppi or greater desktop scanners? Here are two likely scenarios: if you're scanning an image that you'll need to print at much larger than original size—for example, a color slide—you'll need to factor in how much you're enlarging the image and multiply that ratio by two times the line screen. I'll walk through a couple of examples in the next section, under the heading "Scanning Slides," to make this more obvious. Second, if you're scanning line art—such as pen-and-ink drawings, woodcut-type illustrations, or black-and-white logos—you'll need to scan at much more than twice the line screen for optimal results. I discuss line art at greater length in the following section under the "Scanning Line Art" heading.

Changing Resolution and File Size

Doubling the resolution of an image will actually increase its file size four times and contain four times as much information. When you double the number of pixels per inch, you're doubling the dimensions both across and down, for four times as much square pixelage.

Photoshop tracks your image's file size and automatically updates it whenever you change the resolution or color mode. An easy way to illustrate this is to create a new file in Photoshop. For example, a grayscale document measuring 1 inch by 1 inch with a resolution of 150 pixels/ inch will take up 22K.

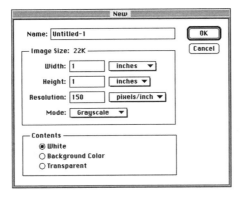

If you choose Image Size from the Image menu and enter 300 as a new value for the resolution, you'll notice that the file size jumps to 88K, or four times 22K.

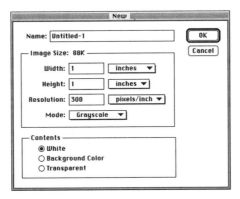

If you then change the mode from Grayscale to RGB using the Mode menu, you'll discover that the file size has jumped threefold—since you're going from an 8-bit mode to a 24-bit one—the next time you call up the Image Size dialog box again.

```
┌─────────────────── New ───────────────────┐
│                                            │
│  Name: Untitled-1                  ┌──OK──┐ │
│                                    └──────┘ │
│  ┌─ Image Size: 264K ──────────┐  ┌Cancel┐ │
│  │   Width:  1      inches  ▼  │  └──────┘ │
│  │                            │            │
│  │  Height:  1      inches  ▼ │            │
│  │                            │            │
│  │ Resolution: 300  pixels/inch ▼          │
│  │                            │            │
│  │     Mode:  RGB Color  ▼    │            │
│  └────────────────────────────┘            │
│  ┌─ Contents ──────────────────┐           │
│  │  ◉ White                    │           │
│  │  ○ Background Color         │           │
│  │  ○ Transparent              │           │
│  └─────────────────────────────┘           │
└────────────────────────────────────────────┘
```

Photoshop also has an "auto resolution" feature for computing your resolution if you just enter the line screen. You can see it in action by clicking the Auto button on the Image Size dialog box. It's interesting to see because it offers three settings for determining what your image resolution should be (Figure 9.3). The double-your-line-screen formula I mentioned earlier is the same that Photoshop uses for its Best setting. Its Good setting multiplies the line screen by 1.5 to determine the resolution. The Draft setting is set to 72 ppi unless you entered an even lower resolution for the image earlier.

For some images the differences between scanning at 1.5 (Good) versus 2 (Best) times the line screen frequency might be negligible, but why take chances? The Auto Resolution dialog box seems designed for users who don't know about the relationship between line screen and resolution, but I wish it were used to inform rather than offer these questionable Draft-Good-Best choices.

Restraining File Size

After you create a new image in Photoshop you can resize it at any time using the Image Size menu item from the Image menu. Experimenting

Figure 9.3

The Auto Resolution dialog box

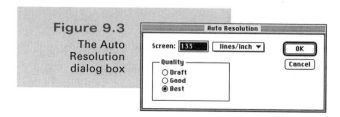

with values in this dialog box should help you understand the relationship between file size, image height and width, and resolution in your graphics.

As you've seen by now, resampling can be detrimental to your image quality. But you can prevent resampling in your image when resizing an existing image by clicking the Constrain File Size check box in the Image Size dialog box. If you increase your image's height and width, the resolution will be lower because you'll have the same number of pixels covering larger dimensions. Conversely, if you decrease your image's height and width, the resolution will increase because you'll be crowding the same number of pixels into a smaller amount of linear distance. If you fail to check the Constrain File Size check box, though, you'll lose some information and reduce the quality of your image.

For example, I frequently take screen shots of what's on my computer screen; these come with the standard Macintosh screen resolution of 72 ppi. At my day job, I work on a magazine that calls for a 133-line screen. Along with converting the mode from RGB to CMYK, the other macro-level change I always need to make is to convert the resolution from 72 to 266; by keeping the Constrain File Size check box clicked, I make Photoshop automatically recalculate the width and height. This nets better results than letting the page layout program access the 72-ppi image and calculating the size percentage based on the lower resolution.

Enlarging Images

If your artwork is going to be enlarged when you scan it—for example, when you're scanning slides—then for best results you're going to need to increase the resolution before you scan. It will help avoid a blocky, pixelated appearance later if the original scan is given the chance to generate plenty of file information early on.

To figure out what resolution to use for a graphic that will be enlarged, just multiply our previously mentioned formula (twice the line screen) by the ratio of the final image dimensions to the scanned image dimensions. For example, let's say you have an image that measures 1 inch by 2 inches, and you want your final image to be three times larger, for a final size of 3 inches by 6 inches. That image's ratio is 3:1, or, after you treat that colon like a division sign, just 3. Now let's say your final

image will print on an imagesetter with a line frequency of 120. To find your ideal scanning resolution, first double the line screen (to 240) and multiply it by the ratio of the final-to-original-dimensions, which we saw was 3. That makes your scanning resolution $240 \times 3 = 720$ ppi.

It's easy to use this ratio method if you need to match a certain height or width for the finished image but don't know what the other final dimension will be. For example, if the artwork needs to fit a hole on page that's 5.5 inches wide, and you have an original slide that measures 1.375 inches by .75 inch, you can do the math (go right ahead and whip out that calculator) and see that the ratio of the final to the original width is 4:1. Thus, the final height will be $.75 \times 4 = 3$ inches. If your line screen frequency in this example is 150 lpi, you can just plug these numbers into the formula: Scan this slide at twice the line screen times the ratio of the final size to the original, or $2 \times 150 \times 4 = 1{,}200$ ppi.

Scanning Line Art

When you scan line art you're using 1-bit scanning, with no colors other than black or white. Since line art scans can't take advantage of anti-aliasing to make smooth transitions between black and white, they are highly prone to "jaggies"—jagged edges around curves—if you scan at anything lower than your scanner's native resolution.

Unlike photos, scanning line art at high resolution is crucial for optimal results. Ideally, you should scan line art at the same resolution as the final output device that will print your job. For example, say you have a line art logo measuring 7 inches by 2 inches that you'll want to appear at the same size in your newsletter, and that you're going to have printed on your service bureau's 1270-dpi imagesetter. Optimally, you should scan it at 1270 dpi for the best appearance. But what if you have only a 300-dpi or 600-dpi scanner and can't afford to send the logo out to a service bureau for scanning? Exercise 9.1 shows how to improve the appearance of your line art scans—surprisingly, you begin by upsampling your image for a worse appearance before it improves.

EXERCISE 9.1

Optimizing Low-Res Line Art Scans

①

②

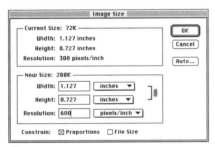

③

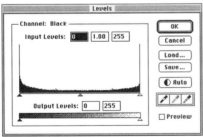

④

1. Scan your line art in grayscale mode at 100% at your scanner's highest resolution settings (for example, 300 dpi). You'll also need to determine ahead of time the dpi used by the imagesetter on which this piece will print. For this example, let's assume the line art will be printed at 600 ppi.

2. Make sure that your Interpolation preferences are set to Bicubic. Choose Preferences from the File menu, then General from the Preferences submenu.

3. Choose Image Size from the Image menu and change the resolution from 300 to 1200—and make sure that the Constrain File Size box is not checked (this is the only kind of situation where it's OK do this!). You'll immediately see the image quality degrade as both the file size and viewing ratio grow significantly. In this example, as the resolution doubled, the file quadrupled from 72K to 288K

4. Now you can use one of two processes—or a combination of the two—to sharpen the image a great deal. The first method involves achieving tonal correction by using either the Levels or Curves commands; you can access either one by choosing Adjust from the Map command under the image menu. This example demonstrates the Levels command. In the Levels dialog box, you can drag the left and right input sliders toward the center to sharpen the edges in your image.

The second, and more flexible, approach is the Unsharp Mask filter. All scanned images can afford some sharpening afterward, and the Unsharp Mask filter is better suited than Sharpen or Sharpen More for improving scans. In this example, I've upped the Amount slider to the highest percentage (500%), set the Radius to sharpen along 1 pixel edge, and a Threshold level of 5 for softening the sharpening in smooth curved areas. You can experiment with other values to see what other kinds of results work for you.

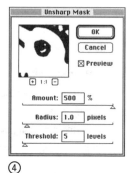

④

5. Next, you can use the Threshold command from the Adjust submenu of the Map menu to adjust the fineness of the lines in the image. Experiment with moving the slider to the left, which thins out and eventually breaks up the fine lines in your image. Moving the slider to the right will produce what I think of as the "mascara effect"—thickening and darkening the individual lines in your image. In this example, reducing the threshold thins out the lines that make up the bird's wing and expands the white spheres that fill the background.

6. The final step is to convert your line art image to Bitmap mode (Figure 9.4). The 50% Threshold usually produces the best results.

tip If your scanned line art is a fairly simple sketch, you can also get good results by saving your line art scan as an EPS file and using an illustration software package's autotracing feature (like Macromedia Freehand's AutoTrace) or a stand-alone tracing program (like Adobe Streamline) to trace the outlines. Then correct as necessary and save the scan as a vector-based drawing.

Figure 9.4
Line art scanned at 300 ppi and upsampled to 600 ppi

Halftone Scanning

Printing presses can't produce continuous tones—that is, pixels in varying shades of gray—the way cameras and scanners can. As a result, most commercial printers translate the continuous tones of photographs and other images into rows of dots in screening patterns called *halftones*. The size, shape, and angle of these halftone dots simulate the continuous effect. Pick up any newspaper or magazine, turn to a page with a printed photo, and hold it right up to your face—the photo that looks like a solid, continuous image at arm's length will reveal row after row of halftone dots.

Halftone dots are a measure of the number of dots you see on the printed page, not the pixels in your document. Your commercial printer's line screen, which I've talked about a lot in this chapter without really defining so far, measures the number of halftone dots per inch.

 note As mentioned earlier, for best results the resolution of your Photoshop images should be set to twice your line screen—and please remember to check the **Constrain File Size** check box in the **Image Size** dialog box.

Full-color print jobs combine four halftone screens, one for each of the CMYK plates. Each of these screens is set at a different angle to help produce consistent color. You can see a rough enactment of this effect with the Color Halftone filter under Pixelate in the Filter menu; experimenting with this filter can also demonstrate how the greater the number of dots in an image, the more realistic (that is, continuous) the halftone effect looks.

If the screen angle of one color plate is not quite right, the halftone dots can clash to create blotchy, funny-looking patterns called moirés. And if you happen to scan an image from a print publication, you'll also unwittingly generate moiré patterns that will interfere with the scanned image. This happens because your printed originals will already have the dot patterns generated in the halftone screen for each color plate before printing.

Using Your Scanning Software to Control Moirés

Most scanner software programs (and their accompanying Photoshop plug-ins) now offer options specifically geared to address moiré problems. For example, all Agfa scanners have a scanning program called FotoLook that offers a Descreen option for removing moiré patterns. Check your scanner's documentation or contact the manufacturer directly to make sure.

note

Be sure to use the word "moiré" when inquiring about options for scanning halftones. Some scanners offer settings for creating your own custom halftone screens, which can produce some nifty patterned effects but are not at all the same thing as moiré problem solvers.

If you're really ambitious—or if you have a lot of high-quality printed images to scan—another thing that could help is to try scanning at a multiple of the line screen of the printed piece. You can find out what that line screen is by obtaining a screen gauge (try asking at art supply stores) to read the screen level, then setting your scanning resolution to two or four times that number.

Using Photoshop Filters to Control Moirés

As noted in Chapter 8, you can use several of the Noise and Blur filters to good effect to help reduce or eliminate moiré effects. Although ordinarily you should probably do most of your image editing in RGB and convert to CMYK afterward, this is one situation where you should convert to CMYK right after scanning. It will usually be easier to edit out the patterns in each separate channel (by pressing ⌘-1 through ⌘-4 for Mac users, Ctrl-1 through Ctrl-4 for Windows users). Experiment with different combinations of applying the Despeckle, Dust & Scratches, Median, and Gaussian Blur filters.

Adjusting Brightness and Contrast

Besides moirés, other common scanning problems include images that scan too dark (poor contrast) or look dull (not enough brightness, or

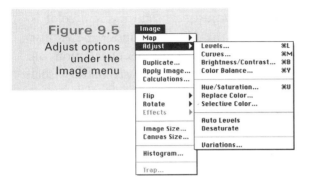

Figure 9.5

Adjust options under the Image menu

reflected light from your image). The scanning process can mute a lot of fine details in your image, especially if your scanner interpolates to attain higher resolution levels.

I mentioned dynamic range very, very briefly earlier in this chapter (see "How Scanners Work, in 250 Words or Less"). Poor contrast in a scanned image can also sometimes happen if your scanner can't handle the dynamic range—the full gamut of light and dark colors in your image.

In this section, we'll look at a few of the options under the Adjust submenu of the Image menu (Figure 9.5) that can help you make dramatic changes in your image's color and tonality.

The simplest way to adjust brightness and contrast is through the Brightness/Contrast dialog box. Be sure to click the Preview box to watch the image reflect changes you make. This dialog box includes two straightforward sliders. Dragging the Brightness slider to the right lightens the image; dragging it to the left darkens the image. Dragging the Contrast slider to the right adds detail by making the whites whiter and the dark portions even darker, and dragging the Contrast slider to the left reduces extremes in light and dark areas, as if a gray smog drifted in front of the image.

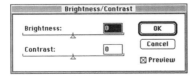

Another very intuitive method for adjusting brightness and color is through the Variations command, the last item under the Adjust submenu of the Image menu. By displaying a number of variations on your original, Photoshop lets you adjust the image based on the visual results you like instead of compelling you to master the formulas yourself. That's also the main drawback with the Variations command—you don't have the precise control here that you do with some of the other Adjust submenu commands.

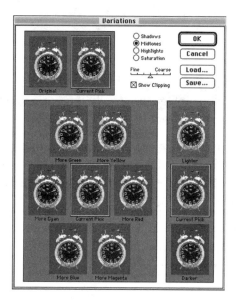

Another way to increase brightness in your image is to try using the Levels command. When you select Levels from the Adjust submenu under Image, you'll see a *histogram*, which is a graphical representation of your image's brightness values. Darker pixel values are shown to the left side of the histogram, while lighter ones appear to the right. You can adjust the gamma of the image—the middle slider under the histogram or the middle number above the histogram—to a higher number to add more contrast to the middle tones. You'll find more information about the Levels command in Chapter 10.

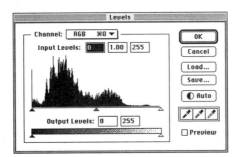

For more finicky adjustments, the Curves command lets you adjust the contrast of the image as a whole or in each individual color channel. If you raise one of the color curves in a region, you increase the contrast there. By sampling the colors in various parts of the image, you may find that one channel doesn't cover its entire range, and you can then adjust its curve to use more contrast for the colors that are actually present. You'll find more information about the Curves command in Chapter 10.

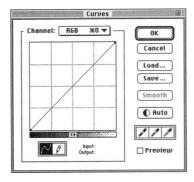

note   **Some designers recommend doing curve corrections in Lab Color mode, especially if you plan to convert your scanned image to CMYK for print use.**

After you adjust levels or curves, you might want to try the Unsharp Mask filter, under Sharpen in the Filter menu. This filter is great for emphasizing the edges of your scanned images, making the image appear sharper to the eye.

Photo CD—an Alternative to Straightforward Scanning

If you've taken photographs that you plan to scan, or if you have slides to digitize but no slide attachment, you might want to take advantage of Kodak's Photo CD format.

Kodak created its Photo CD file format specifically for archiving photographs. You'll need to install a Photo CD plug-in to let Photoshop read Photo CD files, but it's worthwhile. With Photo CD, you can retrieve your files at one of several file sizes and bit depths. They maintain all the fine detail and tonal quality of the originals, because none of the original scan is sacrificed to save space. This can give you a lot of flexibility with images—for example, you can place a low-res version in your layout documents but later link to the high-resolution version when you go to press. Many CDs of royalty-free photos use the Photo CD format too.

If you have slides to digitize, there are a number of services that will scan slides to Photo CD. You'll be able to outsource—have someone else do the scanning for you—and receive your images at several resolutions. Some professional photographers will do this for you, charging around $5–$7 per slide to make high-end Pro Photo CD packs. Consumer Photo CD files are the more common format, and should run you about 75 cents to $1.50 per slide. There are a number of mail order photo labs that will also create Photo CDs for you.

Summary

In this chapter you gained familiarity with scanning, one of the most common ways to obtain images for editing in Photoshop. The next chapter, "Retouching Essentials," will go further in showing you more sophisticated techniques for polishing your images.

10
Retouching Essentials

IN THIS CHAPTER

Saving Photos

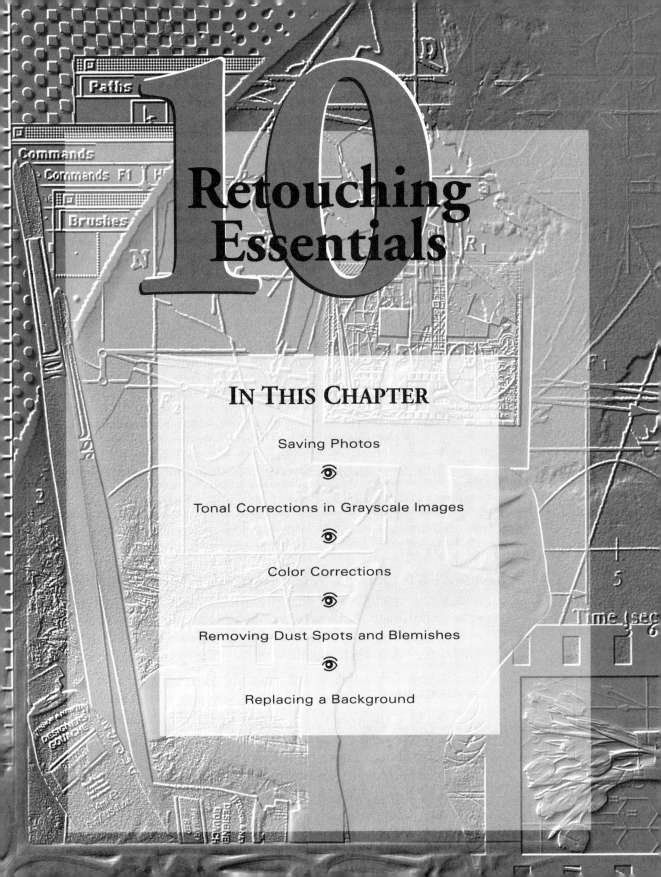

Tonal Corrections in Grayscale Images

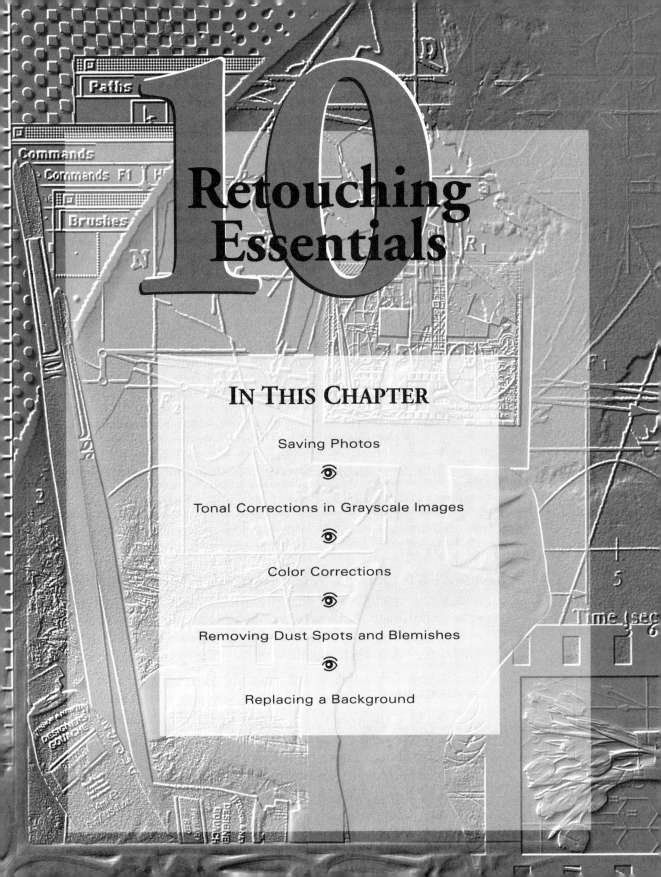

Color Corrections

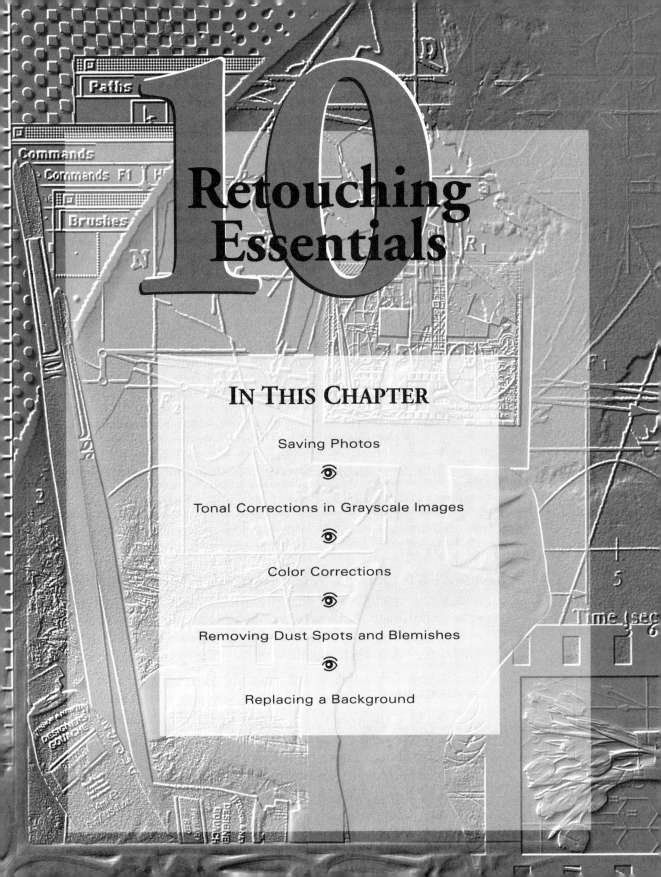

Removing Dust Spots and Blemishes

Replacing a Background

Like a makeup artist or an auto mechanic, a Photoshop designer may be called upon to make defects disappear. In the world of image editing, that includes removing dust spots, eradicating skin blemishes in portraits, or changing a distracting background. You may need to tweak poor lighting or enhance washed-out colors in photographs.

Whether your retouching efforts are going to be an everyday event for you at an advertising job or a once-in-a-while need for salvaging a less-than-perfect photo shoot, you'll need to know how you can retouch and color-correct images in Photoshop.

This chapter takes a good look at the more advanced techniques that you can use to remove defects from photos while maintaining a convincing overall appearance. You'll learn the following techniques:

👁 Assessing an image to determine the best way to correct flaws

👁 Using the Rubber Stamp tool and feathering to eliminate dust spots and blemishes

👁 Using the Levels and Curves commands to correct poor lighting

👁 Using the Dodge and Burn tools to adjust shadows

Taking Stock

As you saw in Chapter 9, "Scanning Essentials," the best predictor for getting good results in your digitized images is using the highest-possible-quality originals. All too often, though, that can be beyond your control. For example, you may wind up with only one blurry or funny-looking head shot that has to run with a magazine profile, or a limited, time-worn selection from a historical archive to illustrate an article that has to have art.

Once you have a digitized version of your original photo, examine it up close in Photoshop at a high magnification to identify any scratches or spots visible on screen that may not have been apparent in the print. If your photos were digitized on a low-end scanner, look for dust spots or other blotches that could have been generated during the scanning process.

Now take a step back to assess your image with an objective eye—you're doing a makeover here, much as if you were a makeup artist or a beauty consultant. Identify which areas are less than perfect, and—more important—what needs changing to suit the context in which you'll use the image. For example, does the photo give the subject's skin a yellowish cast? If you're working on a beautiful-baby photo spread, you'd better retouch that jaundiced look. For any kind of portrait, you want to make sure that your subject is in tight focus and in good lighting; you might also want to remove distracting details in the background.

Using the Eyedropper and the Info Palette

No matter how objectively you search your image for hidden flaws, your eyes can be somewhat limited when you're assessing images for print. Why? You're seeing your image's colors and shadings onscreen in RGB mode instead of how they'll really appear printed in full color. As a result, you should rely on readings you get from the Info palette as a guide to the colors in your image (Figure 10.1). When you have the Eyedropper tool selected and move your cursor over an image, the Info palette will report back the exact color values of the pixels beneath the cursor.

note

You can change the sample size for the Eyedropper tool from the default Point Sample, which takes readings from one pixel at a time, to a 3x3-pixel sample or 5x5-pixel sample. The benefit to this is avoiding being thrown off by chance readings from stray, odd-colored pixels. Double-click the Eyedropper tool in the Toolbox to call up the Eyedropper Options dialog box.

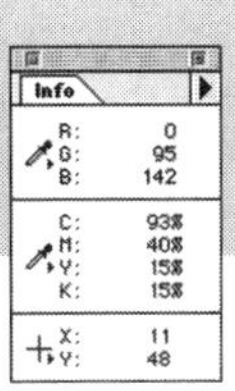

Figure 10.1

The Info palette—small but useful

Info	
R:	0
G:	95
B:	142
C:	93%
M:	40%
Y:	15%
K:	15%
X:	11
Y:	48

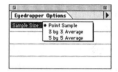

As you'll see later in this chapter, you'll also find Eyedropper tools in the Levels and Curves dialog boxes. You saw these options briefly in the last chapter, but here you'll see how you can really put them to work for you in radically retouching your images.

Keeping Backups Close By

Always use copies of your scanned images when you begin retouching or any other major surgery. If you remove too much detail or change your mind about what parts of the image you want to edit, it's ever so much easier to restore an archived image than to haul out the original again for rescanning.

Similarly, try to save your work at crucial points if you're doing a lot of experimenting in your Photoshop work. Many computer games let you save your position if and when you're about to try something dangerous. Consider approaching your image editing in the same spirit so you won't have to backtrack too much if you change your mind about how you want to proceed.

The Take Snapshot command under the Edit menu lets you keep a *snapshot* in Photoshop's image buffer, giving you a second version of your file that you can revert to if necessary. You can restore specific parts of this snapshot image by using the From Snapshot setting of the Rubber Stamp tool, and you can use parts of the last saved version of the file by using the From Saved setting of the Rubber Stamp tool (Figure 10.2).

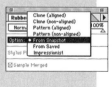

Figure 10.2

Choosing the From Snapshot or From Saved options from the Rubber Stamp tool's options

Send Us
YOUR COMMENTS

Dear Reader:

Thank you for buying this book. In order to offer you more quality books on the topics *you* would like to see, we need your input. At Prima Publishing, we pride ourselves on timely responsiveness to our readers' needs. If you complete and return this brief questionnaire, *we will listen!*

Name (First) _____ (M.I.) _____ (Last) _____

Company _____ Type of business _____

Address _____ City _____ State ____ ZIP ____

Phone _____ Fax _____ E-mail address: _____

May we contact you for research purposes? ❑ Yes ❑ No

(If you participate in a research project, we will supply you with the Prima computer book of your choice.)

❶ How would you rate this book, overall?

❑ Excellent ❑ Fair
❑ Very good ❑ Below average
❑ Good ❑ Poor

❷ Why did you buy this book?

❑ Price of book ❑ Content
❑ Author's reputation ❑ Prima's reputation
❑ CD-ROM/disk included with book
❑ Information highlighted on cover
❑ Other (please specify):_____

❸ How did you discover this book?

❑ Found it on bookstore shelf
❑ Saw it in Prima Publishing catalog
❑ Recommended by store personnel
❑ Recommended by friend or colleague
❑ Saw an advertisement in:_____
❑ Read book review in:_____
❑ Saw it on Web site:_____
❑ Other (please specify):_____

❹ Where did you buy this book?

❑ Bookstore (name):_____
❑ Computer store (name):_____
❑ Electronics store (name):_____
❑ Wholesale club (name):_____
❑ Mail order (name):_____
❑ Direct from Prima Publishing
❑ Other (please specify):_____

❺ Which computer periodicals do you read regularly?_____
_____
_____

❻ Would you like to see your name in print?

May we use your name and quote you in future Prima Publishing books or promotional materials?

❑ Yes ❑ No

❼ Comments & suggestions: _____
_____
_____

8 **I am interested in seeing more computer books on these topics**

❑ Word processing ❑ Databases/spreadsheets ❑ Networking ❑ Programming
❑ Desktop publishing ❑ Web site development ❑ Internetworking ❑ Intranetworking

9 **How do you rate your level of computer skills?**

❑ Beginner
❑ Intermediate
❑ Advanced

10 **What is your age?**

❑ Under 18 ❑ 40–49
❑ 18–29 ❑ 50–59
❑ 30–39 ❑ 60–over

SAVE A STAMP

Visit our Web site at **http://www.primapublishing.com**

and simply fill out one of our online response forms.

PRIMA PUBLISHING
Computer Products Division
701 Congressional Blvd., Suite 350
Carmel, IN 46032

The cool part about using these options is the control you have over making your image restoration look naturalistic. You can use the Brushes palette to choose the thickness and edges of a brush for painting the saved image back in. Back in the Rubber Stamp tool's Options dialog box, you can set the opacity and mode (for example, Overlay, Darken). By tweaking the opacity and brush settings, you wield great control over parts of your image, making the restored bits look realistic, not just pasted in digitally.

Can This Photo Be Saved?

Our lives may be full of Kodak moments, as the ads tell us, but they don't mention the near-misses that get captured on film all too often. Poor lighting, closed eyes, and bad hair days can result in photos you'd sooner toss out than consider for a Page One layout.

Here's a brief rundown of some of the kinds of corrections you may be likely to want to make:

- 👁 **Tonal corrections** These include setting the lightest and darkest points in your image, and adjusting midtone areas and highlights.

- 👁 **Removing dust spots** Scanners capture any dust on the scanning area along with your artwork, and you need to get rid of the spots for a professional-quality image.

- 👁 **Facial fixes** You may find yourself critiquing portrait shots the way you'd scrutinize your own appearance before going out. Things to check for here include dark shadows under the eyes or blemishes on the skin. If you're doing a more radical makeover, you could even remove the subject's glasses or trim facial hair.

- 👁 **Fixing a distracting background** Bystanders, passing cars, or other objects in your image's background can distract from the subject itself. Often you can blur the background or remove intrusive objects from the scene altogether.

We'll tackle these problems one by one, starting with strategies for grayscale tone and color correction. Following that are tips for removing

blemishes and fixing backgrounds. I've included these in the general order in which you'd want to fix up your image—it's easier to take care of the smaller problems, like dust spots, once you've gotten a handle on adjusting contrast and other tonal corrections.

Tonal Corrections in Grayscale Images

In making tonal corrections to your grayscale images, you'll draw out hidden details in the shadows, midtones, and highlights. You'll improve the tonal range so that the lighter tones don't turn completely white when printed.

The most intuitive way to learn how to do tonal corrections is by example, so open up your own grayscale image in Photoshop or follow along with the one shown here. Here, I've opened up a Kodak CD photo of a baker; there are no dust spots or other obvious blemishes, but the image is much, much too dark. As printed here in Figure 10.3, the image's details are mostly lost in the gloom.

The first step on the path to tonal correction is to open up the Info palette and use the Eyedropper tool to take some readings. Notice that in the Info palette you can display readouts in two different modes; this can be very useful when you're working in RGB and want to keep tabs on values for CMYK output or percentages for total ink values. Click the Info palette's pop-up menu to choose the Palette Options command. Click the Show First Color Readout check box and select either Actual Color or Grayscale (Figure 10.4).

What, if anything, should you display for the second color readout? Since you're just working in Grayscale mode here, there's no need to show the CMYK values. If you've managed to wrap your mind around thinking in terms of the 0–255 gray value range, you should choose to show the RGB values for the second color readout; you'll see identical values for the R, G, and B values. Otherwise, keep the Show Second Color Readout check box unchecked.

Figure 10.3
A grayscale image in need of tonal correction

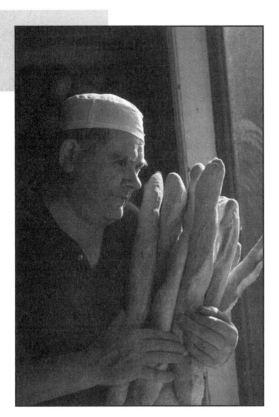

Figure 10.4
The Info Options dialog box. For grayscale images, set your first color readout to either Actual Color or Grayscale.

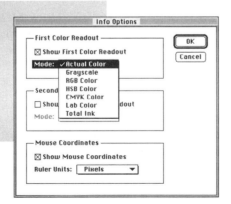

note

If you show a second color readout set to CMYK, you may be wondering why the Info palette will show values for the cyan, magenta, and yellow channels when you're working with a Grayscale image. After all, why isn't black the only channel that registers, since it's really just a Grayscale image? Photoshop is displaying the values it would use if you did convert the mode from Grayscale to CMYK—the program doesn't just translate your grays over to the black channel. It translates them to values in all four channels that would yield a similar gray.

The third check box in the Info Options dialog box controls the mouse coordinates; you can choose your preferred unit of measurement. I usually keep tabs on the mouse coordinates measured in pixels.

Your next task is to take readings of the lightest and darkest points in your image. You should bear in mind that your printer may display much less tonal variation than your monitor does; it will not distinguish between, say, 10 percent black and 13 percent black in a noticeable way. Any values you have in the 1 percent to 5 percent black range will likely print entirely as white. Similarly, any black values over 95 percent may print completely in black because of *dot gain*, or the tendency of a printing dot to spread during the halftone process that produces its final printed version on paper. Dot gain, which you'll see again in more detail in Chapter 12, is most prevalent in offset printing on lower-quality paper like newsprint.

In my example photo, the lightest reading is 7 percent black and the darkest point is 96 percent black. Later, when you start making tonal corrections, you'll find more interesting information here that shows your before-and-after pixel values—so you'll be able to see exactly how much you've lightened or darkened sample areas.

For now, what will be more telling will be readings of the midtone areas, because just from looking at the image it's apparent that the midtones are too dark and will need to be lightened. You can generate readings of your midtone values by analyzing a histogram of the image, which is a graph showing the distribution of gray tones in an image. Histograms are always useful to look at first thing after you scan an image. You can see this graph by choosing Histogram from the Image menu.

If you have an active selection in your image, the histogram will include only the values in your selected area. Here's a sample histogram dialog box, showing the sort of well-balanced chart you'd want to see for your images:

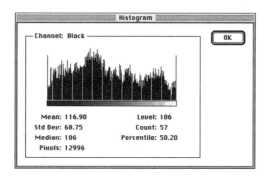

Instead of measuring gray values in percentages of black, the histogram shows how many occurrences there are of each of the 256 possible values in a Grayscale image. Running along the x-axis of this chart you'll see a color bar blending from black to white. Each point along this chart shows one of the gray values between 0 (black) and 255 (white).

This chart can tell you at a glance which direction to go in to correct your image's tones. A high frequency of 0 or 255 values may indicate that your scanner wasn't able to handle the full tonal range of your image and has clipped, or converted to 100 percent black or white, some extreme dark and light values. A histogram with values bunched toward the right side indicates the image is way too light, while a bell-curved histogram (high in the middle) has too many midlevel grays

and needs more contrast. A well-balanced histogram should contain values spread in fairly equal amounts across the length of the chart—that shows the tonal range is just right.

Beneath the graph in the Histogram dialog box you'll find some additional information. You probably won't need to refer to most of it, but it's useful to know what it shows:

- **Mean**   Shows the average brightness value.

- **Std Dev**   Shows how much the brightness values vary. The term is short for Standard Deviation.

- **Median**   Gives the middle brightness value in the image—half the pixels are darker than this point and half are lighter. It's a different value from the average (mean).

- **Pixels**   Tells you the total number of pixels in the image—which you could also figure by multiplying the image's height and width in pixels—or in the active selection.

The next three values change as you move your cursor (a crosshair) across the histogram.

- **Level**   Shows the gray value of the point your cursor is passing over. While it's easy to tell where 0 (black) and 255 (white) fall at the ends of the spectrum, using the crosshair in this way is the best way to see the frequency of other gray values.

- **Count**   Gives the exact number of occurrences of the gray value the cursor is passing over, which you see represented graphically on the chart.

- **Percentile**   Tracks what percentage of the grays in the image are less than or equal to a given value. For example, if you put the crosshair on the median value, the Percentile reading should be equivalent to 50.00; if you put the crosshair at the 255 level, Percentile should read 100.00.

As you make tonal changes to your images, you should take frequent looks at what changes have been wrought on your image's histogram.

Gaps in the histogram indicate *posterization,* or areas where there are sudden jumps in tonal variation.

As anticipated, the histogram for the baker image shows an unevenly balanced histogram (Figure 10.5). The chart is heavily weighted toward the left, indicating that the image is much too dark.

Let's look at ways to correct this image using one or more of the Adjust subcommands under the Image menu for making tonal corrections: Variations, Levels, and Curves.

Variations

As you saw in Chapter 9, Variations offers the most intuitive interface for tonal correction. Although this is the very last option in the Adjust submenu, I've listed it first because it's not a bad place to begin when you're just starting out. Like an interactive kiosk, this option offers you pictures you can click to apply a new variation on your image. You get new options based on your past decisions. You can see your original image next to your "Current Pick" setting in a convenient before-and-after view.

But this same easy-to-use interface prevents you from exerting precise control over changes. In a general way, you can boost contrast by darkening shadows and lightening highlights, and reduce contrast by doing the opposite. The Fine/Coarse slider offers the only control you have here for increasing or decreasing the level of change that takes place as you increase or decrease brightness or contrast. The Variations dialog

Figure 10.5

The histogram for the baker image, before tonal correction

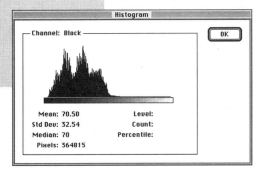

box doesn't let you sample pixels in your image, the way you can with the Levels or Curves commands.

The Show Clipping setting allows your variations to produce areas of flat color—extremes at the 0 (black) or 255 (white) ends of the tonal range. You'll want to avoid these results in general, because they show areas where detail has been destroyed and where your variations have exceeded the tonal range.

In Figure 10.6, I've toyed around with the baker image a bit using the Variations command. I've managed to lighten up the midtones and boost the contrast a bit. I'd like to experiment with a greater level of control, though, so I'm going to cancel these changes without okaying them and move on to the Levels command.

Levels

Now let's look at how you can alter an image using the Levels command, which lets you drag sliders or enter specific values to alter the shadows, highlights, and *gamma* (midtone) settings. For making tonal corrections in grayscale images, Levels is usually the best choice.

Figure 10.6
Using the Variations command to adjust the baker image

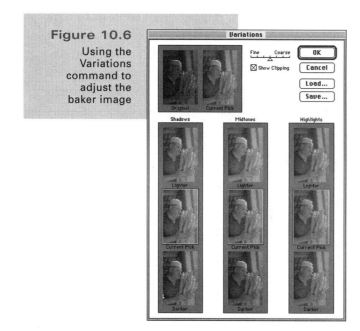

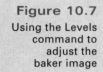

Figure 10.7

Using the Levels command to adjust the baker image

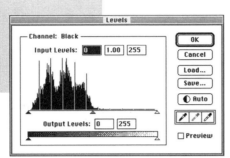

Choose Adjust from the Image menu, then select Levels to display the Levels dialog box. In Figure 10.7, I've displayed the Levels dialog box for the uncorrected baker image.

The main part of the Levels dialog box should be familiar—it'll show the same kind of histogram you saw when you chose Histogram from the Image menu earlier.

Input Levels

Directly beneath the histogram are three slider controls: a black slider for controlling shadow values, a gray slider for controlling gamma values, and a white slider for controlling highlight values. The three Input Levels option boxes next to the Input Levels heading correspond to the black, gray, and white sliders respectively—so you can enter specific values instead of dragging the sliders.

The values for the black (shadows) and white (highlights) sliders use the 0–255 range for measuring levels of gray. You can move the black and white sliders in toward the center to increase the overall contrast; in doing so, you'll change the tonal range in a couple of significant ways. For example, if you move the black slider from its default of 0 up to 50, you'll *clip* all the pixels in the range of 0 to 50 to level 0, or solid black. All the levels to the right of the black slider will be remapped between 0 and 255. Similarly, if you move the white slider from its default of 255 down to 225, all the pixels in the range of 225 to 255 will be *clipped,* or converted, to solid white at level 255, and all values to the left of the white slider will be remapped between 0 and 255. Figure 10.8 illustrates how this works.

Figure 10.8
Moving the black and white sliders in the Levels dialog box turns all values beyond a specified point to solid black or white, and remaps all tones in between.

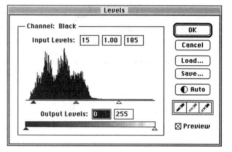

The gray slider lets you change the midtones without affecting either the shadows or highlights. It lets you determine where you want the midtone gray—that is, level 128—to fall. If you move the gray slider to the left, you're lightening the image by reducing the number of pixels that fall between 0 and 128 in value. If you move the gray slider to the right, your image will grow much darker because you're remapping a much lighter gray value down to 128, and increasing the number of pixels between 0 and 128.

Output Levels

Beneath the three Input Levels slider bars is the Output Levels option, which is designed solely to reduce contrast. You can enter values or drag a black or white slider toward the center to control just how much you reduce the contrast. When you drag the black slider to the right, you lighten the image by reducing shadows; moving the white slider toward the center darkens the image by removing highlights.

How does this differ from the way the Input Levels sliders function? Here's an example: as you saw above, if you move the Input Level's black slider to level 50, you'll turn all the pixels that had been in the range of 0 to 50 to level 0, or solid black. With the black Output Levels slider, setting it to 50 tells the program to take all those pixels that had been in

Figure 10.9

Moving the gray slider in the Levels dialog box lightens your image by reducing the number of pixels with values in the darker half of the tonal range.

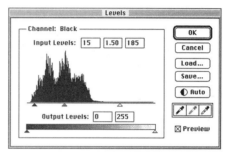

the range of 0 to 50 and make 50 the lowest possible value; those darkest values are remapped to lighter ones. As a result, the image brightens but there's less overall contrast in the range between light and dark.

The other options available to you in the Levels dialog box—including the Load and Save buttons, the Auto button, and the Eyedropper tools—come up later, in the "Color Correction" section of this chapter.

Curves

The Curves dialog box has a somewhat different metaphor for making tonal corrections than Levels does; ultimately it's more powerful, but certainly less intuitive for the uninitiated.

With Curves, you won't see a histogram of the gray values in your image the way you do with the Levels command. Instead, you get a graph that represents the relationship between the values you're starting off with (or *input levels*) and the values that you'll alter (your *output levels*). You can also think of input and output levels as the before and after values in your picture, the way the Info palette showed your starting and ending values when you edited an image using the Levels command.

The input levels are mapped along the x-axis and the output levels along the y-axis. When you first display the Curves dialog box, the

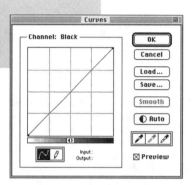

Figure 10.10

The Curves
dialog box

input levels and the output levels have the same values; as a result, the graph maps the simple equation x=y, which produces a straight diagonal line at 45° (Figure 10.10).

The default settings for the gradient bar under the Curves graph blend from white to black, representing the percentage values measured by the graph, from 0 percent black (that is, white) to 100 percent black (solid black). The lower part of the graph represents the lighter, highlight areas or your image; you can reduce highlights by clicking and dragging up along the lower part of this curve. Likewise, the upper part of the graph represents the darker, shadow areas of the image, and you can lighten these shadows by clicking and dragging down at points along the upper part of the curve. Clicking and dragging along the middle of the curve affects the image's midtones.

note

You can reverse the gradient bar under the curves graph; this will let Curves use the model of 256 levels of gray for measuring input and output levels; the lower end of the curve will measure shadows and the upper end of the curve will measure highlights. It doesn't matter which model you use for editing in Curves—just use whichever one you're more comfortable with, percentages of black or the model using 256 levels of gray.

If you move your cursor over different parts of the graph, you'll see Input values increase as you move the cursor to the right, and Output values will increase as you move the cursor up.

You can also track where on the graph any pixel in your image falls by selecting the Eyedropper tool and moving it across your image while the Curves dialog box is onscreen. A circle will appear at the point on the curve that represents the percentage of black for that pixel.

The Curves dialog box gives you a great deal of control over the overall tonal range, allowing you to make very precise adjustments to one part of the curve. When you add a new control point, creating an output level that has either more or less black than the input level at that point, you're actually affecting the slope of the entire curve. If your output level is very different from the input level, you'll see the a dramatic shift in the curve as other points move to new output levels along the curve. You can add multiple control points at any part of the curve to gain further control over the changes you make on the graph in the Curves dialog box.

Any tonal changes you can make with the Levels dialog box you can reproduce in Curves, and then some. For example, to clip all values over a certain value—say, solid black—in Curves, you just need to move the uppermost point on the curve straight to the left, so the highest values are mapped in a straight line. Figure 10.11 shows what a highly posterized curve would look like; as you can see, many output level values in this graph are identical.

From working with the baker image using the Levels command, I know that I want to increase the contrast slightly but focus even more on

Figure 10.11

Posterizing an image with the Curves dialog box

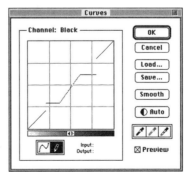

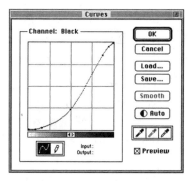

Figure 10.12
Making tonal
corrections
using Curves

lightening the midtones. I can practice achieving contrast by creating a
slight S curve. Here, I'm increasing the highlights by clicking and dragging down a new control point along the lower part of this curve, and
increasing the shadows ever so slightly by clicking and dragging up a
new control point along the upper part of this curve. Next, I'm pulling
up control points along the center of the image to lighten the midtones
significantly (Figure 10.12).

tip   **Resetting the Graph in the Curves Dialog Box**

You can reset the graph in the Curves dialog box to its original straight
x=y function by holding down Option (for Mac users) or Alt (for Windows
users) as you click the Reset button.

At the bottom left of the Curves dialog box, you'll see a curve icon and
a pencil icon; these represent what mode you're working in.

In *curve mode*, you can add, move, and delete the control points as I just
discussed. If you switch to the pencil—in what is called *arbitrary mode*—

you can use the pencil to draw new lines in the graph. Switching to arbitrary mode made it easy for me to create the posterized mode in Figure 10.11; I just drew several straight lines across to map numerous values to the same output level value. If you change the mapping function in this way, you can create your own unusual effects just by doodling.

Color Corrections

You'll need to attend to fine-tuning the shadows, highlights, and midtones in your color images just as you've done by now in grayscale images. In addition, you'll have additional color correction issues to face before you can produce images that will look good in print.

For starters, you may need to correct color casts that the scanning process generated. There may also be color casts in your original transparency or print that you'll want to try to correct.

Just as you tackled tonal corrections in editing a grayscale images before touching up the more nit-picky problems, you should color-correct your image here before worrying about smaller issues.

In anticipating problems that could arise on press, you may need to correct for dot gain the same way you did for grayscale images. Later in this chapter you'll learn about techniques for reducing the overall ink density to compensate for poor *trapping* during printing, which refers to the ink's ability to adhere to another layer of ink as well as it would to paper. When your job has poor trapping, some of the inks will fail to adhere, resulting in color and tonal changes in your final output.

Here, I've opened up a clip art photo of a telephone repair person (Figure 10.13). There are few dust spots or blemishes to change, but I'll walk through making some tonal corrections here.

There are two main ways I'm hoping to manipulate the color for this image. First, I want to tone down some of the highlights; some of the lightest colors have *blown out,* leaving shiny white spots in the folds of the telephone repairman's shirt and wrench. Second, I want to improve the overall contrast between the background sky and the the foreground image.

Figure 10.13
A sample RGB image in need of some tonal corrections and general cleanup

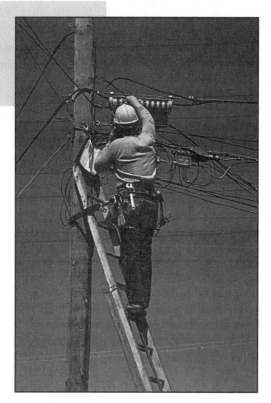

Taking Eyedropper and Info Palette Readings

Now's a good time for you to switch your Info palette first and second color readouts to show both RBG and CMYK values, because the colors you see onscreen may not match their print counterparts very well. *(Pssst— have you calibrated your monitor lately?)* If you're working on images for print publication, you'll want to have your future CMYK values available at a glance so you can guard against out-of-gamut colors (those RGB colors that have no CMYK equivalent) and too-heavy total inking.

Another good reason for keeping both the RGB and CMYK values at the ready in your Info palette is to help you add or subtract colors to produce their complementary colors. Remember way, way back to Chapter 4, "Color Essentials," where you saw that opposite color pairs (like cyan and its opposite color, red) are called *complementary colors.* For example, an image with little cyan in it will have a high percentage of red and vice versa. You might want to get hold of a color wheel or refer back to the color charts in Chapter 4 when you're doing your color correcting, to help keep these relationships in mind. The relationship between adding and subtracting the primary colors (red, green, and blue) and the secondary colors (cyan, magenta, and yellow) is also apparent in the Color Balance dialog box (Figure 10.14), which you can display by choosing the Color Balance command from the Adjust submenu under the Image menu. This is one of the good applications for the Color Balance dialog box; the effects you can produce by moving the sliders can usually be reproduced just as easily—and with even more control—through judicious use of the Curves dialog box.

By selecting the Eyedropper tool and passing the cursor over the image to take some readings, I was able to make some initial suppositions about what colors I needed to add and subtract. For example, the overall image is very dark but also suffers from lack of contrast; there are few highlights or shadows. The image is so blue—because of the deep sky tones—that the denim-clad worker doesn't pop out enough as the subject, the focus moves to the hat and the ladder. Since this clip art image came from a Kodak Photo CD collection, I'm also on the lookout for a way to correct the color cast that permeates it.

Next, we'll turn to the same tools for color correction that we used earlier with tonal correction in grayscale images: histograms and the Variations, Levels, and Curves dialog boxes. Functionally, they'll work the same but can produce much greater effects in three channels (for RGB mode) or four channels (in CMYK) than they did in just one.

Figure 10.14

The Color Balance dialog box

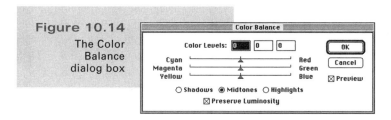

Using the Histogram Command

Just as when you're assessing a grayscale image, you can turn to the Histogram command under the Image menu to assess the tonal range of an RGB or CMYK image. When you look at a histogram for an image in either of these two color modes, you have the option of viewing the histogram for any individual color channel, or a channel called Gray that represents the composite brightness values (Figure 10.15).

Here, I've clicked the Channel pop-up menu to view the Red, Green, Blue, and composite Gray channels for my sample image. In each channel, the histogram is skewed with very high values in the midtones but few in the highlights and shadow areas.

Setting a White, Black, and Neutral Point

When images like the one in Figure 10.13 lack shadows and highlights, it indicates they have compressed tonal ranges. One technique you can use here for expanding a compressed tonal range is to set a white point (for the highlight) and a black point (for the shadow).

You can set the white and black points either automatically (using the Auto button in either the Levels or Curves setting—Figure 10.16) or by choosing colors for the white and black points with the Eyedropper tool. If you've been wondering what the Auto command does, you can see that it only automatically remaps the lightest and darkest pixels to the white and black point—it doesn't automatically fix a bad histogram.

Setting a neutral point helps you eliminate a color cast. For example, if your photo was shot indoors under fluorescent lighting you may notice

Figure 10.15

Checking the Gray histogram in a color image

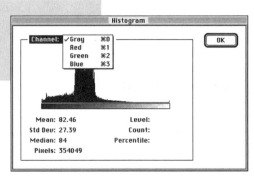

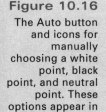

Figure 10.16

The Auto button and icons for manually choosing a white point, black point, and neutral point. These options appear in both the Levels and Curves dialog boxes.

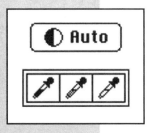

a reddish color cast. There are also different kinds of film optimized for indoor versus outdoor work; if you used the wrong kind of film for your photo shoot, a problematic color cast may arise in the prints. With the neutral point, you can identify a neutral gray for Photoshop to use for its midtone, and with luck correct other off-tinted midtones at the same time.

note — **You can also use the Auto Levels command under the Adjust submenu of the Image menu to set the white and black points in an image. It has the same effect as pressing the Auto button in the Levels dialog box.**

Variations

Just as when you edited a grayscale image earlier, you can probably have fairly good success editing your image to one with a color balance you prefer using the Variations command (Figure 10.17). Note that the dialog box gives you several extra options with a color image; among other things, you can edit the saturation or vividness of the colors used.

Levels

For greater control than Variations allows, you can use Levels (Figure 10.18) to correct a composite color image—or better yet, individual color channels. Here, I used Levels most heavily in the Blue channel, to tone down the highest values while trying to expand the tonal range in the Red and Green channels.

EXERCISE 10.1

Manually Setting the White and Black Points in an Image

1. To select a white or black point manually, move your cursor over your image; notice the cursor changes to an eyedropper. Keep an eye on your Info palette reading to look for the highest RGB levels for the white point, or the lowest RGB levels for the black point.

2. When you're ready to set those levels, double-click the white point or black point icon in the Levels or Curves dialog box. Move your cursor back to the area you identified for the white point and click; the Color Picker dialog box will appear with the words "Select white target color" at the top. You have the option of altering the values in the dialog box if you didn't manually select the exact value you intended to.

3. Repeat these steps for choosing the black point. Note that if you choose solid white and solid black for your white and black points, it has the same effect as if you pressed the Auto button in Levels or Curves.

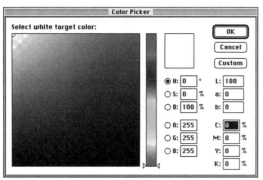

②

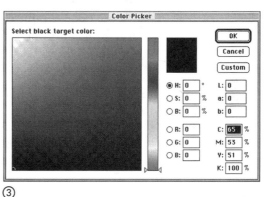

③

With the Save and Load buttons, you can retain and then load settings that you plan to use frequently with these two buttons in the Levels dialog box.

Curves

As with Levels, you can use Curves to edit individual color channels for touching up your color images (Figure 10.19).

Figure 10.17

Using the Variations command with a color image offers controls over saturation as well as shadows and highlights.

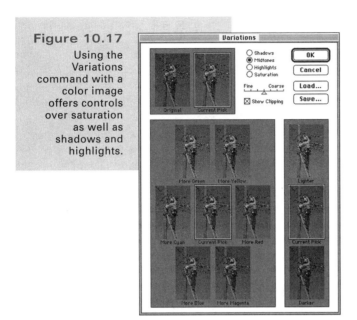

Using the Dodge and Burn Tools

After you've made your tonal corrections, you may still find small areas where you need to tweak some shadows. Here's where the Dodge or Burn tools could come in handy.

Figure 10.18

You can use the Levels command to edit individual color channels.

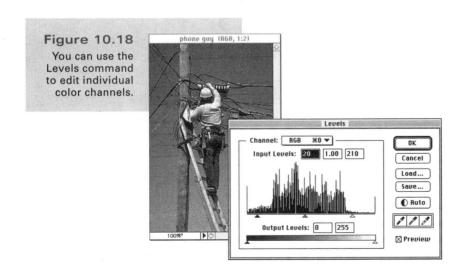

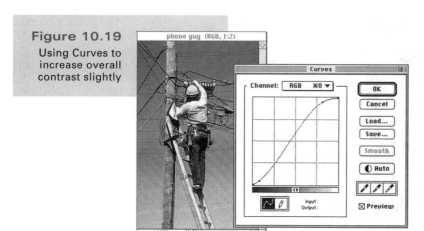

Figure 10.19
Using Curves to increase overall contrast slightly

As mentioned in Chapter 3, the Dodge and Burn tools (which share a spot in the Toolbox) derive from photographic techniques for, respectively, lightening and darkening parts of an image.

The image that I've tweaked here—Figure 10.20—is in much better shape than when you first saw it in Figure 10.13.

Now that you've seen how to get a handle on some of the big tonal and color correction issues, you're ready to sweat the small stuff: fixing dust spots, scratches, and other small imperfections.

Removing Dust Spots and Blemishes

It's easy to find dust spots on any scanned image, but scanned slides are especially prone to dust spots—the enlargement process tends to magnify any imperfections in a slide image. And when you sharpen up the scanned image (which most scans need to improve the focus), you'll enhance those dust spots too (Figure 10.21).

Using the Rubber Stamp Tool

You can usually eliminate small stray blotches easily with judicious use of the Rubber Stamp tool; you can clone another portion of your image and blend it in to replace dust spots or scratches seamlessly.

Figure 10.20

Compare the color-corrected image here with its original in Figure 10.13.

Figure 10.21

This scanned image picked up several dust spots and other blemishes. The digitized image also emphasized a scratch that was not apparent in the print original.

The Rubber Stamp tool has two cloning settings—Aligned and Non-aligned. You can change these settings by double-clicking the Rubber Stamp tool in the Toolbox and choosing a different option in the Rubber Stamp Options dialog box.

Cloning (Aligned)

With the Aligned setting—which is the Rubber Stamp tool's default setting—you identify an originating point, and then click and drag in a different area to duplicate the original area. As you continue to drag the cursor, more of the original area appears. Figure 10.22 illustrates an example of cloning with the Aligned setting chosen.

tip

● ●

Take Care When Cloning

Be sure to keep careful tabs on how wide an area you're cloning. If you clone too broad an area, you might inadvertently replicate other blotches near the source area or other contrasting pixels that would be out of place.

● ●

If you then move your cursor around to click and drag in a different part of the image—say, an inch to the right—you'll start cloning an area an inch to the right of the original source area.

It's usually a good idea to choose a new source area frequently if you're touching up a wide area; using and reusing the same selection can cause noticeable patterns to emerge, which detracts from the realism of your retouching efforts.

If you want to keep cloning the original source area over and over again, you'll need to choose the Cloning (Non-aligned) option from the Rubber Stamp Options dialog box.

Cloning (Non-aligned)

After you identify an originating point, this Rubber Stamp option lets you replicate your source area anywhere else you click. This produces the effect most people think of first when they hear about cloning: multiple copies of the same object. Figure 10.23 illustrates the kind of

Figure 10.22
Cloning with the
Rubber Stamp
tool's Aligned
setting

object you might want to make multiple copies of. Here, I'm cloning a sunflower to create a field filled with flowers, so it will look like I'm a much more successful gardener than I actually am.

The Cloning (Aligned) option is more useful for obliterating dust spots and scratches in an image, while the Cloning (Non-aligned) option is a better choice if you need to embellish an image (say, add more grass to an unkempt lawn, or more leaves to a sparse-looking tree).

tip

Rubber Stamping Across Layers

If you're touching up a scanned photo, your rubber stamping affects a single layer. But what if you've added layers or are working with another Photoshop document with multiple layers? Click the Sample Merged check box in the Rubber Stamp Options dialog box to clone pixels from other layers.

Figure 10.23
Cloning with
the Rubber
Stamp tool's
Non-aligned
setting lets you
produce multiple
copies of the
same image area.

EXERCISE 10.2

Masking Dust Spots and Scratches

Practicing spot-removal techniques is easiest when your subject matter is a human portrait or a prized possession—in other words, someone or something whose appearance you'd normally pay attention to.

①

1. Choose an image for editing, taking care to identify the spots you want to eliminate. Zoom in to a high magnification, one at which you'll be comfortable working at on a pixel-by-pixel basis—for example, a 3:1 or 4:1 ratio.

2. Select the Rubber Stamp tool from the Toolbox. Make sure that it's set to the Cloned (Aligned) option. You can also choose a brush size and set opacity; here, I'm just using the Photoshop defaults of a small brush size and 100 percent opacity.

3. Position your cursor over an area of your image that has similar tones to the area where you want to replace the first dust spot. To select that area as the point of origin, hold down (Option) (if you're a Mac user; use (Alt) if you're a Windows user) as you click over that spot. Notice how your cursor changes while you're selecting a point of origin.

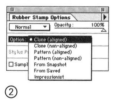

②

4. Now you're ready to start altering your first dust spot. If it's a large area, work from the outside to blend each pixel with the bordering ones. As mentioned before, you should change the point of origin by (Option)-clicking (or (Alt)-clicking) elsewhere as necessary to get a realistic mix of tones.

③

5. Now move on to fixing another spot in your image. You'll almost certainly have to (Option)-click (or (Alt)-click) to choose a new source point. When you finish touching up your dust spots manually, the net effect should look clean and fluid, with no obvious digital futzing.

Using Feathering to Smooth Transitions

Sometimes you may find it easier to replace parts of your image by duplicating and pasting in a selection from another area. *Feathering* is a key part of making this kind of switcharound look more realistic.

You can feather a selection either before or after you actually make the selection. To feather the selection ahead of time, click the Feather check box in whichever selection tool you use—for example, the Lasso or Rectangular Marquee tool. Or to feather after you've made a selection, just choose Feather from the Select menu.

When you duplicate the selection by copying and pasting—or as a shortcut, (Option)-dragging (for Mac users; (Alt)-dragging for Windows users)—the feathered edges will help obscure the boundaries of the pasted selection and add to the realistic effect.

Using Modes to Eliminate Lots of Spots

If you have an area of an image so riddled with small spots that rubber stamping them out doesn't seem feasible, try this powerful technique for eliminating multiple spots at once. Make a selection of the area—remember, feathering the edges will help make your retouching blend in better—and turn it into a floating selection by choosing Float from the Select menu. As a floating selection, your selection is on its own layer and can make use of the mode settings in the Layers palette. If the spots are whitish in color, choose the Darken mode in the Layers palette; if the spots are dark in color, choose the Lighten mode. Now you can offset the selection slightly—use the arrow keys on your keyboard to nudge the selection a pixel at a time—mask the original spots (Figure 10.24). Voilà—no more spots! Don't you wish your dishwasher detergent could do that?

There's one major drawback to this technique, though, as you'll see if you study the face in the the right-hand image of Figure 10.24. This method of eliminating lots of spots is best for background areas, but not areas where important detail can be lost. Here, for example, the eyeglasses are starting to break up. A better way to edit this image would have been to apply the mass spot-elimination technique only in the background areas, and to eliminate the spots in the main subject areas on an individual basis.

Figure 10.24
You can cover up a myriad of spots at once by duplicating the area, then changing the mode of the selection's layer to Darken or Lighten as necessary.

Making Wrinkles Vanish

By now you've seen how to remove flaws introduced during the printing or scanning process, but what about touching up real facial characteristics like wrinkles or freckles? With Photoshop, you can perform a digital facelift or wipe away a faceful of freckles with a few artful moves.

The first step, if the subject of the photo is the one urging you to make these corrections, is to point out reassuringly that physical appearance is no measure of real worth despite society's messages. Most real-life facelifts look a lot scarier than the untouched originals, anyway.

If and when you do pursue improving on a person's looks in Photoshop, remember to emphasize naturalism above all else. A digital facelift doesn't mean removing all facial lines—everyone has *some* of those—but just blending them into lighter skin tones so they're less prominent.

Just as when you're removing dust spots, the Rubber Stamp tool can be most useful in clearing up a complexion. Make sure you change your source point frequently—no one's skin tone is very uniform. For the most realistic blended effects, choose a slightly larger brush size and lower the opacity slightly, so there are no sudden changes between pixels.

The Smudge or Airbrush tools are other useful tools to use; just like applying concealer or other cosmetics in real life, you can dot on a perfect skin tone color and Smudge or Airbrush to blend it in.

Replacing a Background

Editing the background—that is, what's going on behind your image's subject—can help you establish the subject as the main focus. As described earlier in this book, you can select the background area and Gaussian Blur it slightly to add an extra degree of separation between it and the image subject.

But details can lead the viewer's attention astray, so you may want to wipe out distractions in the background. For example, other people walking behind your subject—especially if they're partially cut off by the photo—can make your otherwise good photo not so good anymore.

Selections, Revisited

You'll need a good grasp on how to make selections if you want to drop an entirely new background behind your subject and make it look realistic; Chapter 7 covered how to create some intricate selections. If your background is truly a distracting one, it may take a number of cumulative selections with the Magic Wand tool to select the entire background area you want. Remember that if the contrast is greater in one channel than in others, it may be easier for you to make your selection in a single color channel before returning to the full image. Creating a path with the Paths palette's Pen tool and converting the path to a selection is another good way to create a selection—and one you can feather at the same time—for use in a composite image.

Judge if the subject itself might be easier to select, because then you need only choose Invert from the Select menu to choose everything that's not the subject.

Don't forget to feather your selection before you paste it in elsewhere. Since you'll probably go to some lengths to get the exact selection you want, it makes more sense to feather afterward instead of before. When you've made your selection, just choose Feather from the Select menu and add a value for the number of pixels deep for feathering.

Summary

In this chapter, you've learned some advanced techniques for retouching flaws and correcting color casts in images using the Rubber Stamp tool and the various Map and Adjust subcommands. With the information covered here, you'll be well-equipped to optimize your images for print—the topic of Chapter 12. Up next in Chapter 11, though, you'll learn methods for creating 3-D shapes and text, beveled edges, and other special geometric effects.

11

3-D Rendering Essentials

IN THIS CHAPTER

From plain geometric shapes to raytraced effects, there are many three-dimensional effects you can create within Photoshop. Three-dimensional shapes let you dress up bullets and icons, or add depth when embellishing print pieces. They're also great for creating clickable buttons in online presentations and Web pages.

In this chapter, you'll learn the basic techniques and some jumping-off points for creating variations on the following effects:

- Spheres, cubes, and cones

- Textured surfaces on 3-D shapes

- Beveled edges on objects and type, for a clickable button effect

- Shadows to enhance 3-D effects

Geometric Shapes

Let's start off with something simple—the basic kinds of geometric shapes that even people-who-can't-draw can draw. Below I've included mini-exercises for creating spheres, cubes, and cones with gradient fills, followed by a section on adding textures and mapping images to these kinds of shapes.

If you want to create a cube with a flat front face, the steps to follow are even simpler. Follow the first step of Exercise 11.2 to create a square selection using the Rectangular Marquee tool. Save the selection to a channel, and then convert the selection to a path. To do that—remember back to Chapter 6—you just choose Make Path from the Paths palette's pop-up menu. You can then draw a second side and the top side using the Pen tool in the Paths palette. As you create the second and third sides, save those paths as selections by choosing the Make Selection option in the Paths palette's pop-up menu. You can then save those selections to a second and third channel, where they'll be ready for you to load into separate channels and apply textures or blends individually (Figure 11.3). You can even stroke each selection to further distinguish them.

EXERCISE 11.1

Creating Spheres

I described a simple way of creating spheres back in Exercise 3.2, but now that you've learned how to use layers, channels, and filters we can create a version that will be easy to edit later:

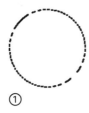

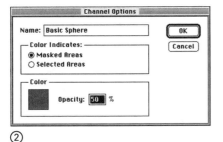

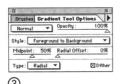

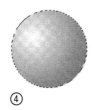

1. Launch Photoshop and create a new document. It's a good idea to either use a transparent background or create a new layer for your sphere—this'll make it easy to place your completed sphere in other images without copying over a solid background. Now choose the Elliptical Marquee tool and hold down [Shift] as you click and drag to form a perfect circle. Remember that if you want, you can draw a circle from the center outward by holding down [Option] (for Mac users) or [Alt] (for Windows users) while you're pressing [Shift].

2. Now let's save this selection in its own channel. As you've seen, there are a couple of ways to do this. You could choose Save Selection from the Select menu or use one of the options for making a new channel in the Channels palette. Here, I clicked the Selection icon (   ) at the bottom of the Channels palette, then double-clicked its row to name it Basic Sphere. Click the RGB icon in the Channels palette to return to the composite view.

3. Set the foreground color to white for the highlights on the finished sphere. Click the background color icon; when the Color Picker dialog box displays, choose a bright color; the color you select here will be the main color of your sphere. Double-click the Gradient tool (   ) to select it and call up the Options palette. Select a value for Radial Offset—higher values will apply more of your foreground color—and make sure the Style reads Foreground to Background. Set the Opacity to 100% and the mode to Normal, then click OK.

4. Position the cursor inside the sphere where you want the highlight to be brightest and drag diagonally to apply the gradient fill. The first place you click will be where the white color is most highly concentrated, blending into the solid background color at the position where you release the cursor.

⑤

⑥

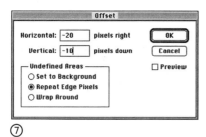

⑦

5. Now, let's create a duplicate of the sphere to use in adding a realistic-looking shadow. Drag the Basic Sphere channel's row down to the New Channel icon ( ) at the bottom of the Channel palette. This will create a new channel called Basic Sphere copy. You can double-click the channel's row to rename the channel Sphere Shadow.

6. Next, we're going to blur and offset this channel to create a shadowy selection for the composite image. Choose Gaussian Blur from the Filter menu and enter a value to generate a fairly pronounced shadow effect, as shown. The exact value you should enter will depend a lot on how big your original sphere is and how deep a shadow effect you want. The higher the value you enter, the more pronounced the offset effect will look.

Next, choose Other from the Filter menu, and then choose Offset from the Other submenu. Here we want the blurry shadow edge to move a little upward and to the left, so we need to enter negative horizontal and vertical values in the Offset dialog box. The basic rule to remember: offset your shadow the opposite of the way you created your gradient. Earlier we added a gradient fill by dragging to the right and down, so we need to move this shadow area up and to the left. In this example, I entered values of -20 and -10 pixels.

7. The next step is to carve out just the little half-moon of shadow we want from this blurry channel. Essentially, you want to load your Basic Sphere selection into the Sphere Shadow channel and subtract the overlapping parts. (We used this method to some extent back in Exercise 7.2, Creating Recessed Text Using Channels.) The way I'm going to spell out here, though, is to use Calculations from the Image menu, which you first saw in Chapter 9. Since the Calculations dialog box has kind of a confusing interface, I wanted to make sure I showed you a straightforward, real-world use of Calculations.

Choose Calculations from the Image menu. Select the Sphere Shadow channel as your Source 1 and the Basic

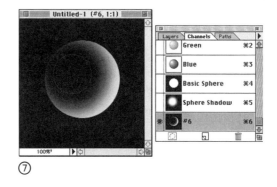

⑦

⑦

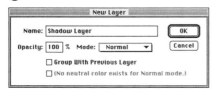

⑧

Sphere channel as Source 2. Choose Subtract for Blending, and choose to send the results to a new channel.

Your new channel's default name is #6. The image should look like the figure directly above.

8. We're almost done now; we just want to save this channel in its own layer so you can edit it independently of the sphere itself. Click the RGB channel's row in the Channels palette to return to the composite view. Create a new layer by pressing the New Layer icon in the Layers palette; here, I've called it Shadow Layer.

With the Shadow layer targeted, choose Load Selection from the Select menu and load channel #6. Or use the shortcut instead: (Option)-click ((Alt)-click, for Windows users) the #6 channel's row in the Channels palette to load it.

9. Fill the shadow selection with any color you like. Here, I've added a dark brown shadow to my yellow sphere. Since the sphere and its shadow are on different layers, you can change the colors any time you like without having to redraw your sphere (Figure 11.1).

Figure 11.1
A sphere with its shading on a separate layer to facilitate future editing

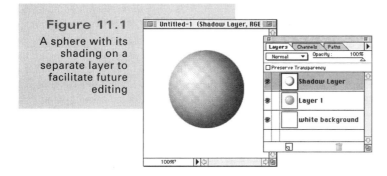

EXERCISE 11.2

Creating Cubes

Cubes are an especially useful design element; for example, you can map a different photo image to each face. Here's one way to create a cube that can be edited later on; in the following mini-exercise, you'll place each side in a separate layer for future use.

①

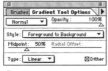

②

②

②

②

③

1. Create a new document. Just as in the sphere exercise, it's a good idea to either use a transparent background or create a new layer for your cube. Now choose the Rectangular Marquee tool and hold down (Shift) as you click and drag to form a perfect square. Remember that if you want, you can draw a square from the center outward by holding down (Option) (for Mac users) or (Alt) (for PC users) while you're pressing (Shift).

2. Now let's add a gradient fill to this first square. Set the foreground colors to black and white, or any two other contrasting colors with the darker color in the foreground. Choose the Gradient tool and make sure it's set to a Linear blend.

   Drag diagonally down and to the right across the selection, as shown here.

   The resulting fill should look like this:

3. Now you'll want to create a duplicate of this layer; this lets you keep a copy of your square in reserve while you assemble the left and right sides of the cube. Choose Duplicate Layer from the Layer palette's pop-up menu. I've named the new layer Top Edge. Hide this duplicate layer by clicking off its eye icon in the Layers palette; we'll use the Top Edge layer later to create the top edge for the cube.

4. With the square in the visible layer still selected, choose Effects from the Image menu and then choose Skew. Small square handles will appear at all four corners of your selection; drag down the one at the bottom right to create a skewed shape. Click inside the selection to effect the change. Save the selection to an alpha channel by pressing the Selection icon at the bottom of the Channels palette.

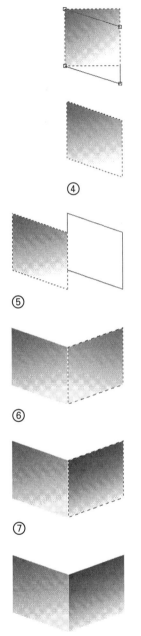

5. Now you need a duplicate of this selection for the right edge of the cube. Hold down Option (for Mac users) or Alt (for Windows users) to create duplicate of your selection; continue to hold down Option (or Alt) as you click and drag to the right. Keep dragging until the duplicate selection is aligned with the original skewed shape's right edge, like this:

6. Select Flip from the Image menu, then choose Horizontal. The skewed right edge selection flips horizontally to create a wide V-shape with the skewed left edge selection. Save the right edge selection to an alpha channel by clicking the Selection icon at the bottom of the Channels palette.

7. The shape of these two edges is fine, but the gradation in the right edge selection is a little off since you flipped it. Apply the same kind of gradient fill to this selection that you used in step 2.

8. Now you're ready to bring your Top Edge layer back into view and place the top edge on the cube. Click the eye icon next to the Top Edge layer and target that layer. Use the Move tool to position the square over the other two sides in the cube.

9. Select Rotate from the Image menu, then choose Arbitrary. Set the angle of rotation to 45° clockwise. Use the Move tool to reposition the square's bottom corner to the junction where the other two sides meet.

10. Choose Effects from the Image menu, then choose Scale. You need to drag the square handles on all four sides so that the lower two diagonal edges align perfectly with the top edges of the other two cube sides. Click inside the selection to effect the change.

When your top edge selection is perfectly in place, save it to an alpha channel so you can reselect it whenever you like. As Figure 11.2 shows, your cube is now complete!

You should save the image you just created here because you'll have another use for it a little later in Exercise 11-4.

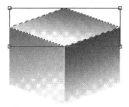

Figure 11.2
A cube with each side available for further editing via alpha channels

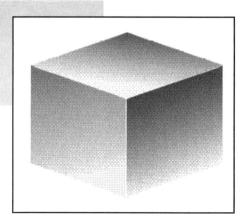

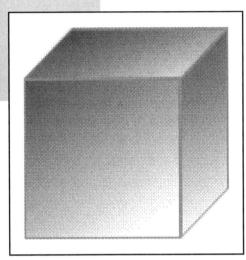

Figure 11.3

A front-facing cube; alpha channels let you select each side separately.

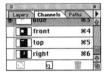

EXERCISE 11.3

Creating Cones

To round out our collection of geometric shapes, the mini-exercise below shows how to create a shiny, metallic-textured cone.

①

1. Create a new Photoshop document with a white background. The exact dimensions aren't important, but make sure it's square; for this example, I created a document measuring 450 by 450 pixels.

2. With the Rectangular Marquee tool selected, click and drag to select the leftmost third of your image.

3. We're going to add a gradient fill from left to right in this first selection. Set the foreground/background colors to black and white, or any two other contrasting colors with the darker color in the foreground. Choose the Gradient tool and make sure it's set to a Linear blend. Press [Shift] and drag straight across your selection from left to right.

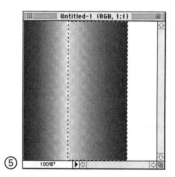

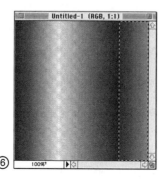

4. Now you'll need to make a second selection, sectioning off most of the remaining white background.

5. This time, you'll need to apply a gradient fill going in the opposite direction. We're trying to create the illusion of depth by creating two opposing lighting effects. With your Gradient tool still selected, press (Shift) and drag straight across your selection from right to left. Alternatively, you could reverse your foreground and background colors before dragging from left to right.

6. Now you should select the untouched white portion of the image and reverse the lighting effect again. Apply the same kind of gradient fill that you used originally in step 3.

7. Select your entire image by pressing ⌘-Ⓐ (for Mac users) or (Ctrl)-Ⓐ (for Windows users). Select Effects from the Image menu, then choose Perspective from the Effects submenu. A small square handle should appear at the corner of the image. Click one of the upper handles and drag straight across to the center of the image; this will create the pointy head of your cone. You can also drag downward if you want the cone to be more squat.

You can make the cone narrower by clicking one of the lower handles and dragging straight across to the center of the image. When you finish shaping your cone, click your cursor inside the selection to effect the change.

8. Now we're going to give the cone a rounded edge at the bottom. Choose the Elliptical Marquee tool and create a long, oval ellipse near the bottom of the cone, extending from edge to edge. The bottom part of this ellipse will form the rounded bottom part of the cone.

9. To select the sides of the triangle, you can create a path using the Paths palette. First, make sure the Paths palette is on the screen; if necessary, choose Palettes from the Window menu, then choose Show Paths from the Palettes submenu. Use the Pen tool to draw a triangle tracing from the point of the cone down the left side, straight across the

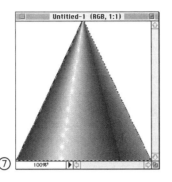

middle of your elliptical selection, and back up the right side, as shown at the bottom of this page.

Zooming in on the cone shape with the Magnifying tool could help you place your points with the Pen tool more easily.

10. Now convert the path to a selection by choosing Make Selection from the Paths palette's pop-up menu. Click the Add to Selection radio button, and your new selection will include both the area covered by your ellipse and the converted path. Save your cone outline to an alpha channel for future use as necessary. You can drag the Work Path row in the Paths palette to the palette's Trash icon.

11. Set the background color to white if it shows a different color. Now choose Inverse from the Select menu and press Delete, as shown in Figure 11.4. Congratulations—you've got a cone!

Figure 11.4
Creating a
3-D cone

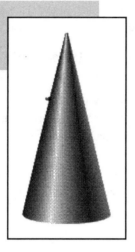

Creating 3-D Shapes with Realistic Textures

By now you've seen how to create some basic geometric shapes—but what if you want to apply a texture or image to the face of one of these images? If you're starting from scratch, you just need to fill your original selection—created with the Rectangular Marquee tool for a cube or the Elliptical Marquee tool for a sphere—with your pattern or image, then follow the steps outlined in the exercises for creating a sphere or cube, respectively. The only other difference is that you'll need to change the Gradient tool settings when you go to apply a gradient fill—an important step in creating both spheres and cubes in Photoshop. You may want to reduce the gradient's opacity so that the shadows you add don't obscure the texture or image itself; additionally, you should set the Gradient to Darken mode instead of Normal.

But what if you've come up with a texture or image you want to apply to a 3-D object you already have? While that's often a simple task in a rendering program like Adobe Dimensions, it's more cumbersome in Photoshop. The next exercise shows you how to overlay an image on each face in the cube we created earlier in this chapter.

EXERCISE 11.4

Overlaying Images on 3-D Graphics

① cube template (Layer 1, RGB, 1:1)

1. Open the image of a 3-D cube you created in Exercise 11.2. The important part to remember here is to have each side saved in an alpha channel.

If you skipped that exercise or want to work with another geometric shape you've obtained from elsewhere, you've got more work to do. Before proceeding with this exercise, use the Pen tool in the Paths palette to trace each side and convert it to a selection, then save the selection in an alpha channel. Sorry about that!

2. Create a new layer for pasting in the image you want to go on the left edge of the cube; you'll probably want to make the mode either Overlay or Multiply to let any gradient fill on the left edge show through. Here, I've named my new layer Left Edge.

After you create the new layer, load the selection for the left edge. Here's an easy way to do this via the palette views: From the Layers palette, click the New Layer icon at the bottom. Next, toggle over to the Channels palette by clicking its tab. Hold down (Option) (or (Alt)) as you click on the row for the left edge's alpha channel. Next, toggle back over to the Layers palette by clicking its tab.

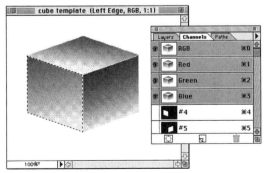

② cube template (Left Edge, RGB, 1:1)

③

3. Now let's open the image you want to paste into the left edge. For this example, I'm going to paste in a likeness of Albert Einstein. Make sure that the new image is in the same color mode as your 3-D graphic and is an appropriate size for the selection area you want to paste it into. Select the entire image, or copy just the part that you want to overlay on the cube.

4. Return to your 3-D image and choose Paste Into from the Edit menu. Pretty snazzy, right? You can reposition the image if you want using the Move tool.

5. Examine the perspective here; you may want to rotate the pasted image to match the angle of the left edge. To do so, choose Rotate from the Image menu and then choose Free. You can rotate the outline of the pasted image until it's parallel with the angle of the left edge. When you're satisfied with the new angle, click inside the box to effect the change.

Now let's save this selection and its contents as a layer mask—do you remember those? Make sure your Left Edge layer is still the targeted layer, and choose Save Selection from the Select menu. Choose Left Edge mask from the Channel pull-down menu.

6. Repeat steps 2 through 5 to create new layers and paste in images for each of the other sides in your object. Figure 11.5 shows my finished cube with a different view of the Einstein image on each side.

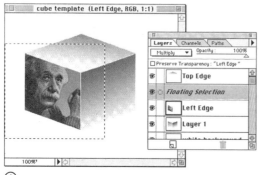

④

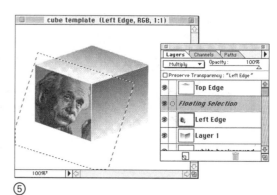

⑤

Save Selection

┌ **Destination** ─────────────
 Document: cube template ▼
 Channel: *Left Edge Mask* ▼

 [OK]
 [Cancel]

┌ **Operation** ─────────────
 ◉ **New Channel**
 ○ Add to Channel
 ○ Subtract from Channel
 ○ Intersect with Channel

⑤

Creating Buttons with Beveled Edges

Beveled edges are what give clickable buttons in online and on-screen presentations the illusion of depth; even ATM machines use them for on-screen keypads. For raised buttons, the edges of the top and left-hand sides have light-color highlights; the bottom and right-hand sides have dark shadowed edges. Reverse the colors, and the button will look recessed instead of raised (Figure 11.6).

It's easy to create soft beveled edges—where each side's highlights blend at the corners instead of at a sharp angle—using the Airbrush tool.

Figure 11.5
A do-it-yourself
photo cube

Figure 11.6
Raised and recessed button graphics

EXERCISE 11.5

Beveling a Button

①

1. Open the image you want to which you want to add beveled edges. Here, I've used a pink granite texture.

2. Set the foreground and background colors to black and white by clicking the Default Colors icon. Select the Airbrush tool. Set the mode to Darken because we're going to add the shadowed edge first. I've reduced the Brush Pressure setting down to 20%; you can experiment with how heavy you want the airbrushed color to look.

②

   Now display the Brushes palette by choosing Palettes from the Window menu, then choosing Show Brushes from the Palette submenu. Choose a brush to use with the Airbrush tool; the size should depend on how deep an edge you want to create. Here, I'm using one set to 35 pixels.

③

3. Now hold down (Shift) as you click the lower left corner of your image, then click the lower right corner of your image. Holding down (Shift) will cause a straight line to appear between the two points you click.

   Continue by clicking the upper right corner of your image. The Airbrush tool will draw another straight dark, airbrushed line from the lower right to the upper right corner.

4. To apply the highlighted beveled edge to your button, you'll first need to reverse the foreground and background colors

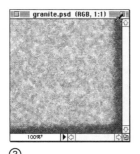

③

④

⑤

by pressing the Switch Colors icon on the Tool palette. You'll also need to switch the Airbrush tool's mode from Darken to Lighten. Keep the Airbrush pressure and the brush size the same; these should match whatever you used for the shadow edge.

5. Now press ⌈Shift⌋ again as you click the upper right corner of your image, then click the upper left corner of your image.

Continue by clicking the lower left corner of your image. You're back to where you started clicking, but, as Figure 11.7 shows, you've now added the illusion of depth to your image.

Figure 11.7
Adding a soft beveled edge using the Airbrush tool

tip

Creating Beveled Edges Using Third-Party Photoshop Filters

There are a couple of third-party Photoshop filters that take all the grunt work out of creating beveled edges. On the commercial side, there's the Drop Shadow filter in Alien Skin's Black Box 2 filter collection. One wonderful freeware filter for creating beveled edges is in the Sucking Fish Filters series called Deko-Boko; check the vendor listings in Appendix B and the plug-in listings in Appendix C for where-to-get-'em information.

Creating 3-D Lettering

Just as the beveled edges on buttons can be concave or convex, you can add such edges to text to create raised lettering or recessed type. By now we've looked at other ways to create these kinds of type effects—most notably in Exercise 7.2 when you were learning about real-world uses for channels—but I've included this section here as an at-a-glance reference with the other 3-D effects.

tip

Using Third-Party Filters Makes Rendered Text a Cinch

TypeCaster from XAOS Tools is a commercially available Mac-only Photoshop filter for creating 3-D type effects; updates are available on their Web site (see the vendors listings in Appendix B). With TypeCaster, you can create concave and convex bevels, control light sources and 3-D rotation, and map textures to the face, edges, or on the bevel. It ships on a CD-ROM with over 100 different textures (in PICT format), and users can apply their own textures as well. It only works when rendering text, not other objects. Check the vendor listings in Appendix B and the plug-in listings in Appendix C for further information.

EXERCISE 11.6

Raised Text

In this mini-exercise, we're going to add raised text to a clickable button, the kind just created above in Exercise 11.5.

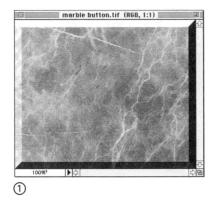

①

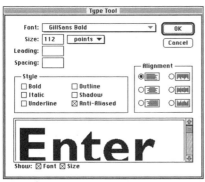

①

1. Open the button image you want to use as the background.

   Select the Type tool and enter the button text in the Type dialog box; click OK when you're done. Make sure the anti-aliased button is clicked. (Note that for on-screen reading, sans serif typefaces tend to be more readable.) Click OK when you finish.

2. Reposition the type to center it on the button. Display the Layers palette; your type should currently appear as a floating selection.

3. Choose Stylize from the Filters menu, then choose Emboss. Set the angle to 135°. Here, I've left the offset at 3 pixels; you might want to change that, depending on how large your type is. Let the preview image be your guide.

4. Drag the Floating Selection row in the Layers palette down to the New Layer icon to place this embossed layer on its own layer. Set the mode to Overlay; the gray text filling your letterforms should vanish, but the highlights and shadows should remain (Figure 11.8). Your work is done here!

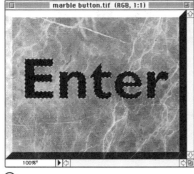

②

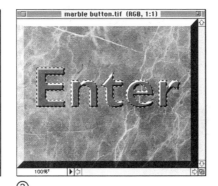

③

Figure 11.8

Adding embossed text to a clickable button

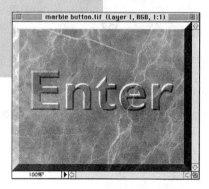

EXERCISE 11.7

Recessed Text

Back in Exercise 7.2, you saw one way to created recessed lettering by adding shadows within the letterforms. Here, I'm going to show you how to enhance that effect by adding embossed highlights and shadows.

①

②

1. Open the image that you created back in Exercise 7.2.

2. Create a new layer. Load the alpha channel for the type selection in your new layer. Choose Stylize from the Filters menu, then choose Emboss. Set the angle to 315°. Here, I've set the offset to 10 pixels; you should set the value to whatever looks best for your type size, letting the preview image be your guide.

3. Set the mode for your new layer to Overlay. The gray text filling your letterforms should vanish, but the highlights and shadows should remain (Figure 11.9). This effect is the opposite of that shown in the raised text exercise just above. Your recessed text is really enhanced now, don't you think?

Figure 11.9
Embellishing recessed text with shadows and highlights

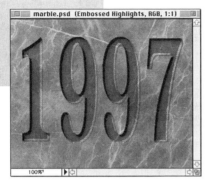

marble.psd (Embossed Highlights, RGB, 1:1)

100%

Shadows

Shadows are an important accessory for 3-D objects because they help enhance the illusion of depth. As you saw back in Chapter 5 when you encountered Photoshop's Layers feature for the first time, it's easy to add shadows to type by creating a duplicate of the layer containing your text, then darkening, blurring, and offsetting the shadow text from the original.

Adding realistic shadows to 3-D objects is only slightly more complicated. At the most basic level, you'd follow the same steps I just described for adding shadows to type, with one added step—distorting the shadow outline to simulate a light source.

Here are a few pointers I've collected for enhancing the realism of your shadow effects:

👁 **Vary the shadow's darkness with its width**   The narrower a shadow, the darker it should be. Longer shadows—which simulate more space between the object and its background—should be lighter in color, because it should reflect (no pun intended!) the illusion of more space between the two.

👁 **Create more than one shadow**   One way to make your drop shadows look more realistic is to make the scene look as if it has more than one light source—so that things in it cast more than one shadow. Experiment with creating a darker, shorter shadow

EXERCISE 11.8

Adding Drop Shadows to Objects

①

1. Open the image to which you want to add the drop shadow. You'll need to select the object by itself, apart from any background layer.

2. Create a duplicate of the object and place it in a new layer called Shadow. If you had previously saved the object's outline to an alpha channel, create a Shadow layer and then load the outlined image from the alpha channel. Make the Shadow layer your target layer.

③

3. With the shadow outline still selected, fill the selection with a dark color for the shadow.

Click the Shadow layer's row in the Layers palette and drag it below the original object's layer. (This is another reason to create objects on their own layers—if your object is on the Background layer, you won't be able to move the Shadow layer behind it.) Keep the Shadow layer targeted, though, with its row appearing in gray in the Layers palette. This way, you can distort the shadow and blur its edges while seeing how it looks in place as a shadow.

④

4. Choose Effects from the Image menu, then choose Distort. You could also choose Skew, but Distort lets you lengthen or shorten the shadow as well as skewing the outline diagonally. When you've reshaped the outline to your heart's content, click inside the selection to effect the change.

⑤

5. Choose Blur from the Filters menu, then choose Gaussian Blur. Use the preview box as your guide for blurring the shadow object's edges an appropriate amount.

6. As a final touch, you can reduce the opacity of the Shadow layer to make the background texture (if there is one) pop out a bit more.

combined with a lighter, longer one. Use the Lighting Effects filter in the Render submenu under the Filter menu to try out different effects.

👁 **Use black ink only for shadows in CMYK mode**   This removes any potential for trapping problems in simple shadows.

Summary

This chapter was very hands-on, with plenty of exercises so you could try out the different special effects for yourself. I hope it helped turn some wheels in your head for coming up with ways to use these techniques in your own work!

Next up in Chapter 12 are some need-to-know guidelines for tackling thorny print production issues. Take a deep breath and dig in!

12
Print Production
Essentials

IN THIS CHAPTER

Preparing Graphics for
Page Layout Programs

Helping Your Service Bureau

Process Color vs. Spot Color

Common Printing Problems on the Press

For many designers, their work isn't complete until they see the finished result—the printed piece, the Web page, or the multimedia presentation. Displaying your graphics in their final form is the last step in the design process, and this book wouldn't be complete without coverage of your output options. This chapter will help you prepare your documents for print production, while the final two chapters will cover Web graphics and multimedia design, respectively.

With desktop publishing, you will usually import your images into a page layout program like QuarkXpress or Adobe PageMaker, which will incorporate them with the publication's text and other page elements. You then send application files—or PostScript files generated from those application files—to a service bureau to output film and (perhaps) color proofs. The film and accompanying proofs then go to your commercial printer, who uses them to produce your final print job. As you'll see in the pages ahead, preparing your files correctly for print output and maintaining a good working relationship with a service bureau are crucial to getting your work to print the way you expect it to.

This chapter will focus on good strategies for the following:

- Creating images that your page layout software can import and print correctly

- Working with a service bureau

- Getting the most out of your images for 1-, 2-, or 4-color print jobs

- Compensating for press conditions like dot gain

Preparing Graphics for Page Layout Programs

Page layout programs have a wide range of image-handling capabilities—you can resize your graphics, rotate or crop them any number of ways, apply new colors, or change the contrast. But how do you decide which features to tweak in Photoshop and which you should leave for your page layout program? Your priorities here are twofold. First, you want to preserve the quality of your image, and second, you want to use each of your applications—Photoshop and your page layout program—to best advantage.

Here are a couple of examples of print issues best handled by page layout software:

⊚ **Rotating graphics** Rotating an image in Photoshop degrades its quality, so if you have an image you need to rotate slightly in your document you should use your page layout software's rotation capabilities instead of modifying your original graphics files in Photoshop. However, graphics that are rotated in page layout programs take a long time to process, so you should check with your service bureau to see what they recommend for your particular print job.

⊚ **Matching colors** If you have an image that uses only a single color (line art) or shades of a single color (like a grayscale image), you can apply a color to a TIFF within QuarkXpress or other page layout programs. This is helpful if you want to match the color of an icon or other graphic to text in your page layout file. Since the color of the graphic and the color of the text—defined in Quark—are the identical, you won't have to take any chances that the color you defined as 100C 40M in Quark would look any different from that same shade used in an image imported from Photoshop. (This is only important if you're printing in CMYK; you shouldn't have any color-matching problems if your Photoshop spot colors have the correct names.)

In both these cases, the original images remain untouched and you can use them just as easily for other purposes.

And here are some issues best handled by Photoshop before you import your graphics into your page layout program:

⊚ **Converting from RGB to CMYK mode** I've mentioned this a couple of times by now, but it always bears repeating—supplying your images in CMYK rather than RGB will ensure that your pictures separate on film the way you want them to. If you wind up printing separations of pages with RGB images embedded in

them, you'll find out the hard way—and the expensive way—that these images will print on just one plate without separating.

👁 **Setting the resolution before resizing** It's important to change the resolution of your image in Photoshop to twice the line screen you'll be printing at.

note **When you change the resolution of a Photoshop image you've already placed in a page layout application file, remember to go back and update the page layout file; the percentage at which the image should appear will change.**

You also want to avoid drastically resizing your images in your page layout program—especially resizing upward, say, at 200 percent—because this could adversely affect the quality of your images. Your images will take on a pixelated look in print if you need to enlarge them significantly, which is another good reason to pay for high-resolution scans if high quality is the most important factor in your print work.

Another good reason to resize in Photoshop is because scaling in page layout programs will compel the imagesetter to use much more processing time, sometimes called *RIP time,* after the raster image processor that does the deed. Some service bureaus will charge you for excessive RIP time—or if they haven't so far, they might if your jobs start encroaching on their ability to do business.

Changing from RGB to CMYK

Forgetting to convert all your images from RGB mode to CMYK is a common mistake—but it can be a very expensive one if your service bureau winds up outputting a lot of film you can't use because the images didn't separate. Your service bureau could also hold up your job until you submit new CMYK images, resulting in great time delays.

Converting an RGB image to CMYK mode is a one-step process, but if you have a lot of images to convert this can eat a lot of time. Luckily, there are a couple of good batch conversion utilities you can use with Photoshop to speed up this kind of routine task. DayStar Digital's

Photomatic is a Photoshop-specific automation utility for performing certain processes on your graphics. Gryphon Software Corp. makes Batch-It, another batch processing program; see Appendix B for all vendor contact information. Adobe is also likely to include a scripting language in version 4.0.

If, as in the RGB-to-CMYK conversion example above, you have a number of images that need the same process performed on them, a Photoshop batch processing utility can really help you speed up your bulk Photoshop work. You can also use general batch processing utilities, like CE Software's QuicKeys (for the Macintosh) and create a custom shortcut for any routine Photoshop task.

● ●

**Save Photoshop Shortcuts as
Application-Specific Macros**

I feel obliged to include this tip here because I'm guilty of doing the opposite—that is, I tend to create keyboard shortcuts for performing certain Photoshop chores, but forget to limit the QuicKeys macro to work only when I'm in Photoshop. As a result, when I happen to use a proprietary shortcut in another program that requires the same key commands, out pops an error message about why that Photoshop task didn't work.

● ●

Changing File Formats

TIFF and EPS are the most commonly used graphic file formats in electronic print production. As with converting color modes, it can be time-consuming to convert a whole bunch of images from another file format to TIFF. The batch-processing utilities I just mentioned will work great for changing file formats too.

For most of your print production needs, you'd do well to just use TIFF. By now you've seen one big exception—saving a clipping path with a graphic so you can silhouette it against another graphic or other elements in a page layout program file—where you have to use EPS. Another exception where EPS is your only option is if you want to save halftone screening with an image—which is something you may want to do with your duotones, tritones, or quadtones.

Figure 12.1
DCS options in
the EPS Format
dialog box

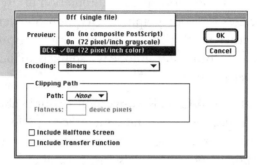

Another common use for EPS files is when your service bureau makes high-resolution scans of your artwork and returns the low-res version to you. When you save a CMYK file in EPS format, you have the option to save it as one file (like any other graphics format) or as five different files—one for each color channel, and a low-resolution, composite file. The composite file is the one your service bureau returns to you to work with. You won't have to worry about swapping the high-res file with the low-res one; your service bureau will take care of that for you.

This type of EPS file uses a format called DCS (Desktop Color Separation), which you'll see options for when you save a file as an EPS. Choosing the Off option keeps your graphic in a single file; turning DCS to On is what saves your graphic in five separate files (Figure 12.1).

As helpful as it is to use EPS in this way to work with low-res files while your service bureau keeps the high-res ones, you have to be careful when you later archive all your images. If you lose one of the five files, you'll be in a jam if you ever need to restore that image.

note

This discussion of DCS has focused only on DCS 1. The later version—DCS 2—has capabilities for storing numerous spot colors as well as process colors. Photoshop has no built-in support for the DCS 2 format, but you can add this capability with the Platemaker plug-in from A Lowly Apprentice Production, Inc. Both QuarkXpress and Adobe Pagemaker support DCS 2, so this offers one of the few ways you can import images with spot colors into a page layout program.

Helping Your Service Bureau— and Yourself, Too

Planning ahead is the rule to live by when you're supplying your service bureau with everything they'll need to run your job.

For completeness, I've included a run-down-the-list approach to making sure the folks at your service bureau have everything they need to output your job. It includes far more than just the admonition to send all the necessary graphics—but since when have you had a graphics project where you only had to send a couple of images? Usually your assignment is a little more complicated, so here's a checklist to help you make sure everything goes the way you want it to.

- 👁 A transmittal form specifying the services you need—for example, color-separated film output. Your service bureau probably has its own form it wants you to use. List by name all your application files, fonts, and graphics. Include appropriate information about line screen and printing resolution, emulsion specifications (for film), billing, and when you expect to have the work delivered.

- 👁 A copy of every graphic imported in your application file. List on the transmittal form the file formats of the graphics you're sending—for example, so many TIFF files and so many EPS graphics.

- 👁 Your page layout file.

- 👁 A hard copy final proof of every page in your job. If you have any additional comments to mark on the laser proofs, use a brightly colored pen or marker so the folks at the service bureau won't miss them.

- 👁 Any additional artwork or transparencies that have not yet been scanned. Label each piece of original art with page and column numbers, and write on the laser proofs indicating where you want the service bureau to scan an image and drop it in.

If you don't send page proofs, your printer won't accept responsibility if, for example, text reflows around images in your application file and changes all the page breaks.

note

Some desktop publishing applications have *pre-flighting* options that help you assess whether you have all the resources you need to print your job. For example, this is what QuarkXpress's Collect for Output option does—it simplifies gathering all the graphics, fonts, and other needed elements. And there's even a pre-flighting program that you can use with Photoshop EPS files called FlightCheck from Markzware; check the vendor listings in Appendix B for vendor contact information.

Here are some further tips that, from the service bureau's perspective, should make you a joy to do business with:

- 👁 **Send color-separated laser proofs** Time permitting, it's a good idea to send color-separated proofs if you're asking for film separations; your service bureau may even require them. Printing color separations is another way for you to check to make sure everything shows up on different plates the way it should.

- 👁 **Flag all FPO (for position only) images** Be sure to point out loud and clear if you expect your service bureau to put in some high-resolution images for the low-res versions in the document. That way, your vendor won't have to waste any time looking for files that you never intended for final output. Similarly, you should never change the name of any FPO file that your service bureau gives you.

- 👁 **Update all modified graphics in the page layout file** This includes any image whose name you may have changed, as well as images where you changed the resolution or color mode at the last minute.

- 👁 **Match the names of spot colors in your Photoshop images with their counterparts in your page layout file** You'll have printing problems if the two names don't match exactly. This shouldn't be a problem with predefined PMS colors in QuarkXpress or Adobe PageMaker.

- 👁 **Use clipping paths when you need to images with a transparent background to overlap other page elements** Setting an image's background fill to "None" in a page layout program can often produce undesirable results. Create a clipping path around the image in Photoshop if the image will overlap other graphics, rules, or type on the page. For other situations, it's a good idea to set the image's background fill to white or 0% black instead of "None."

👁 **Delete all unused colors in your page layout file's color palette.**

How Your Service Bureau's Imagesetter Works

After you submit your application files to your service bureau, they'll use them to generate PostScript files. If your company is trying to save money, you may be responsible for generating those PostScript files yourself, although that opens up possibilities for errors on your end. PostScript-based imagesetters have a raster image processor (or RIP) that translates the instructions in the PostScript files to dot patterns for each separate color. A recorder in the imagesetter uses a laser beam to reproduce the dot patterns on the film or paper loaded in the machine.

Halftone Screening

These imagesetter dots are organized into a system of halftone cells. The more imagesetter dots that can fit into one of these cells, the larger the printed halftone dot will look in print. These varying sized dots help create the appearance of continuous tone in your printed images.

I've already described elsewhere how halftoning works so I won't try your patience with an elaborate description; I just wanted to emphasize that the imagesetter dots are not one and the same with the halftone dots you'll see on the printed page.

Stochastic Screening

Besides halftoning, you can also simulate the appearance of continuous tone with *stochastic screening*. In stochastic printing, the dots are all the same size. The distance between the dots, not their varying size, is what helps create a realistic-looking image.

Figure 12.2
Halftone
screening (left)
compared with
stochastic
screening (right)

To create stochastic screens in Photoshop, you can use a third-party plug-in like the Second Glance LaserSeps Pro export filter. You can also, however, create a not-bad stochastic effect when you convert an image from Grayscale to Bitmap if you choose the Diffusion Dither option. You may have to play with increasing the resolution to get it right.

Process Color vs. Spot Color

Whatever form your print project will take, you'll want to plan well ahead of time how you'll be using color in the job. For example, will you use process color (CMYK) or spot color?

Since commercial printers will charge you for each ink that you use for printing, you or your company will save money by choosing spot color if you're printing only a small number of colors—three or fewer. A typical 2-color job uses black ink and a spot color, such as an ink from a predefined color system like the Pantone Matching System (PMS).

Even though you're just using two inks, you can stretch your color range by making use of varying percentages of both those inks, blends, and duotones—areas where both inks will print.

Duotones

A duotone is like a grayscale image, except that two inks—usually black and a PMS color—print over the same area. This added color depth can create some really interesting images, and add interest to a 2-color print job where all other elements appear in just one ink or the other. When you're ready to save a duotone for use in a print job, you'll need to save it in EPS format.

● ●

Use Short Pantone Names

Be sure that the Short Pantone Names check box in Photoshop's General Preferences (click the More... button to see the More Preferences dialog) is clicked. This addresses one problem that can come up with PMS color names in Photoshop not matching their counterparts in page layout programs. PMS colors defined in PageMaker come up with two-letter suffixes, as in Pantone 199 CV; but by default, Photoshop will name that same color Pantone 199 CVC. If you check the Short Pantones Names check box, you can stave off this miscommunication between the programs. This won't be a problem for you if you're a QuarkXpress user, as the program will figure out that these misnamed colors refer to the same color.

● ●

Check this box to ensure your page layout program will recognize your PMS spot colors.

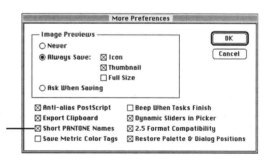

Printing Spot Colors from Photoshop

What if you're fine-tuning some images for a two-color print job and want to print spot colors, not duotones, from Photoshop? Your options for doing this are actually pretty limited.

To create spot-color images, you have to use the Platemaker plug-in from A Lowly Apprentice Production, Inc. First, you'll need to save your the spot color portion of your image in an alpha channel. Then, with Platemaker, you can save your Photoshop image in DCS 2 format, which supports multiple spot colors in extra channels. Since both QuarkXpress and Adobe Pagemaker support DCS 2, you'll be able to include images with spot colors that are not duotones.

On the Press

Up until now I've focused only on how to prepare your work for imagesetter output, but you should also know about the kinds of printing problems that could come up.

Dot Gain

When your job is on press, the neat little halftone dots the imagesetter puts on film for you may show up as much bigger dots of ink on your paper (Figure 12.3). *Dot gain* is the term used to describe an increase in the dot size; as a result, your job could print too dark or intense. It's attributable in part to what kind of inks or what kind of paper the job involves; newsprint, for example, is especially absorbent, so it may print darker than you intended.

Photoshop has a built-in method for safeguarding against dot gain on press. Choose Preferences from the File menu, then Printing Inks Setup

Figure 12.3

An example of dot gain: Halftone dots on film used for making printing plates can vary in size and shape from the corresponding dots printed on paper.

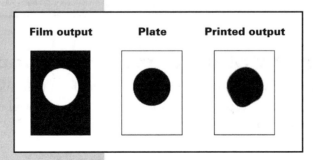

Figure 12.4
Photoshop's
Trap options

from the Preferences submenu. The Printing Inks Setup dialog box will display a value for the percentage of dot gain expected during printing.

Trapping

If you've ever seen slight gaps between colors in a document, then you've seen what poor trapping does—it's a result of misalignment between printing plates.

Like many desktop publishing programs, Photoshop has its own method of trapping. It can print one color slightly larger so as to overlap another color; this way, the telltale white gap won't appear even if the press gets the two colors slightly out of register. This technique is also known in printing circles as *spreading and choking.* Photoshop's trapping method spreads lighter colors under darker ones.

You can launch Photoshop's Trap dialog box by choosing Trap from the Image menu. You can then select a unit of measurement and enter a value for the width of the trap (Figure 12.4).

note

Bear in mind that trapping is only an issue when you've got solid tints that meet—for example, stripes made up of solid magenta only and solid yellow only. For most of your Photoshop imagery, such as photographs, this should not be a cause for concern.

Summary

The strategies covered here should help you work better with your service bureau and get the kind of results that you're after in your print production. In the next chapter, you'll get a chance to focus exclusively on creating graphics for Internet publishing.

13
Web Graphics Essentials

Whether you're supplying artwork for your company's new site or serving up examples of your work for a personal online gallery, it's easy to get excited about what you can do on the World Wide Web. Graphical Web browsing—which lets users take in the visuals as well as text information—has been the driving force behind the Web's explosive growth, making it the fastest-growing Internet service and creating almost overnight a vast, uncharted industry for content providers, programmers, advertisers, and artists. Well-designed graphics are almost a necessity for impressing visitors to your site and capturing their attention—and this chapter aims to show you how to do that.

For your Web graphics to have the greatest impact, you'll have to take into account—or is that grudgingly accept?—the differences between designing for online viewing and designing for print publication. Some users will have monitors that can display thousands or millions of colors—but most will see only 256 colors or fewer. Will your images look as good to users on other computer platforms as they do to you? You'll also need to balance the goals of offering great-looking images and of keeping file sizes low so users don't have to wait around too long for the graphics files to download.

As an artist and information designer, you'll probably find many ways to use graphics on your Web site—from the all-important logo or imagemap on your main page to those good-looking interactive buttons and icons to the coordinated look you present from page to page. But unlike print publishing where you can specify pretty much everything the reader will see, a lot of online presentation factors are difficult—if not impossible—for you to control. You usually can't anticipate how wide your users' browser windows will be, for example, or determine if their browsers will display transparent backgrounds or if text will wrap around graphics they way you intended.

That said, it's still incredibly easy to incorporate graphics into a Web page. Photoshop has a lot of features that are very handy when you're developing graphics for the Web: you can easily control pixel size, number of colors in an image, and specific colors used in the color palette, and you can convert a variety of file formats to GIF or JPEG. It won't take long for you to have a potential worldwide audience ready to appreciate your creations. This chapter will focus on the following topics:

👁 Exploring why file size is such a large concern for Web graphics, and optimizing your images for faster downloading

👁 Choosing file formats for Web graphics

👁 Creating graphics for specific Web site purposes: background tiles, navigation buttons and icons, and imagemaps

👁 Resolving color management issues, including browser palettes and RGB-to-hexadecimal color conversion

👁 Creating special effects, including transparent backgrounds

👁 Creating additional Web graphic effects with browser plug-ins and related programs

File Formats Revisited

Photoshop supports both GIF and JPEG, the only graphics formats most Web browsers can display as *inline images*. These are images that show up in the body of your Web page without requiring a separate program (called a *helper application)* or a separate browser window to display them.

Deciding whether you should save your Web graphics as GIFs or as JPEGs should largely depend on what kinds of graphics they are. The JPEG format is the best choice for photographic-quality images or graphics with a lot of color blends. GIF is an 8-bit color format, so it can only contain up to 256 colors. These differences between these file formats were discussed at greater length back in Chapter 2. For graphics that use less than 256 colors—especially icons, logos, or navigational graphics—GIF should be just fine.

GIF is the most widely used format on the Web. In Photoshop you can save files in the standard GIF87 version, which the program calls "CompuServe GIF." There's also another variation of the GIF format called GIF89a that supports special features like transparent backgrounds and interlacing (also called progressive display). You can use Photoshop to save GIF89a files—and thus create these special effects—

with the GIF89a export filter Adobe added to Photoshop in version 3.0.5. There are also GIF89a plug-ins available if you're using an earlier version of Photoshop. You'll find more detailed info about the GIF89a format and these added capabilities later in this chapter, in the "Web Special Effects" section.

One other graphics format that's gotten some attention as a potential up-and-coming Web standard is PNG (Portable Network Graphics). Pronounced "ping," PNG began to take shape after the patent controversy over the GIF format in 1994 seemed likely to threaten GIF's widespread use (see Chapter 2). Although GIF is still with us, PNG format development is continuing. PNG has a lot of the same features as GIF including indexed color palettes, interlacing and transparency (in GIF89a), and lossless compression. It also has some features that GIF doesn't, like support for 48-bit color and an alpha channel for masks. PNG also automatically adjusts graphics for gamma correction to compensate for cross-platform differences in brightness and contrast—a major bonus for Web graphics, since many Photoshop designers who use Macs forget that their GIFs will look much darker to Windows users.

Adobe plans to include native support for the PNG format in an up-coming version of Photoshop. Until then, you can save Photoshop files in PNG format by using a third-party plug-in like Ian MacIntosh's free PNGForm. PNGForm is available online at **ftp://ftp.asi.com/pub/ photoshop/filters-pc/pngform.zip** or **http://www.asi.com/psarchive/ pcplugs.html**.

Minimizing Download Times

On one hand, some aspects of designing graphics for the Web are much more liberating than designing for print; for example, you aren't limited to using just a certain number of inks (as for 1-color or 2-color printing), and you don't have to worry about dot gain, ink density, or bad trapping. On the other hand, it's not unusual to create Photoshop images for print publication that are 1MB to 10MB in size—but on the Web, every byte counts. In this medium, even a 70K file can be unforgivably huge.

If your graphics take too long to load on your pages, chances are your visitors will grow tired of waiting and link somewhere else instead. As a Web graphics designer, you'll have to work at keeping your graphics small in size without losing too much image quality. There are a couple of ways you can actively try to reduce the file size of your graphics—for example, you can reduce the number of colors in your GIFs or increase the compression in your JPEGs. I'll discuss these techniques next, and then provide some tips for giving your visitors options for viewing low-resolution versions of your complex graphics.

Using Fewer Colors

Reducing the number of colors in a GIF is one way to make that file smaller. (Reducing colors in a JPEG is less important, because its file size will depend more on its level of compression.) In Photoshop, you can set the number of colors used when you convert a file to Indexed Color mode, which is what you'll do when you save it in GIF format. Exercise 13.1 will show you how to experiment with reducing the number of colors in a GIF to reduce its file size without reducing its quality too much.

note You can really reduce graphics loading time if you save all the images on your Web pages using the same color look-up table— for example, the Netscape CLUT used here—or another custom color table you create.

Maximizing Image Compression

Both GIF and JPEG have built-in compression schemes for reducing file size, which will help your images download faster.

As you saw in Chapter 2, "File Format Essentials," one of the big differences between GIF and JPEG is the way the two formats use compression. A JPEG reduces file size by using a lossy algorithm, losing some of the information that we can't necessarily see. This loss of visual detail—usually slight changes in pixel color and brightness values—is virtually unnoticeable. GIF uses a lossless algorithm, so it keeps all the visual data. The compression method GIF uses takes advantage

EXERCISE 13.1

Reducing the Number of Colors in a GIF

①

1. With your image open on screen, select Indexed Color from the Mode menu. If your image is in CMYK mode, you'll need to convert to RGB mode first, then convert to Indexed Color. If your image is in Indexed Color mode, you'll need to convert to RGB mode and then back to Indexed Color again. The original GIF used here is 46.3K.

2. Look at the Indexed Color dialog box that appears. If your original graphic had fewer than 256 colors, you'll see the exact number listed next to the Other button in the Resolution section. The Einstein image, for example, had 197 colors.

   Click one of the radio buttons under the Resolution section to reduce the bit depth, or type in a specific number. In the

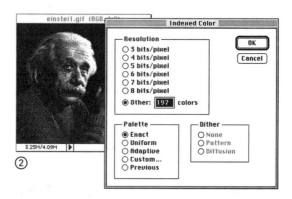

②

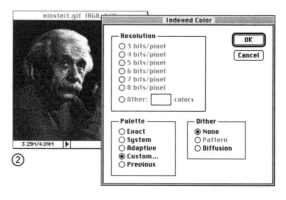

②

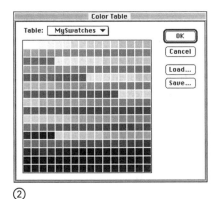

②

Palette section, you can click Adaptive to let Photoshop choose replacement colors for you as necessary.

Better yet, if you have the Netscape custom color palette on your hard drive (see Chapter 4's exercise for creating that), click the Custom radio button instead and choose the Netscape palette for your color look-up table. This will use only values from the 216 colors displayed by Netscape on both the Windows and Mac platforms, so that you can be sure that both Mac and Windows users with 256-color monitors will be able to display those colors in your image. Here, I used my Netscape color palette. (Remember back to Chapter 4, when we created this color look-up table.)

In the Dither section of the dialog box, I almost always choose None. The Diffusion setting, which injects combinations of the available colors in areas of your image to recreate missing colors, usually seems to harm more than help. I make an exception and use the Diffuse dithering option if most of the colors in an image seem to fall outside the 216-color palette, making the remaining patches of color look too blocky. You may have to use some trial-and-error here to get an effect you're happy with.

3. Click OK and evaluate the results (Figure 13.1). If you want to try another value instead, choose Undo from the Edit menu. Choose Indexed Color from the Mode menu to try again. Here, I reduced the Einstein picture down to 16 colors (4-bit). For a lot of images that'll be too much of a reduction, but you should continue to experiment with your own images to see how far you can reduce the number of colors without adversely affecting image quality.

Figure 13.1
Reducing the number of colors specified in Indexed Color mode reduces the overall file size of your GIF files.

of large areas of similar color—so you can see how reducing the colors in an image can help with compression too. JPEG can often create smaller file than GIF, but it's still only worth using JPEG on photographic-quality images. Simpler images tend to lose too much detail in the compression process, so any savings in file size wouldn't make up for the loss in image quality.

In Photoshop, you can save JPEG files with one of four levels of compression, as shown in Figure 13.2. The higher the amount of compression you use, the more information you lose.

Which of these levels of compression will work best for your Web graphics? The best way to find out is through experimentation—a lot depends on how much degradation in quality you can get away with, considering the graphic's purpose. Just make sure to do your experimenting on a copy of your original file; once you compress a JPEG, you can't retrieve the visual information you've lost.

Cropping Your Graphics

It may seem obvious, but it's worth mentioning that cropping the dimensions of your graphics will reduce their file size. If you originally designed your images for print publication, for example, you might have kept them at a larger-than-necessary size to allow them to *bleed,* that is, to run past the edges of the printed page. You don't have to think about that on the Web, so you can crop down your graphics to a smaller size.

Creating Thumbnails

If your graphics are still unavoidably hefty, you might want to consider embedding smaller—and faster-downloading—thumbnail sketches of your images in your pages, including just a link to the larger images.

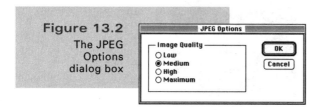

Figure 13.2
The JPEG
Options
dialog box

This way, you can let users decide whether they want to see the bigger images. You'll probably want to save the small thumbnail versions in GIF and the high-resolution images in JPEG format.

Here are the steps to making a thumbnail version of any Photoshop graphic:

1. With your image open on screen, select the whole image by pressing ⌘-A (for Mac users) or Ctrl-A (for Windows users).

2. Select Effects from the Image menu, then choose Scale. Hold down Shift to preserve the image's proportions when you scale it. Click one corner of the image and drag toward the center to reduce the image's size.

3. When you've reduced the selection to a suitable size, release Shift and stop clicking and dragging. Click once inside the image to cause the scaling to take effect.

4. Your resized image should still be an active selection with a marquee border. Choose Crop from the Edit menu to reduce the overall image dimensions. Click the Mode menu and convert the color mode to Indexed Color. Choose Save As from the File menu to save the thumbnail as a GIF, and save the file under a different name.

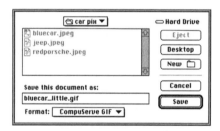

tip   Another way to use thumbnail versions of your images without any scaling on your part is to use the thumbnail sketches that Photoshop automatically generates for your files' icons. You can copy these thumbnails and paste them into a new Photoshop document. For example, on a Macintosh, just locate the graphic you want on your hard drive and choose to view it by icon. Press ⌘-I to call up the Get Info dialog box. Click the thumbnail image shown and press ⌘-C to copy it. Now return to Photoshop, create a new document, and press ⌘-V to paste in the icon from the clipboard's memory. Voilà!

Creating Low-Resolution Versions of Images

It's also possible to let visitors load a small, low-resolution version of your image on a page before they get the full-resolution one. After all the other elements on your page appear, the high-res image will load and cover up the low-res version. (Visitors to your Web page will need to use a browser that supports this Netscape-invented LOWSRC attribute in the IMG tag.)

This effect is very considerate for users who have slow Internet connections because it will give them a sense of your page's overall layout and text to read while the larger image loads. It can also help you keep visitors on your site who would otherwise grow impatient enduring a long wait for a high-res image to load ahead of other information.

The low-res image you use doesn't need to be black-and-white—for example, you could load a 256-color image over a 16-color, low-res version—but it should have the same dimensions as your high-res graphic. Once your visitors have your page's images cached in browser memory, though—which means the graphics file is saved on the users' hard drives for fast reloading upon return visits—they'll only see the high-res image load and appear when they come back to your page again.

To create a low-resolution version of one of your graphics, open the image, convert to Indexed Color mode, and reduce the number of colors, just as described in the "Reducing Your Graphics' File Size" section of this chapter. To create a grayscale or black-and-white version of one of your images, just convert the image to Grayscale or Bitmapped by choosing the appropriate menu item under the Mode menu. Choose Save As from the File menu to save the new low-res file under a different name. Figure 13.3 shows how a high-res image will appear on a Web page after the low-res version and all other page elements come in.

tip

• •

Another good way to reduce download time for graphics is to reuse graphics whenever possible on a site. It's much kinder to your visitors to use just one bullet icon instead of five in different colors, for example. A general rule: give some thought to whether the additional graphic adds anything to your page's message.

• •

Figure 13.3
Displaying a low-resolution version of an image, followed by the final, high-resolution one

The Bandwidth Conservation Society offers additional tips on its Web site on how to make your images download faster without affecting their quality. Check out **http://www.infohiway.com/way/faster/**. Their site includes some wonderful online tutorials covering many Web graphics issues.

note

I've also included URLs in Appendix A—but those are mostly pointers to general Photoshop resources. The URLs included in this chapter specifically address various Web graphics issues.

Functions of Web Graphics

You can use graphics on your Web pages for all kinds of purposes. They can serve as logos, navigational aids, hyperlinks, section dividers, icons and bullets, or as the content material itself.

The rest of this section will focus on editing your images with their intended Web purpose in mind. Your challenges here are to create graphics that are small and easy to download, and yet are visually striking and communicate essential information about your site.

 note   **Broad issues about Web site design are really beyond the scope of this book, but I've recommended several books on Web graphics in Appendix A's Bibliography.**

Your graphics for print publication often communicate a message as well as—or better than—the accompanying text, but that's just not always the case on the Web. You also need to take into consideration that not all visitors to your Web site will be able to see your graphics— some users will have nongraphical browsers while others, tired of enduring long download times, will have turned off automatic image loading. As a result, it's important to avoid putting crucial information in graphics unless it will also appear in the body of the page's text. If you're coding up your own pages as well as supplying the graphics, give some thought to entering text in your image tag's ALT attribute that lets users know what they're missing.

 note   **In this chapter, I occasionally refer to the HTML tags you'd use to reference graphics or colors in Web pages, but learning how to use HTML is really beyond the scope of this book. For Photoshop designers who are just starting to learn HTML, I always recommend Laura Lemay's introductory book, *Teach Yourself Web Publishing with HTML in a Week* (SAMS.net Publishing).**

Background Patterns and Colors

Some Web browsers, notably Netscape Navigator and Microsoft Internet Explorer, let Web designers display a background pattern on their pages.

You can achieve this through HTML coding by adding additional attributes in a document's <BODY> tag: BACKGROUND IMG specifies a background image, and BGCOLOR lets you name a background color. If you specify an image for a background pattern, you should also specify a background color in case your users have automatically turned off image loading.

You can even use an image with a transparent background as a background image; the BGCOLOR you specified (or the default background color) will fill in anywhere transparent color is specified.

note

If you want to change the color of your Web pages' text to complement your image, note that you must specify both a background image and color. If your viewers have automatically turned off image loading, the browser won't change the default text colors unless you've also specified a new BGCOLOR. This is good to know—and logical to boot—because if your image and specified BGCOLOR require type in a light-colored hue to make your pages readable, you'll want the right colors to appear. So if you want your page's words to be white or yellow, make sure you specify a dark-hued BGCOLOR in addition to serving up your background image.

The design considerations for background images and colors are similar to what you'd keep in mind for images in print publications that require type overlays. You want to make sure that the background image isn't so intricate or dark that the overlying text is unreadable. No matter what you use for a background image, reducing its opacity is sure to help with readability. In your Web page, you can specify light-colored type to run over the background, but bear in mind that while readable it'll strain your readers' eyes after a while.

Background Images and Tiling

You can use any inline graphic for your background image; the user's browser will tile the image repeatedly to fill the browser window. Conduct a little Web browsing of your own to see how other designers use background patterns—you'll probably find many good (and bad) examples.

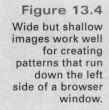

Figure 13.4

Wide but shallow images work well for creating patterns that run down the left side of a browser window.

Many Web designers design tiling patterns to be viewed in one of two ways. The first involves creating a very wide but thin graphic, intended to repeat over and over down the page, but so wide as to prevent any horizontal tiling. Typical dimensions for such graphics might be 1,024 pixels wide by 1 pixel deep.

This will produce a vertical pattern that wends its way down the page. You can use graphics with this shape to create background designs that run flush against the left side of the browser window.

note

It's not practical to create patterns that run down the center or flush right with the browser window, because you can't control the width of your users' browser windows—or their monitors, for that matter.

The second—and, I think, more common—method, involves creating small, square graphics (generally, from 16 by 16 pixels up to 96 by 96 pixels) that tile across and down the user's browser window, as shown in Figure 13.5.

For these kinds of tiling graphics, you'll probably want your tile pattern to appear seamlessly—meaning that viewers won't notice where the image's edges end and where the tiling effect begins.

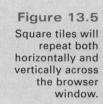

Figure 13.5
Square tiles will repeat both horizontally and vertically across the browser window.

How do you go about doing this? A lot depends on what your background image is going to look like. If you want to use a picture that has well-defined edges—say, a floating logo or object—you could create a borderless tile so that all edges use the same solid color, as in Figure 13.6. If your image already has its own border—like a bathroom tile bordered by grout—your image is ready-made to appear as a square tile, as shown in Figure 13.7.

Figure 13.6
A borderless tile and the background pattern it creates.

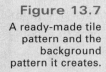

Figure 13.7
A ready-made tile pattern and the background pattern it creates.

Using the Define Pattern Command to Evaluate a Background Tile

Don't fire up your Web browser just yet to test out your patterns—there's a very easy way within Photoshop to anticipate how an image will look as a background tile. After you create a graphic you want to use as a repeating background pattern, like the one in Figure 13-7, select the whole image by pressing ⌘-Ⓐ (for Mac users) or Ctrl-Ⓐ (for Windows users). Select Define Pattern from the Edit menu. Create a new image that's at least several times large than your new pattern image. Choose Fill from the Edit menu, and select Pattern from the pull-down menu next to Use. You should see your pattern image repeat over and over, filling in the entire image area both horizontally and vertically.

But let's say you want to create a completely blended seamless tile—to create a giant abstract pattern, or the overall jumble of a starry night sky or a million M&Ms. Exercise 13.2 will show you how to accomplish this using Photoshop's Offset filter.

tip

• •

For Kai's PowerTools Users Only

There's also a useful plug-in in Kai's PowerTools called Seamless Welder, which makes creating seamless tiles—by algorithmic displacement—a breeze.

• •

Background Colors

Instead of using a background pattern, you could specify a hexadecimal color to replace your browser's default background color. It's especially important to do this if you're using a tiling background graphic, in consideration of Web visitors who have disabled image loading. You can add a background color to your Web pages with the BGCOLOR attribute in the <BODY> tag. First introduced by Netscape, the BGCOLOR attribute is now also supported by some other browsers. See "Using Color Palettes Throughout a Site" later in this chapter for more information about choosing background colors.

There are a few other design guidelines you should keep in mind when choosing graphics and colors to use for your Web page backgrounds:

👁 **Keep the pattern or design simple and light in color**   Your pages' text will appear on top of this image, so you want to maximize readability.

👁 **Use a small color palette in background graphics**   The more colors that need to load, the longer it takes for your page to appear—and the more likely that impatient users will tire of waiting to read the document and click elsewhere.

👁 **Don't go overboard in dramatic color changes**   White or yellow type on a multicolored background pattern is a striking effect that'll get people's attention, but please keep readability in mind if you have a lot of text on your pages.

EXERCISE 13.2

Creating a Seamless Tile Graphic for a Background GIF

①

1. Open an existing RGB or Indexed Color image you want to modify for a Web page background pattern. The image should be a perfect square; check Canvas Size under the Image menu to make sure its height matches its width. Here, I'm going to edit an image of some bulk candy; as pretty as it is, it doesn't tile well in its current form.

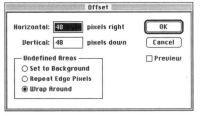

②

2. Next, you'll need to choose Other from the Filter menu, then choose Offset to offset the graphic by half its size both horizontally and vertically. My graphic is 96 by 96 pixels wide, so I've specified in the Offset Options dialog box that the image should be moved 48 pixels to the right and 48 pixels down. Make sure that the Wrap Around radio button is checked. This will move what was formerly the upper left quadrant to the lower right, and reposition the other quadrants accordingly.

As you can see, the image has been offset half its length across horizontally and vertically. The seam you see running across the middle is what would have appeared had you used your original image as your final tiled graphic.

②

③

3. Now we'll edit the middle of the graphic using the Rubber Stamp tool to blend away the seam. Remember to Option-click (for Mac users) or Alt-click (for PC users) to select small portions of the image to paint over the seam. Take care with this step, because it's important to cover up the seam well while keeping the transitions natural-looking.

The new edges you've created with the Offset filter will be seamless because they'll run into the adjacent quadrant from the original graphic.

Your image should tile very well now—but will text on top of it be readable? If you're not sure, you can follow the next step.

4. I wanted to reduce the opacity for this image so overlaid text would be readable, but I also wanted to let the pattern

④

④

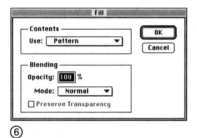

⑥

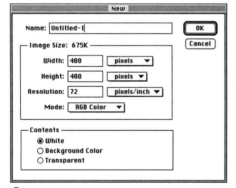

⑥

show through. First, I added a second layer by choosing New Layer from the Layers palette's fly-out menu. I filled it with white and adjusted the Opacity slider.

5. Choose Save or Save As from the File menu to save your new background pattern image. Save as either a GIF or JPEG as you deem necessary.

6. If you like, you can try out the tip given just before this exercise about viewing multiple renditions of your patterned image within Photoshop. First, select your whole image and choose Define Pattern from the Edit menu.

   Create a new image that's somewhat larger than your pattern image. Here, I've made the new image 480 by 480 pixels, or five times wider and deeper than my original.

   Now choose Fill from the Edit menu and select Pattern from the pull-down menu next to Use. As the pattern image fills in across and down, you'll see that the seam that marred the original image is gone; the edited image now blends seamlessly.

Figure 13.8 shows what this image looks like as a background pattern in a Web page.

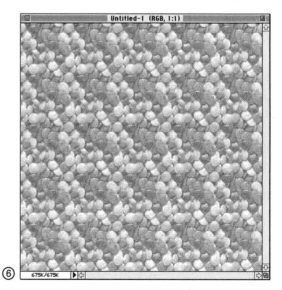

⑥

Figure 13.8

The finished repeating tile pattern in action on a Web page

👁 **Keep an eye out for good and bad backgrounds on other Web pages** Even through casual Web surfing, you'll find many other examples of how other designers have handled this challenge. Observation helps you get a sense of what works and what doesn't.

Icons

Icons can liven up your Web pages by drawing the reader's eye to important lines of information and navigational links. They are typically very small GIFs, measuring 32 by 32 pixels or at most 64 by 64 pixels and containing only a few colors—although there are no hard-and-fast rules. Icons afford great opportunities for getting very creative in a small space. With only a few pixels to work with, for example, how would you represent navigational arrows—say, back to the previous page, go right for the next page—in an interesting way?

As mentioned earlier, you can also create thumbnail images of highly detailed graphics that you can embed in your pages as icons that link to their larger, longer-to-download versions.

There are many freely downloadable icon archives available on the Web; I've included a few URLs for them in the "Acquiring Web Graphics" section. But they're much like commercial clip art collections: after much searching, you may find a few icons that are perfect for your needs, some that'll inspire you to create better-looking versions, and a whole bunch that you'd never find a use for.

Imagemaps

Clickable imagemaps contain *hot spots* that link the user to different URLs at the click of a mouse button (Figure 13.9). This added capability lets your images also serve as a visual index for your site's content or directory structure.

You can use Photoshop to create and edit the images that will serve as your clickable maps, but you'll need extra Web graphics software and scripting skills to implement a *server-side imagemap.* These require you to create a map configuration file to identify the boundaries of each hot spot; when a user clicks an area of your imagemap, the request goes to the server that hosts your site. I've listed pointers to imagemap utilities at the end of this section. Ask your Internet service provider what Web server they're using (probably NCSA or CERN), which map file format they support, and how to devise and place on the server a script that will make your imagemap work.

An exception is *client-side imagemaps*—these imagemaps work with no scripting and no separate map configuration file (the hot spots are specified in your HTML), and you don't have to worry about what Web

Figure 13.9

This image on Adobe's main page functions as an imagemap, redirecting readers to different parts of the company's site depending on which part of the picture they click.

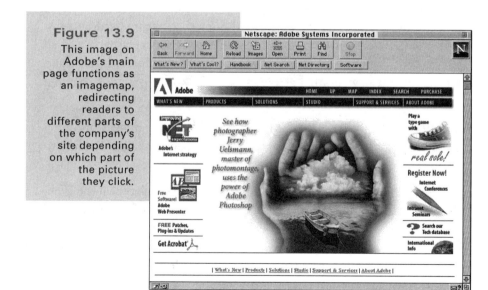

server your provider is using. The catch is that only certain browsers support client-side imagemaps, so they won't work, for example, for visitors using a version of Netscape Navigator earlier than 2. But if you can ensure that everyone in your audience uses a browser that supports the feature—for example, if your client is a company developing an internal Web site (or *intranet*) and all employees are using Netscape 3—then client-side imagemaps are definitely the easy way to go.

Imagemaps use the Cartesian (x-y) coordinate system to identify on what part of the image the user's cursor clicks. Just like the default coordinates in a Photoshop image, imagemaps place the point of origin (0, 0) in the upper left corner of an image. If you're creating a server-side imagemap, I recommend you use one of the imagemap editing programs listed at the end of this section to activate the hot spots. If you're making a client-side imagemap, though, guess what? Photoshop is all you need to define your hot spots!

Defining Hot-Spot Coordinates for a Client-Side Imagemap

You're going to use the Pen tool in the Paths palette to click and place points to identify the x-y coordinates of the image's hot spots. After you open an image to use for a client-side imagemap, you should make sure the Info palette is showing. Choose Palettes from the Window menu, then choose Show Info. In this palette, you'll see the x-y coordinates of your cursor change as you move it around.

You should also display the Paths palette by choosing Palettes from the Window menu, then choosing Show Paths. You can then use the Pen tool (⬗) to place points in squares or polygons. Note the x-y coordinates as you place each point; you can also reselect each point with the Arrow tool (⬈) to view its x-y coordinates again.

note   **Netscape's version of client-side imagemaps does not (yet, anyway) support circular hot spots.**

When you finish identifying the coordinates of each hot spot, you can delete the path altogether before closing the file—you don't want or need to save it with your imagemap image.

Putting these client-side imagemap coordinates to work takes you back to writing some HTML—again, a little beyond the scope of this book. But here are some good online resources I suggest you check out for further information about client-side imagemaps and the syntax to use in your HTML documents.

👁 **Netscape's Extensions to HTML 3**
   http://home.netscape.com/assist/net_sites/
   html_extensions_3.html

👁 **Microsoft's HTML Support—Client Side Images**
   http://www.microsoft.com/intdev/author/html30/
   imagemap.htm#Area

Even if you don't consider yourself at all technically inclined or Web-oriented, you can still implement client-side imagemaps without writing a single line of code in Perl (or any other scripting language). The HTML for identifying the hot spots in client-side imagemaps is quite straight-forward, and the online resources mentioned here should be a great help to you in implementing them.

Design Considerations for Imagemaps

From a design standpoint, you'll need to make each hot spot visually discrete in your image, to avoid confusing users about the boundaries of where they should click. It's very frustrating to the user to misclick an imagemap and wind up at a URL other than the one intended. Besides making them very visible, consider interlacing your imagemap graphics; if your visitors can find the right spot to click without endur-ing a long wait for the entire imagemap image to load, they'll be happy to move to another part of your site that much more quickly.

Additional Software for Creating Server-Side Imagemaps

👁 **MapEdit 2 (for Windows users)**
   http://www.boutell.com/mapedit/

👁 **WebMap for Macintosh**
   http://www.city.net/cnx/software/webmap.html

Animated GIFs

An animated GIF can present a no-hassle way to add animation to your Web pages, using a single GIF89a file with multiple images overlaid within it and set controls for looping, timing, and backgrounds. The image looks like a simple flip-book animation. The animating effect takes place within the file itself, so there's no additional HTML coding on your end; you can embed the graphic in a Web page with a simple <IMG> tag, the way you place an ordinary GIF.

Netscape Navigator and Microsoft Internet Explorer support animated GIFs, but not all browsers can display them in motion; sometimes only your first frame will appear as a static image.

At the time of this writing, there are not yet any commercially or publicly available plug-ins for creating animated GIFs within Photoshop. However, you can certainly use Photoshop to create the images that make up the individual frames in an animated GIF, and use one of the programs listed here to put them together.

👁 **GIFBuilder** (for Macintosh users; freeware)
   http://iawww.epfl.ch/Staff/Yves.Piguet/clip2gif-home/GifBuilder.html

👁 **GIF Construction Set for Windows** (from Alchemy Mindworks)
   http://www.mindworkshop.com/alchemy/alchemy.html

Using Color Palettes throughout a Site

As you saw in Chapter 4 and earlier in this chapter, it's pretty easy to create a color look-up table that you can load when you save a graphic in Indexed Color mode. You can use the Netscape color palette (with 216 colors) to ensure that your Web visitors on Windows and Mac platforms see your images using the same colors. You could also create your own

custom look-up table by modifying the Swatches palette for all your Web graphics, to set a color-coordinated look to your Web pages.

To further the impression of color coordination, you could use some of the colors in your indexed color palette to set the colors of your links and the background color on your pages. When you specify these colors in your HTML documents, though, you can't use RGB values; you need to specify the colors in hexadecimal format, which uses three 2-digit (or 2-letter) couplets to represent the red, green, and blue values of that color. It sounds confusing—and Photoshop has no built-in method of converting between RGB and hexadecimal—but there are a number of online resources for converting RGB values to hexadecimal on the fly, including:

- **Beach Rat**
  http://www.novalink.com/hex

- **Color Ramper**
  http://www.netcreations.com/ramper/index.html

- **DesignSphere Online**
  http://www.dsphere.net/rgb2hex.html

- **InfiNet's background colors page**
  http://www.infi.net/wwwimages/colorindex.html

- **RGBtoHex**
  http://www.lne.com/Web/Examples/rgb.html

A number of Web sites also include color swatches for hexadecimal colors to make the process easier: you look at all the samples, pick a shade that appeals to you, and copy the hexadecimal number.

Special Effects

Transparency and interlacing are two of the most popular techniques that you can use to dress up your Web graphics.

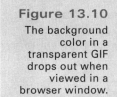

Transparency

Transparent images look like they blend in smoothly with the Web page's background, no matter what color or pattern appears as the background in the browser window (Figure 13.10). On your Web page, your image will look like it's floating over the background color or pattern.

Some Web graphics utilities let you assign just one color in your original GIF to become transparent, but the cool thing about Photoshop's GIF89a filter is that you can select numerous colors in your image and declare them all to be transparent. This frees you up from having to edit your images' backgrounds down to a single solid color.

The JPEG format doesn't currently allow for transparency. It doesn't sound like a logical development, either; because JPEG compression causes some data loss, a pixel designated the transparent color might change to another color—potentially producing results that would undermine the purpose of the transparent effect. Nevertheless, there are efforts underway to create a transparent JPEG format. JPiG is a proposed transparent JPEG format initiated by Ed Scott and Thomas Lindström, an effort that they admit began as a joke. You can find more information about this project at **http://www.algonet.se/~dip/**.

When you're deciding whether to give an image a transparent background, remember that the ones that work best have an isolated background using a single color. If the background is gradated or has several colors, it may be more difficult to knock out several background

Figure 13.10

The background color in a transparent GIF drops out when viewed in a browser window.

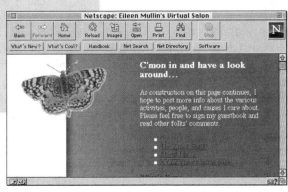

colors without inadvertently knocking out some colors in the main area of the image as well.

note **Not all Web browsers support transparency; if the browser doesn't, the user will see your original background color in place instead.**

You can download Adobe's GIF89a export filter from the Adobe Technical Support File Library; go to **http://www.adobe.com/supportservice/custsupport/tsfilelib.html** and check the Photoshop libraries by platform. Even after you install the filter, the transparent GIF option won't show up with other filter plug-ins under the Filter menu. Instead, when you're ready to save a file in GIF89a format, you'll find the option by choosing Export under the File menu.

There are also third-party Photoshop plug-ins for creating transparent GIFs. For example, BoxTop Software offers a shareware plug-in called PhotoGIF that will fill the gap here; as of this writing, it's only available for the Macintosh, but a Windows version is in development. See the vendor listings in Appendix B to find out where you can download PhotoGIF and all the other third-party plug-ins mentioned in this chapter. After you download and decompress PhotoGIF, place it in the folder that contains the rest of your Photoshop plug-ins and relaunch Photoshop.

Exercise 13.3 shows the steps you should follow to create a transparent GIF within Photoshop.

note **If you can't identify for sure a color that doesn't appear elsewhere in your image, here's one way to test it. Click the Magic Wand on your background color, then choose Similar from the Select menu. If you see any other areas of your image become surrounded by a marching ants border, you'll know that your background color does appear elsewhere in your image.**

EXERCISE 13.3

Create a Transparent GIF with Photoshop 3.0.5's GIF89a export filter or BoxTop Software's PhotoGIF

①

②

③

If you're using Photoshop's GIF89a export filter:

1. Open the image file that you want to save as a transparent GIF.

2. Now choose Export from the File menu, then GIF89a Export from the Export submenu. You'll see a different set of options depending on whether or not you've already saved the image in Indexed Color mode. If you haven't, you'll see a dialog box prompting you to load a color look-up table, or use the System or an adaptive palette.

   If you have already saved in Indexed Color mode, you'll see the GIF89a export dialog box (Figure 13.11).

3. You can now choose one or more colors—as many as you want, really—to drop out as transparent colors by selecting the eyedropper tool in the GIF89a export dialog box and clicking the appropriate miniature color swatches at the bottom of the dialog box. Every color that appears in the image will show up at the bottom of this GIF89a export dialog box. If the image uses fewer than 256 colors, the swatch boxes at the end will be black.

   When you finish choosing transparent background colors, click OK. You'll then see a dialog box prompting you to give the file a name and save it.

If you're using BoxTop Software's PhotoGIF plug-in:

1. Open the image file that you want to save as a transparent GIF. Make sure you've saved the image in Indexed Color mode.

2. With your image open onscreen, fill the background area with the color you want to use for the transparent color. Unlike Photoshop's GIF89a export filter, you can only choose one color here as the transparent background color. Use a color that you can tell doesn't appear elsewhere in the

image. Make sure the background color in your tool palette is set to this color value.

3. Choose Save As from the File menu, then choose GIF89a from the format pop-up menu.

Enter a filename and click the Save button.

4. In the resulting BoxTop PhotoGIF dialog box, make sure the GIF89a radio button is selected. The PhotoGIF plug-in will default to using your background color as the color to drop out as transparent. You could also click the color swatch labeled "Current" to see the color palette in use by your graphic.

5. Click the OK button when you're done.

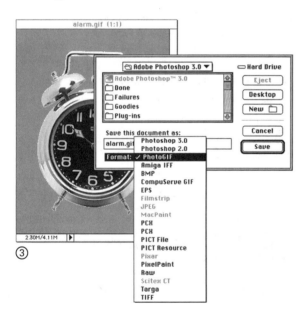

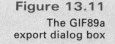

Figure 13.11
The GIF89a export dialog box

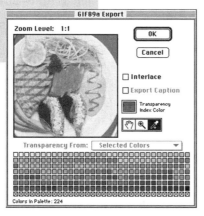

Interlacing

Interlaced (or interleaved) graphics begin to appear as blurred, low-resolution shapes and then gradually appear in sharper focus, instead of appearing line-by-line from top to bottom (Figure 13.12). As a result, your Web visitors will be able to get a sense of the graphic's content while they wait for the rest of the image to load.

The total amount of time it takes an interlaced graphic to appear won't be any faster than a noninterlaced one, but it can give the impression

Figure 13.12
An example of an interlaced graphic gradually appearing in sharper focus

that it is. Your visitors can click elsewhere if they realize they don't care to see the rest of the image.

To interlace your graphics, you'll need to save them in GIF89a format. You've already seen how to do this when saving images with transparent backgrounds—you need either Adobe's GIF89a export filter or BoxTop Software's PhotoGIF plug-in. Interlacing is even easier than saving a transparent file in Photoshop:

With Photoshop's GIF89a Export Filter

Choose Export from the File menu, then GIF89a Export from the Export submenu. Click the Interlaced check box option and press OK.

With BoxTop Software's PhotoGIF Plug-In

Choose Save As from the File menu and pick GIF89a from the Format pop-up menu. Enter a filename and click the Save button. In the resulting dialog box, click the Interlace check box and then click OK.

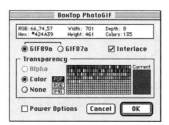

There is also a variant of the JPEG graphics format called progressive JPEG (or p-JPEG) that produces the same result as an interlaced GIF. In Touch Software makes a Photoshop plug-in called JPEG Transmogrifier that can save JPEGs with this interlacing effect; Progressify is another Photoshop plug-in that does the same thing. On your end, these plug-ins function in much the same way as the PhotoGIF one demonstrated here. See the URLs listed in Appendix C to find out where you can download JPEG Transmogrifier, Progressify, and all the other third-party plug-ins mentioned in this chapter.

tip

• •

If you create graphics that will be both interlaced and transparent, be sure to set the interlacing first and then the transparency. Otherwise, you may see some oddly colored pixels appear in the transparent area as the image starts to appear more clearly in multiple passes.

• •

Acquiring Web Graphics

Here are but a few of the many online graphics archives you can find on the Web:

Resources for Background Textures

👁 **KPT Online: The Backgrounds Archive**
    http://the-tech.mit.edu/KPT/bgs.html

👁 **Netscape's The Backgrounds Sampler**
    http://home.netscape.com/assist/net_sites/bg/backgrounds.html

👁 Backgrounds 4 Us
http://www.ecnet.net/users/gas52r0/Jay/backgrounds/back.htm

👁 Truman's Texture Woild
http://www.websharx.com/~ttbrown/how2tile.html

Icon Graphics

👁 Anthony's Icon Library
http://www.bsdi.com/icons/AIcons

👁 Graphic Element Samples
http://www.gsia.cmu.edu/gifs/index.html

👁 YorkWeb Icon Library
http://www.york.ac.uk/icons/

Animated GIFs

👁 The 1st Internet Gallery of GIF Animation
http://members.aol.com/royalef/galframe.htm

👁 Interdine Designs' Collection of Animated GIFs
http://www.interdine.com/agif/related.html

👁 The MicroMovie MiniMultiplex
http://www.teleport.com/~cooler/MMMM/

General Image Archives

👁 Rob's Multimedia Lab's GIF Directory (also has links to other archives)
http://www.acm.uiuc.edu:80/rml/Gifs

👁 Smithsonian Image Archive
http://sunsite.unc.edu/pub/multimedia/pictures/smithsonian/

👁 **Yahoo's Computers and Internet: Multimedia: Pictures: Archives** (lists many collections)
http://www.yahoo.com/Computers/Multimedia/Pictures/ Archives/

Summary

Photoshop is really useful for just about anything you'd want to do with Web graphics. The material here will no doubt need updating sooner than just about anything else in this book, but that's the great thing about Web resources—you can find information updated more quickly there than you will in magazines and books. You can keep up-to-the-minute on Web graphics technology with the URLs given here and in Appendixes A and B.

Gear up now for our final chapter: creating and editing images in Photoshop for multimedia applications.

14

Multimedia
Essentials

IN THIS CHAPTER

Saving Photoshop Images as
QuickTime Movie Frames

Video Editors

Acquiring Good Source Images

Video Filters

Interactive Presentations

By using Photoshop in conjunction with multimedia authoring programs like Adobe Premiere or Macromedia Director, you can animate your still images and add a soundtrack to create a video presentation. You can also approach video editing from the other end—taking an existing computer movie and editing specific frames in Photoshop to create your own custom effects.

You can show these video presentations either on a computer screen or—if you use the right equipment—on a TV set. In this way, you can take the kind of online presentation skills you first saw in the last chapter on Web graphics and extend them further to cover a vast array of interactive presentations—from slide shows and kiosk displays to movies on CD-ROM or online games.

Even if you've never thought about creating multimedia presentations before, there are good, easy ways to get started without investing a lot of money or brainpower—for example, you can create slide shows of your still images. This gives you a lot of flexibility, actually, because you can mix and match slides to suit any particular client pitch or presentation as necessary.

What's involved in creating and editing graphics in Photoshop for use in your multimedia projects? You'll find that many of the design and color decisions you face with multimedia projects are similar to those you saw in creating Web graphics—you need to think about creating an engaging interface while bearing in mind the limitations of your users' equipment. It doesn't matter how snazzy your images are if your potential viewers can't see them, or won't wait around long enough to look at them!

This chapter will cover the following issues related to graphics for multimedia presentations:

- 👁 Importing and exporting movie frames between multimedia authoring programs and Photoshop

- 👁 Acquiring video stills

- 👁 Examining and making use of Photoshop's video filters

- 👁 Designing for interactive presentations

Saving Photoshop Images as QuickTime Movie Frames

Apple's QuickTime is a versatile, cross-platform video format that's commanded popularity as both a desktop video and Web video format (see Figure 14.1). It can include embedded text and MIDI soundtracks. You can play QuickTime movies at several different sizes. The small standard frame size (160 by 120 pixels) offers the best playback quality for all users, although any PowerPC-based Mac can accommodate at least 320 by 240 pixels. High-speed Pentiums can also accommodate larger QuickTime movies.

If you're brand-new to multimedia graphics and video editors, you might want to start small. Here's how to create a QuickTime movie frame-by-frame just by using Photoshop images—no extra software required:

After you launch Photoshop, create and save a PICT file, displaying any kind of image you want. Launch your QuickTime player—I use Apple's own MoviePlayer—and choose Import from the File menu. Toggle through your menu hierarchy until you select your PICT file, then click the Convert button and give the new movie a name. This will create a one-frame QuickTime movie based on your single PICT image; at this point, you can go back to Photoshop and create a number of similar PICTs—making sure they're the same size as your original—that you can copy and paste into your new QuickTime movie. To create a very, very, basic simulated animation, you can create an object in your first PICT file, then use the Offset filter repeatedly to create subsequent frames in which the object moves in one direction, then another.

Figure 14.1
A QuickTime movie opened in Apple's Movie Player

You can follow this procedure in reverse to pluck a frame out of a Quick-Time movie and edit it in Photoshop; just use your system's Copy and Paste features to save a single frame as an image in Photoshop. You should isolate the frame you want to export, select Copy, and then launch Photoshop. Create a new document within Photoshop; the suggested dimensions of the new document will match the still frame you have saved in your system's clipboard. You can now apply any kinds of effects or filtering you want and save it in a file format that's useful for you.

Video Editors

Moving up the value chain, there are a number of other video editing software packages that you can explore for creating professional-quality computer video. Just as with QuickTime, you can edit in Photoshop individual frames or groups of frames from movies you create in programs like Adobe Premiere or Macromedia Director.

Using Photoshop with Adobe Premiere

With Adobe Premiere, a leading video editor and authoring tool, you have a vast resource at your fingertips for creating video editing and transitioning effects (see Figure 14.2).

You can use Photoshop to edit Premiere movies—converted to Film-strip format—frame by frame, using all the effects and filters you can apply to other still images.

 *tip*

• •

Copying a Selection to the Same Location, Frame-By-Frame

If you want to add a selection to the same place in more than one consecutive frame in your Premiere movie, here's how to make sure it falls in the same spot in each frame: After you position your selection where you want it in your first frame, press Ctrl-Option-Shift and press ↓. The selection will propagate to the same spot in the next frame down; repeat as desired.

• •

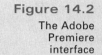

Figure 14.2

The Adobe Premiere interface

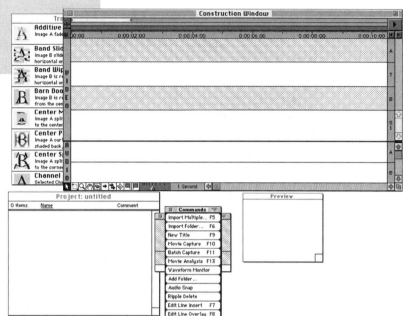

Using Photoshop with Macromedia Director

Macromedia Director dominates the CD-ROM multimedia category (see Figure 14.3). With its own scripting language, Lingo, Director really constitutes a full-fledged development platform.

As in Premiere, you can apply cool filtering and other effects to PICT files in Photoshop and then import them to Director.

tip

Check Distribution Curves in Photoshop

Most video editors will offer options for compressing, and video compression technology works best with images that have good brightness and saturation (or what videophiles describe as *luminance* and *chroma*). You can check on this by opening a sample frame in Photoshop and checking its histogram to make sure it's well-distributed.

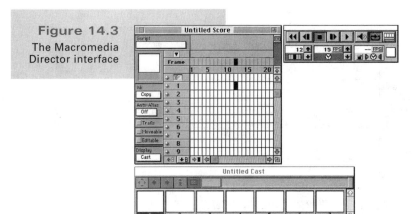

Figure 14.3
The Macromedia Director interface

QuickTime VR Authoring Kit's Stitcher

A QuickTime supplement-on-steroids, QuickTime VR adds a panoramic perspective to your desktop video; users can redirect the point-of-view in a QuickTime VR movie to zoom in, out, and around in a 360° view (see Figure 14.4). The program that fuses together the images-in-all-directions in a QuickTime VR movie is called the Stitcher; as you'll see, it creates a composite PICT that's warped-looking but completely editable in Photoshop.

You can use Photoshop to open and edit a Stitcher PICT to correct the color balance, touch up flaws, or even remove objects from the movie. The part I think the most interesting is that you can create interactive hot spots for the movie within Photoshop by painting the spot with a solid color. If you're including more than one hot spot, you paint them different colors so the program can distinguish among them. This is quite different from the way you'd create hot spots in other video edit-

Figure 14.4
A QuickTime VR Stitcher PICT opened in Photoshop.

ing programs like Macromedia Director, or in utilities for creating Web imagemaps. After you paint in all the hot spots you want, you'll need to erase the rest of the picture—so it's easiest for you if you create your hot spots on separate layers. Use the Save As command to save the hot-spot-only image in its own file.

During a later part of the QuickTime VR movie creation process, the program will combine the hot-spot-only image with the original Stitcher PICT you opened in Photoshop. The colored spots you painted in will be invisible; your users will only see that the cursor changes when it crosses those areas—indicating places to click to make something happen.

This method of adding interactive capabilities to a desktop video requires more time and effort than the same task in Macromedia Director, for example, but I think it's a lot more fun. You can paint in very tiny hot spots—as small as a single pixel if you want, say, a secret door that's likely to remain secret for a long time. This method also allows for some unusual effects—for example, you could have the entire image disappear except for the hot spot itself when somebody clicks just the right place.

Acquiring Good Source Images

Many of the guidelines in Chapter 9 for getting good images from scanners also apply to optimizing images for use in your multimedia presentations. You can get images from a variety of sources, from images you create yourself in Photoshop to images you lift from videotape, from canned images on CD-ROM to images captured via digital camera.

Potential sources for multimedia images fall into one of two categories: analog or digital. All the video and audio we see and hear we interpret as analog signals. More pristine images come from completely digital sources like laser disc or CD-ROM and are superior for creating desktop video; pure digital video also won't degrade from original to copy. When we watch a movie on laser disc or presentation on CD-ROM, we're listening to an analog signal that comes from a digital source; if we record what we're listening to, the copy won't be quite as good. If we make a digital copy of that master CD-ROM, however, the information it contains will be just as sharp as the original.

The best source material for your projects really depends on your purpose at hand, though, so pure digital video may cost too much—overkill for what you need. Depending on your end use, you'll probably find that analog sources and signals are more than fine for most of your desktop digital video work. If you're interested in making stunning QuickTime videos for your Web site, for example, there won't be a noticeable difference between images captured with a digital camera and those you've put together from other video sources.

Many modern Macintoshes come with good video capture capabilities. For example, Apple's PowerPC AV series has built-in video digitizers so you can attach a video camera directly to the computer. You could also use an AV to capture and edit high-quality QuickTime movies from videotape or laser disc. For Windows users, using a video camera with the Snappy device from Play, Inc. gives good results for sharpening video stills as you capture them. Connectix offer its Color QuickCam for both platforms, available for about $200.

You may also find third-party plug-ins that can help you with your video captures. For example, Photoshop AV-Capture2 (available on the Info-Mac archives; see Appendix A) is a shareware Photoshop plug-in that lets you acquire still images via the AV/TV-Videocard or any other QuickTime-compatible video card. The Plug-in Digitizer is another shareware plug-in (Mac only, also available on the Info-Mac archives) that lets you capture images from any QuickTime-compatible video digitizer. With this plug-in, you can capture any depth and size independently of the current monitor setting.

Video Filters

We passed by these filters in Chapter 8's filter overview because they're really only something you need to know about when you're ready to work with video stills. Only two video filters come with Photoshop—NTSC Colors and Deinterlace—but there are a couple of useful third-party video filters as well.

NTSC Colors

If you intend for your multimedia project to wind up on videotape, you'll want to use this filter to constrain your images to NTSC-standard colors. Applying this filter is akin to using an indexed-color palette; it cuts back the available colors in your image to comply with the acceptable color gamut for television. Unlike an indexed-color palette, though, it doesn't block your image from further filtering—if you make subsequent changes with other filters or effects, it could reintroduce colors outside the acceptable color range.

De-interlace

This filter is useful if you're working with a single video frame snapped in the middle of interlacing, where the scan lines are still visible. The filter's dialog box lets you opt for using duplication or interpolation to eliminate the scan lines.

Third-Party Filters

Photoshop guru Chris Cox included three video filters in his Chris's Filters collection. All three—FastKey, ColorKey, and ChromaKey—can help you with video compositing (see Figure 14.5). After using the filters, which let you create different kinds of masks, you would use the Composite command (under the Image command's Calculate menu) to composite the filtered image with other ones.

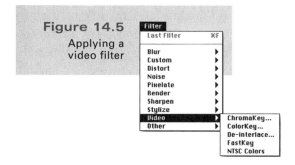

Figure 14.5
Applying a video filter

Design Considerations for Interactive Presentations

Some of the issues I touch on here will be familiar to you from last chapter's discussion of how to work around the limitations of your users' systems. But although you may be designing for a lowest common denominator in making your multimedia presentations, note that this doesn't mean meeting the same minimum expectations you had in designing for an online audience. With a presentation, you may well know exactly what kind of equipment you're designing for, so you can do a little more than when you're working blind. At the same time, the absolute requirements are different when you're working on a large scale. For example, if what you're working on is a presentation for a freestanding kiosk at a trade show, you have to catch people who have a lot of distractions. Make any interactive elements like clickable buttons very prominent and put them in the same spot on every screen. Some further design tips are included below.

Building an Interactive Display

Much like on a Web page, adding buttons with beveled edges to your display will make it easy for a broad audience to recognize the active areas of your screen—the hot spots they can interact with by touching them (on a kiosk) or clicking them (with a mouse).

Limiting Color Ranges

Again, just as in Web design, you can't assume much about the computer systems your users will have or the size and quality of their monitors. If you're designing an on-screen presentation—say, a trailer for a CD-ROM—you can make use of the same indexed color palette that won't dither for Windows or Mac users that you created in Chapter 4. If you know that the presentation will be platform-specific—for example, it'll be on a Mac-only CD-ROM—then you could use the appropriate system palette for slightly more range than the cross-platform, nondithering palette we used earlier in making Web graphics.

Creating Readable On-screen Text

It takes some thought to create text in your images well-suited to on-screen reading. Make sure you click the Anti-Aliased check box in the Type dialog box if you include text in your Photoshop images before including them in a movie file. Since your users will read your text at low screen resolutions—no better than 72 dpi or so—you're better off using simple typefaces, especially sans serif ones. Some other factors for improving screen readability include:

- **Avoid long blocks of text**   In a multimedia format, you can require users to click a button to indicate they want to see certain text—instead of dumping it all on them at once. Just as on a Web page, vast amounts of text can be daunting—not to mention tiring—to read.

- **Choose contrasting type and background colors carefully**   Light-colored text on a dark background is the most dramatic, so it's a good choice for titles. For reading more extensive amounts of information, though, it can be a strain on the eye. Black text on a light background is also easier for most people to read because that's what they're familiar with.

- **Crank up the point size**   Your readers will thank you for using larger type whenever feasible. Try to limit the width of your columns too, even if you know that your presentation will be seen on a wide monitor or overhead projection.

Summary

With this chapter's coverage of using Photoshop to edit multimedia presentations, you've made it through 14 chapters of need-to-know information for gaining Photoshop expertise. You should be very proud of yourself—you've taken the initiative to become proficient in a high-profile, essential skill for graphic designers today. From here, you'll have many doors open to you—professionally, you can use your Photoshop skills to build up your portfolio and command a better position; for fun, you can entertain your friends and family with bizarre composite images worthy of the supermarket tabloids. But most of all, for yourself, you've demonstrated you're a successful self-motivator. Let me congratulate you on your perseverance, and I wish you all the best in your graphics ventures!

A

Sources for Further Information

Books

Adobe Systems Inc. *Adobe Photoshop: Classroom in a Book*. Indianapolis, Ind: Adobe Press/Hayden Books, 1994.

Adobe Systems Inc. *Advanced Adobe Photoshop: Classroom in a Book*. Indianapolis, Ind: Adobe Press/Hayden Books, 1994.

Bouton, Gary David, and Barbara Bouton. *Inside Adobe Photoshop 3*. Indianapolis, Ind: New Riders Publishing, 1995.

Blatner, David, and Bruce Fraser. *Real World Photoshop 3*. Berkeley, Calif: Peachpit Press, 1996.

Day, Rob. *Designer Photoshop*, 2nd ed. New York: Random House, 1995.

Greenberg, Adele Droblas, and Seth Greenberg. *Fundamental Photoshop*, 2nd ed. San Francisco: Osborne/McGraw-Hill, 1995.

McClelland, Deke. *MacWorld Photoshop 3 Bible*, 2nd ed. Foster City, Calif: IDG Books, 1994.

Periodicals

Computer Shopper, One Park Avenue, 11th Floor, New York NY 10016; phone 303-665-8930; **http://www.zdnet.com/cshopper/**

How, 1507 Dana Ave., Cincinnati, OH 45207; 513-531-2690 ext. 344; **http://www.plannetonline.com/HOW**

MacWEEK, 301 Howard St., 15th Floor, San Francisco, CA 94105; phone 415-243-3500; **http://www.macweek.com/**

PC Graphics & Video, 201 E. Sandepointe Avenue, Suite 600, Santa Ana CA 92707; phone 714-513-8400

PHOTO>Electronic Imaging, 57 Forsyth Street N.W. Suite 1600, Atlanta GA 30303; phone 404-522-8600 ext. 257; **http://www.peimag.com/**

Publish, 501 Second Street, San Francisco CA 94107; phone 415-243-0600; **http://www.publish.com/**

Step-by-Step Graphics, 6000 N. Forest Park Drive, Peoria IL 61614; phone 800-255-8800

Related Usenet Newsgroups

alt.design.graphics   A range of computer graphics questions and discussion, some Photoshop-related.

comp.compression   Includes discussion of graphics compression issues (JPEG, MPEG, etc.).

comp.graphics.apps.photoshop   Discussion of Adobe Photoshop techniques and problem solving.

comp.graphics.misc   Various issues in computer graphic design and questions about graphics file formats.

comp.infosystems.www.authoring.images   Discussion of Web graphics.

comp.publish.prepress   Covers electronic prepress issues.

comp.sys.mac.graphics   Broad discussion of Macintosh graphics programs, including painting, drawing, 3-D, and animation tools.

Mailing Lists

Photo

This is a replacement list for the former Photshop List—that's Photshop—not Photoshop; what's one missing O?—that lasted from June 1993 through June 1996 at ecn.bgu. The purpose of this list is to provide a forum for discussion of the Adobe Photoshop application and issues related to its use in both the Mac and PC environments.

To subscribe, send e-mail to listserv@westwater.com with:

    subscribe photshop <your-name-here>

Substitute your real name for <your-name-here> in the body of the message.

To unsubscribe, send e-mail to listproc2@bgu.edu with:

    unsubscribe photshop

Do not include your name with requests to unsubscribe in the body of the message.

Requests should have no subject or signature and should appear exactly as listed here with no additional words or punctuation.

The Graphics List

The Graphics List is for professionals and amateurs to discuss all issues related to the theory, techniques, history, and practice of graphic design.

To subscribe, send a message to listserv@ulkyvm.louisville.edu with:

> subscribe graphics <your-name-here>

in the body of the message.

To unsubscribe, send a message to listserv@ulkyvm.louisville.edu with:

> signoff graphics

in the body of the message.

The Graphics List also has a Web site:

http://www.nothingness.org/graphicsweb/

Photoshop-Related Web Sites

Adobe's Official Photoshop Pages

What's New

> **http://www.adobe.com/prodindex/photoshop/main.html**

Free Updates & Patches/Technical Support File Library

> **http://www.adobe.com/supportservice/custsupport/
> tsfilelib.html**

Adobe Photoshop Details (system requirements)

> **http://www.adobe.com/prodindex/photoshop/details.html**

General

The Graphics List

>**http://www.nothingness.org/graphicsweb/**
>(also mentioned in "Mailing Lists" section of this appendix)

Sumex Info-Mac archives

>The site's maintainers ask that you use one of the dozens of
>mirror sites instead of the actual archives because of the heavy
>load placed on the server. Here's one:
>**http://hyperarchive.lcs.mit.edu/HyperArchive.html (mirror)**

Michael J. Sullivan's Scanning Tips

>**http://www.hsdesign.com/scanning/**

PHOAKS: Resources for comp.graphics.apps.photoshop

>**http://www.phoaks.com/phoaks/comp/graphics/apps/
>photoshop/**

PC Resources for Photoshop

>**http://www.netins.net/showcase/wolf359/adobepc.htm**

Windows Photoshop Resources

>**http://www.winternet.com/~faz/pshop/**

Tips and Techniques

Adobe's Tips & Techniques page

>**http://www.adobe.com/studio/tipstechniques/main.html#
>photoshop**

Alf's Photoshop Site

>**http://www.fns.net/~almateus/photos.htm**

Colleen's Photoshop Plug-in Page

http://www-leland.stanford.edu/~kawahara/photoshop.html

Kai's Power Tips and Tricks for Adobe Photoshop

http://the-tech.mit.edu/KPT/

MetaTools University

http://www.metatools.com/metatoolsuniv.html

Raytracing in Photoshop

http://www.rahul.net/natpix/RayPS.html

Ticks on Trips

http://www.iserv.net:80/~rtideas/

Frequently Asked Questions (FAQ) Lists

Color FAQ

http://www.inforamp.net/~poynton/notes/colour_and_ gamma/ColorFAQ.html

Photoshop FAQ

http://www.cybercomm.nl/~muller/photoshop/

Gamma FAQ

http://www.inforamp.net/~poynton/notes/colour_and_ gamma/GammaFAQ.html

Graphics File Formats FAQ

http://www.cis.ohio-state.edu/hypertext/faq/usenet/ graphics/fileformats-faq/top.html

JPEG FAQ

**http://www.cis.ohio-state.edu/hypertext/faq/usenet/
jpeg-faq/top.html**

List of Graphics FAQs on Usenet

**http://www.cis.ohio-state.edu/hypertext/faq/usenet/
graphics/top.html**

Unisys FAQ on the LZW Patent

http://www.unisys.com/LeadStory/lzwfaq.html

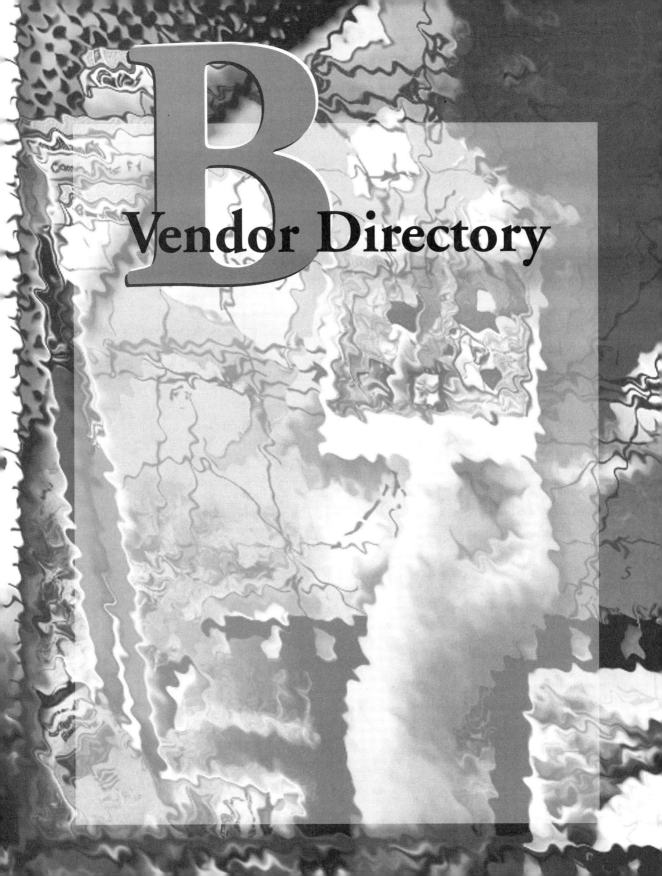

B

Vendor Directory

Here are a bunch of outlets–mostly commercial–who have products that you can use with Photoshop. If the vendors have links to freeware and demo software on their Web sites, I've put in a note about what they offer.

Adaptive Solutions, Inc.
1400 N.W. Compton Drive, Suite 340
Beaverton OR 97006

PHONE: (503)690-1236 or (800)48-CNAPS
FAX: (503)690-1249
E-MAIL: *info@asi.com*
URL: **http://www.asi.com/**
(PowerShop prepress accelerator board for Photoshop)
FREEWARE: Links to plug-ins and kernels available at **http://www.asi.com/psarchive**

Adobe Systems Incorporated
P.O. Box 7900
1585 Charleston Road
Mountain View CA 94039-7900

PHONE: (408)961-3769 or (800)833-6687
FAX: (800)235-0078
CUSTOMER SERVICE: (800)628-2320
MACINTOSH TECHNICAL SUPPORT: (206)628-3955
WINDOWS TECHNICAL SUPPORT: (206)628-3956
E-MAIL: *adobe@adobe.com*
URL: **http://www.adobe.com/**
FREEWARE: Patches and plug-ins are available at **http://www.adobe.com/supportservice/custsupport/tsfilelib.html**.
(For a complete roundup of Adobe products, try the Adobe Products and Applications Index at **http://www.adobe.com/prodindex/main.html**.)

Alien Skin Software LLC
800 St. Mary's Street, Suite 100
Raleigh NC 27605-1457

PHONE: (919)832-4124
FAX: (919)832-4065
E-MAIL: *alien-skinfo@alienskin.com*
URL: **http://hoople.catalogue.com/alienskin/**
(Black Box 2 collection of Photoshop filters)
DEMO SOFTWARE: **http://hoople.catalogue.com/alienskin/demopage.html**

Andromeda Software Inc.
699 Hampshire Road, Suite 109
Thousand Oaks CA 91361

PHONE: (800)547-0055 or (805)379-4109
FAX: (805)379-5253
URL: **http://www.andromeda.com/**
(Andromeda series of Photoshop filters)

Apple Computer, Inc.
1 Infinite Loop
Cupertino CA 95014

PHONE: (408)996-1010 or (800)SOS-APPL
URL: **http://www.austin.apple.com/macos/**
(ColorSync 2 plug-ins for Photoshop)

Ares Software Corp.
561 Pilgrim Drive, Suite D
Foster City CA 94404

PHONE: (800)783-2737
(FontMinder 2.5 font tracking software for Windows)

Artbeats Images, Inc.
Box 709
Myrtle Creek OR 97457

PHONE: (503)863-4429
FAX: 503/863-4547
E-MAIL: *artbeats@pioneer-net.com*
URL: **http://www.artbeats.com/**
(Collections of backgrounds and seamless textures)

BoxTop Software
P.O. Box 2347
Starkville MS 39760

PHONE: (601)324-7352
URL: **http://www.aris.com/boxtop/**
(HVS WebFocus Toolkit, GIFmation, ProJPEG, and PhotoGIF plug-ins)
FREEWARE: PhotoGIF (for Mac users), at **ftp://aris.com/boxtop/PhotoGIFv1.1.4.sit.hqx**; ProJPEG (for Mac users), at **ftp://aris.com/boxtop/ProJPEGv1.0.1.sit.hqx**; HVS Color, Mac version at **ftp://aris.com/boxtop/HVSColorDemov1.2.5.sit.hqx** and Windows version at **ftp://aris.com/boxtop/HVSCOL12.ZIP**.

Connectix
2655 Campus Drive
San Mateo CA 94403

PHONE: (415)571-5100 or (800)950-5880
FAX: (415)571-5195
E-MAIL: *info@connectix.com*
URL: **http://www.connectix.com/**
(QuickCam cameras, RAM Doubler)

Corel Corporation
1600 Carling Avenue
Ottawa, Ontario
Canada K1Z 8R7

PHONE: (613)728-3733
FAX: (613)761-9176
URL: **http://www.corel.com/**
(Corel Professional Photos CD-ROM collections)
FREEWARE: **http://www.corel.com/freefunfantastic/freebies/index.htm**

Cytopia Software
PHONE: (415)364-4594
FAX: (415)364-4592
E-MAIL: *prdmgmt@cytopia.com.*
URL: **http://www.cytopia.com/**
(CSI PhotoLab color-correction filters)
DEMO SOFTWARE: follow links from main Web page

Daystar Digital
5556 Atlanta Highway
Flowery Branch GA 30542

PHONE: (770)967-2077
E-MAIL: *support@daystar.com*
URL: **http://www.daystar.com/**
(Daystar Genesis MP, PhotoMatic)
FREEWARE: PhotoMatic batch processing software; download it from **http://www.daystar.com/PhotoMatic_FnB.html**.

DesAsc
702 Wrightwood Avenue
Chicago IL 60614

PHONE: (312)404-7888
FAX: (312)472-8834
E-MAIL: *daccess@interaccess.com*
URL: **http://www.desacc.com**
(ImportAccess 1.1 plug-in for accessing medical imaging data)

Diaquest, Inc.
PHONE: (510)526-7167
FAX: (510)526-7073
E-MAIL: *sales@diaquest.com*
URL: **http://www.diaquest.com/**
(DQ-Animaq Video Animation Controller)

Digital Frontiers, LLC
1019 Asbury Avenue
Evanston IL 60202

PHONE: (847)328-0880
FAX: (847)869-2053
URL: **http://www.digfrontiers.com/**
(HVS Color plug-in)

Eastman Kodak
Digital Imaging Support Center

PHONE: (716)726-7260 or (800)235-6325
URL: **http://www.kodak.com/**
(PhotoCD, digital cameras, scanners)

Extensis Corporation
55 S.W. Yamhill, 4th Floor
Portland OR 97204

PHONE: (800)796-9798
URL: **http://www.extensis.com/**
(Intellihance plug-in for batch-correcting scanned
images, for Windows users)
FREEWARE: PhotoNavigator plug-in downloadable
from **http://www.extensis.com/Demo.html**;
demo versions of other products available ttoo.

Gryphon Software Corporation
7220 Trade Street
San Diego CA 92121

PHONE: (619)536-8815
FAX: (619)536-8932
URL: **http://www.gryphonsw.com/**
(Batch It! batch processing software for
Photoshop, for Mac users; Morph 2.5 for Mac/
Windows users)

Human Software
PHONE: (408)399-0057
(AutoMask plug-in, Squizz distortion filter, Select
filter, Swap color-editing filter, CD-Q plug-in for
producing color separations from Photo CDs)

**Image Club Graphics, a division of Adobe
Systems Incorporated.**
729 Twenty-Fourth Avenue Southeast
Calgary, Alberta
Canada T2G 5K8

ORDERS: (800)661-9410
CATALOG REQUESTS: (800)387-9193 (in North
America)
OUTSIDE NORTH AMERICA: (403)262-8008
FAX: (403)261-7013
E-MAIL: *rsixto@adobe.com*
URL: **http://www.imageclub.com/**
(Adobe Photoshop Plug-in catalog; clip art
collections)

ImageXpress
PHONE: (770)564-9924
E-MAIL: *ImageXpres@aol.com*
URL: **http://gracenet.com/IX/SCANPREP.html**
(ScanPrep Pro)
FREEWARE: Trial version of ScanPrepPro, scanner
plug-ins; follow links from main Web page

inTouch Technology Corp.
1383 Washington Street
Newton MA 02165

PHONE: (617)332-6800
FAX: (617)332-1685
E-MAIL: *gyld@in-touch.com*
URL: **http://www.in-touch.com/**
(JPEG Transmogrifier, Transmogrifier plug-in)
DEMO SOFTWARE: 30-day trial version of the
Transmogrifier plug-in at **http://www.in-touch.com/pjpeg2.html**

Light Source
17 East Sir Francis Drake Blvd., Suite 100
Larkspur, CA 94939

PHONE: (415)925-4200
FAX: (415)461-8011
(Colortron Color System, Ofoto scanning
software)

Markzware Software
1805 E. Dyer Road, Suite #101
Santa Ana, CA 92705

PHONE: (800)300-3532
FAX: (714)756-5108
E-MAIL: *info@markzware.com*
URL: **http://www.markzware.com/**

(FlightCheck prepress application, works with
QuarkXPress, Adobe's Pagemaker, Illustrator, and
Macromedia's Freehand 5.5)

MetaTools, Inc. (formerly HSC Software)
6303 Carpinteria Avenue
Carpinteria CA 93013

PHONE: (805)566-6200
FAX: (805)566-6385
URL: **http://www.metatools.com/**
(Kai's PowerTools filters, KPT Convolver 1,
Bryce, Kai's Power GOO, Power Photos Vol. 1—
4 royalty-free images)
DEMO SOFTWARE: follow links from main Web page

Pacific Coast Software
11770 Bernardo Plaza Court, Suite 462
San Diego CA 92128

PHONE: (619)675-1106
FAX: (619)675-0372
E-MAIL: *info@pacific-coast.com*
URL: **http://www.pacific-coast.com/**
(PhotoMill image browsing application with Web
capabilities for Macintosh users)

PhotoDisc
2013 Fourth Avenue, 4th Floor
Seattle WA 98121

PHONE: (206)441-9355 or (800)528-3472
FAX: 206-441-4961
URL: **http://www.photodisc.com/**
(PhotoDisc royalty-free digital stock photography)
FREEWARE: Free image offer at **http://204.162.146.3:16003/free/index.htm**.

Play, Inc.
2890 Kilgore Road
Rancho Cordova CA 95670

PHONE: (916)851-0800
FAX: (916)851-0801
URL: **http://www.play.com/**
(Snappy video capture device)

Radius Inc.
215 Moffett Park Drive
Sunnyvale CA 94089-1374

PHONE: (408)541-6100
E-MAIL: *support@radius.com*
URL: **http://www.radius.com/**
(Radius PhotoEngine, ThunderColor 30, NuBus
graphics cards, SuperMatch monitor calibration
program)

Specular International
7 Pomeroy Lane
Amherst MA 01002

PHONE: (413)253-3100
FAX: (413)253-0540
E-MAIL: *support@specular.com*
URL: **http://www.specular.com/**
(Collage, TextureScape)

Total Integration, Inc.
334 E. Colfax Street, Suite A
Palatine IL 60067

PHONE: (847)776-2377
FAX: (847)776-2378
URL: **http://www.totalint.com/**
(ColorMatrix, Epilogue, FASTedit/IVUE,
FASTedit/Deluxe filters, IRIS/CT plug-in
module)

Ultimatte Corporation
20554 Plummer Street
Chatsworth CA 91311

PHONE: (818)993-8007
FAX: (818)993-3762
E-MAIL: *ultimatte@ultimatte.com*
URL: **http://www.ultimatte.com**
(PhotoFusion for Macintosh, Ultimatte for
Macintosh, Ultimatte video hardware)

Wacom Technology Corporation
501 S.E. Columbia Shores Blvd., Suite 300
Vancouver WA 98661

PHONE: (360)750-8882 or (800)922-9348
FAX: (360)750/8924
E-MAIL: *support@wacom.com*
URL: **http://www.wacom.com/**
(Wacom graphics tablets)

Xaos Tools, Inc.
600 Townsend Street, Suite 270E
San Francisco CA 94103

PHONE: (415)487-7000
FAX: (415)558-9886
URL: **http://www.xaostools.com/**
(TypeCaster, Paint Alchemy 2, Terrazzo, Fresco)

Index

Available Now!

Access for Windows 95: The Visual Learning Guide	$19.95
ACT! 2.0: The Visual Learning Guide	$19.95
Build a Web Site: The Programmer's Guide to Creating, Building, and Maintaining a Web Presence	$34.95
The CD-ROM Revolution	$24.95
CompuServe Complete Handbook & Membership Kit, Second Edition (with CD-ROM)	$24.95
CorelDRAW! 5 Revealed!	$24.95
Create Wealth with Quicken, Third Edition	$21.95
Cruising America Online 2.5	$21.95
Cruising CompuServe	$21.99
Cruising The Microsoft Network	$21.95
Data Security	$34.95
Discover What's Online	$24.95
DOS 6.2: Everything You Need to Know	$24.95
Essential Book for Microsoft Office	$27.99
Excel for Windows 95: The Visual Learning Guide	$19.95
Excel 5 for Windows By Example (with 3½-inch disk)	$29.95
Excel 5 for Windows: The Visual Learning Guide	$19.95
Excel for the Mac: The Visual Learning Guide	$19.95
IBM Smalltalk Programming for Windows & OS/2 (with 3½-inch disk)	$49.95
Interactive Internet: The Insider's Guide to MUDs, MOOs, and IRC	$19.95
Internet After Hours	$19.95
Internet After Hours, 2nd Edition	$21.99
Internet for Windows: America Online 2.5 Edition	$19.95
Internet for Windows: The Microsoft Network Edition	$19.95
Internet Information Server	$40.00
The Internet Warp Book: Your Complete Guide to Getting Online with OS/2	$21.95
Introduction to Internet Security	$34.95
Java Applet Powerpack (with CD-ROM)	$30.00
JavaScript (with CD-ROM)	$35.00
KidWare: The Parent's Guide to Software for Children	$14.95
Lotus Notes 3 Revealed!	$24.95
LotusWorks 3: Everything You Need to Know	$24.95
Mac Tips and Tricks	$14.95
Macintosh Design to Production: The Definitive Guide	$34.95
Making Movies with Your PC	$24.95
Making Music with Your PC	$19.95
Managing with Microsoft Project	$30.00
Microsoft Office in Concert	$24.95
Microsoft Office in Concert, Professional Edition	$27.95
Microsoft Works for Windows By Example	$24.95
Microsoft Works for Windows 95: The Visual Learning Guide	$19.95
Migrating to Windows 95	$39.95
Moving Worlds (with CD-ROM)	$35.00
OS/2 WARP: Easy Installation Guide	$12.95
PageMaker 5.0 for the Mac: Everything You Need to Know	$24.95
PageMaker 5.0 for Windows: Everything You Need to Know	$19.95

PC DOS 6.2: Everything You Need to Know	$24.95
PowerPoint for Windows 95: The Visual Learning Guide	$19.95
PROCOMM PLUS for Windows: The Visual Learning Guide	$19.95
Professional Web Design	$40.00
Quicken 3 for Windows: The Visual Learning Guide	$19.95
Quicken 5 for Windows: The Visual Learning Guide	$19.95
QuickTime: Making Movies with Your Macintosh, Second Edition	$27.95
Researching on the Internet: The Complete Guide to Finding, Evaluating, and Organizing Information Effectively	$29.95
Smalltalk Programming for Windows (with 3½-inch disk)	$39.95
The Software Developer's Complete Legal Companion (with 3½-inch disk)	$32.95
Software: What's Hot! What's Not!	$16.95
Sound Blaster: Making WAVes with Multimedia	$19.95
Stacker Multimedia	$19.95
Symantec C++: Object-Oriented Programming Fundamentals for the Macintosh (with 3½-inch disk)	$39.95
Think THINK C! (with two 3½-inch disks)	$39.95
Thom Duncan's Guide to NetWare Shareware (with 3½-inch disk)	$29.95
UnInstaller 3: Uncluttering Your PC	$19.95
The USENET Navigator Kit (with 3½-inch disk)	$29.95
Visio 4: Drawing Has Never Been Easier!	$19.95
Visual Basic for Applications Revealed!	$27.95
The Warp Book: Your Definitive Guide to Installing and Using OS/2 v3	$24.95
Web After Hours	$22.95
Web Browsing with America Online	$22.95
Web Browsing with Netscape Navigator 1.1	$24.95
Web Browsing with NETCOM NetCruiser	$24.95
Web Browsing with Prodigy	$22.95
Web Browsing with The Microsoft Network	$22.95
WinComm Pro: The Visual Learning Guide	$19.95
Windows 3.1: The Visual Learning Guide	$19.95
Windows 95: The Visual Learning Guide	$19.95
Windows 95: A to Z	$34.95
Windows 95: Easy Installation Guide	$12.95
The Windows 95 Book: Your Definitive guide to Installing and Using Windows 95	$24.95
WinFax PRO 7 for Windows: The Visual Learning Guide	$19.95
Word 6 for the Mac: The Visual Learning Guide	$19.95
Word for Windows 95: The Visual Learning Guide	$19.95
WordPerfect 6.1 for Windows: The Visual Learning Guide	$19.95

Fill in and Mail Today

PRIMA PUBLISHING

P.O. Box 1260BK
Rocklin, CA 95677

USE YOUR VISA/MC AND ORDER BY PHONE
(916) 632-4400 (M-F 9:00-4:00 PST)

Please send me the following titles:

QUANTITY	TITLE	AMOUNT
_____	_____	$ _____
_____	_____	$ _____
_____	_____	$ _____
_____	_____	$ _____
_____	_____	$ _____

Subtotal $ _____

Postage & Handling *($6.00 for the first book plus $1.00 each additional book)* $ _____

SALES TAX

7.25% (California only) $ _____

8.25% (Tennessee only) $ _____

5.00% (Maryland, Indiana only) $ _____

7.00% General Service Tax (Canada) $ _____

TOTAL *(U.S. funds only)* $ _____

❏ Check enclosed for $ _____ (payable to Prima Publishing)

Charge my ❏ Master Card ❏ Visa

Account No. _____ Exp. Date _____

Signature _____

Your Name _____

Address _____

City/State/Zip _____

Daytime Telephone _____

Satisfaction is guaranteed—
or your money back!
Please allow three to four
weeks for delivery.

**THANK YOU
FOR YOUR
ORDER**